FAREWELL
TO THE
SELF-EMPLOYED

**Recent Titles in
Contributions in Labor Studies**

FAREWELL
TO THE
SELF-EMPLOYED

Deconstructing a Socioeconomic
and Legal Solipsism

MARC LINDER

Contributions in Labor Studies, Number 41

GREENWOOD PRESS
New York • Westport, Connecticut • London

Library of Congress Cataloging-in-Publication Data

Linder, Marc.
   Farewell to the self-employed : deconstructing a socioeconomic
and legal solipsism / Marc Linder.
     p. cm.—(Contributions in labor studies, ISSN 0886-8239 ;
no. 41.)
   Includes bibliographical references and index.
   ISBN 0-313-28466-0 (alk. paper)
   1. Self-employed. I. Title. II. Series.
HD8036.L56 1992
331.12—dc20   91-39643

British Library Cataloguing in Publication Data is available.

Library of Congress Catalog Card Number: 91-39643
ISBN: 0-313-28466-0
ISSN: 0886-8239

First published in 1992

Greenwood Press, 88 Post Road West, Westport, CT 06881
An imprint of Greenwood Publishing Group, Inc.

Printed in the United States of America

The paper used in this book complies with the
Permanent Paper Standard issued by the National
Information Standards Organization (Z39.48-1984).

10 9 8 7 6 5 4 3 2 1

A poor independent workman...in his separate independent state, is less liable to the temptations of bad company, which in large manufactories so frequently ruin the morals of the other.

ADAM SMITH,
AN INQUIRY INTO THE NATURE AND CAUSES
OF THE WEALTH OF NATIONS
83-84 (E. Cannan ed. 1937 [1776])

This Bill is a helpful measure, under which anyone can agree with his employer that he or she is henceforth to be treated as self-employed merely by completing a simple form.... Self-employment is one of the most obvious escape routes from that sterile employee culture which was recently condemned by His Royal Highness the Prince of Wales. ... Employers will be able to employ people...without the fear of becoming locked in by employment protection laws and the other burdens on businesses.

91 PARL. DEB., H.C. (6th ser.) 147 (1986)
(Michael Forsyth, M.P.)

In German Idealism and in Marx, self-consciousness, self-determination, and self-realization qualified as the concepts in which the normative content of modernity was summarized. The meaning of the prefix "self" has, to be sure, been distorted in the wake of a possessive individualism and under the banner of sheer subjectivity. We must give back to this "self" its intersubjective meaning. ... No one is a subject who belongs only to himself.

JÜRGEN HABERMAS,
DIE NACHHOLENDE REVOLUTION
35 (1990 [1988])

Contents

Tables

Acknowledgments

To **Gail Hollander,** who, in addition to never sounding bored as a sounding board, without ruth or wrath exposed an embarrassing number of facile arguments; **Larry Ward** and **Peter van Zante** for discussing arcane aspects of tax, pension, and corporation law; **Andy Morriss** for insisting on the need to address recent developments in economic theory; **Julius Sensat** for sharpening the overall focus; **Frank Allen,** whose computerlike mastery of government documents facilitated access to many of them; and André Gorz for ADIEUX AU PROLÉTARIAT (1980).

FAREWELL
TO THE
SELF-EMPLOYED

1

Introduction: The Transvaluation
of a Real Self-Contradiction

"At least you're your own boss."
"To be a boss of nothing is nothing."[1]

Being self-employed...is for workers a less efficient substitute than
placing money in the bank is for investors.[2]

The notion that a worker can--and would want to--"employ"
himself is a curious one. After all, given the ideological
freight of alienation[3] and exploitation associated with
"employment," why would a worker do unto himself what
capitalists do unto others?[4] And even granting the
socioeconomic, epistemological, and psychological possibility
of self-employment, how does a self-employer/self-employee[5]
differ from an other-directed employee, and why does that
difference make a difference?

Because economists and sociologists of the left and the
right have persistently treated self-employment as a black
box, the recent wave of literature devoted to counting or
commenting on the alleged growth in the number of self-
employed[6] since the mid-1970s has submerged the
formulation of these vital questions. Consequently, the
deployment of an arsenal of sophisticated statistical
techniques may be projecting shoddy ordnance.[7]
Paradoxically, then, precisely at the moment of its renewed
zenith, the category of self-employment is ripe for

dismantling.

This perception of an increase in the number of self-employed[8] can most adequately be studied in the context of the contemporaneous[9] proliferation of diverse forms of employment that deviate from the modern capitalist model of "total employment."[10] Abandoning that paradigm of the full-time, permanent, on-location, exclusive relationship of a worker to one enterprise, the subsidiary regime embodies a temporal casualization and physical externalization of employment relationships.[11] Whether they involve part-time, temporary, home, leased, subcontracted, or contract labor or self-employed workers, all of these forms effect significant reductions in wages, fringe benefits, and the costs of unionization by forging just-in-time work forces.[12] In the case of firms most blatantly intent on realizing these cost savings, "the self-employed workers were former employees who were asked back to work on a special project."[13]

Whereas these disemployment strategies are typically imposed unilaterally, regardless of the workers' preferences, a more subtle technique addresses the aspirations of the mass of dependent contractors who may no longer be satisfied with the "veritable Eden of the natural human rights...Freedom, Equality, Property" that is the labor market.[14] Pursuing a consensual tack, some employers and state bureaucracies have dangled before workers the prospect of trading their merely formal independence for real independence from the traditional other-directed workplace. Instead of being confined to owning and negotiating the best terms for the sale of their labor power,[15] they urge workers to take control of the circumstances under which they transform that ability to work into actual labor. Hence the slogan of a large temporary employment agency in France: "'Soyez propriétaire de votre travail.'"[16]

This book argues that the socioeconomic theory of self-employment is rooted in a misconceptualization and that the formulation of public policy toward the self-employed is misguided and dysfunctional. The book begins with an analysis of the methodological basis of the most important mode of enumerating the self-employed, which reveals defects so fundamental as to render the commonly used data virtually worthless. In this connection sociologists and economists are taken to task for their penchant to count before knowing what it is they are studying (see chapter 2). Chapter 3 develops a class-rooted analysis of self-employment focusing on the latter's hybrid character, which makes it, at least as an ideal type, extraterritorial to capitalist production. The question of economic and personal independence--the holy grail of self-employment--forms a crucial link in this discussion. Chapter 4 is devoted to several currently prominent substantive aspects of the self-employed: where they work, how much they earn, and what inferences can be drawn from the dramatic rise in the number or share of self-employed women. In chapter 5 the relationship between self-employment and unemployment and the legislative and judicial revaluation it is undergoing are examined. Underlying this change is an appreciation of the self-employed as tendentially overlapping with the dependent employed population. Contrary to the claims of some researchers that the official statistical account of self-employment is flawed because it ignores those who have incorporated (themselves), an examination of tax, pension, and corporation law in chapter 6 explains why this approach cannot save the thesis of a renaissance of the self-employed. The last chapter offers a political-economic explanation of the need to dismember the category of the self-employed and to redistribute its constituent parts to the capitalist and working classes, where they objectively--and increasingly subjectively--belong.

NOTES

1. BERNARD MALAMUD, THE ASSISTANT 30 (n.d. [1957]).

2. Daniel Fischel, *Labor Markets and Labor Law Compared with Capital Markets and Corporate Law*, 51 U. CHI. L. REV. 1061, 1066 (1984).

3. The locus classicus of the discussion of alienated labor and self-alienated workers in capitalist societies is still Karl Marx, *Ökonomisch-philosophische Manuskripte (Erste Wiedergabe)*, in I:2 KARL MARX [&] FRIEDRICH ENGELS, GESAMTAUSGABE (MEGA) 187, 234-47 (1982 [1844]). For a brief discussion

of the results of an empirical study of alienation among farmers in the process of becoming subordinated to agribusiness capital, see William Heffernan, *Social Dimensions of Agricultural Structures in the United States*, 12 SOCIOLOGIA RURALIS 481, 487-88 (1972). Self-employment should not be confused with so-called autonomous activities standing outside the sphere of commodities and exchange, which have figured prominently in Gorz's recent work. *See, e.g.,* André Gorz, *Allocation universelle: version de droite et version de gauche*, 41 LA REVUE NOUVELLE 419, 424-26 (1985); ANDRÉ GORZ, MÉTAMORPHOSES DU TRAVAIL (1988).

4. *But see* Mervyn Rothstein, *From Cartoons to a Play About Racism*, N.Y. Times, Aug. 17, 1991, at 11, col. 1: "'I had this boss who was an alcoholic jerk...and he was so bothersome and so difficult to be around that I quit and swore I was never going to work for anybody else again; I was going to be self-employed'" (quoting Lynda Barry).

5. That these terms--instead of the drab past participle *self-employed*--have never caught on, may have to do with embarrassment at the starkness of the paradox that they express.

6. For an international overview, see THOMAS HAGELSTANGE, DIE ENTWICKLUNG VON KLASSENSTRUKTUREN IN DER EG AND IN NORDAMERIKA (1987).

7. Perhaps the best example is an older effort by STANLEY LEBERGOTT, MANPOWER IN ECONOMIC GROWTH: THE AMERICAN RECORD SINCE 1800, at 364-84 (1964), who devotes twenty pages to his statistical methodology without ever discussing what defines the self-employed--other than "being one's own boss...sitting under one's own fig tree and having no one to say him nay." *Id.* at 30. Within a much briefer quantitative compass, even Marxist sociologists unthinkingly identify the self-employed with the "independent petty bourgeoisie." *See, e.g.,* ALBERT SZYMANSKI, CLASS STRUCTURE: A CRITICAL PERSPECTIVE 164-66 (1983). *See also* JOACHIM BISCHOFF ET AL., JENSEITS DER KLASSEN? GESELLSCHAFT UND STAAT IM SPÄTKAPITALISMUS 81-84 (1982) (uncritical acceptance of West German census data on *Selbständige*). The first scholarly monograph on the self-employed to appear in the United States in thirty years, while vaguely aware of these fundamental socioeconomic and conceptual problems, also perpetuates this hypostatizing tradition. ROBERT L. ARONSON, SELF-EMPLOYMENT: A LABOR MARKET PERSPECTIVE 2 (1991) ("ambiguity in the definition of self-employment itself"). For further critique, see Marc Linder, Book Review, 98 AM. J. SOC. ___ (1992).

8. As ARONSON, SELF-EMPLOYMENT at 26, observes, whereas the earlier literature stressed the irrationality of self-employment, those writing in the 1980s, impressed by the apparent increase in self-employment and thus viewing it in the most favorable light, have reached for a rational motivation and located it in nonpecuniary advantages such as control and time flexibility, which Aronson characterizes as exercises in circularity.

9. On the evolution of the temporary employment regime, see Mack Moore, *The Temporary Help Service Industry: Historical Development, Operation, and Scope*, 18 INDUS. & LAB. REL. REV. 554 (1965).

10. *See* Jean-Jacques Dupeyroux, *Et maintenant?* DROIT SOCIAL, July-Aug. 1981, at 486; Efrén Córdova, *From Full-time Wage Employment to Atypical Employment: A Major Shift in the Evolution of Labour Relations?* 125 INT'L LAB. REV. 641 (1986); Robert Moberley, *Temporary, Part-Time, and Other Atypical Employment Relationships in the United States*, 38 LAB. L.J. 689 (1987).

11. *See* U.S. GENERAL ACCOUNTING OFFICE, WORKERS AT RISK: INCREASED NUMBERS IN CONTINGENT EMPLOYMENT, LACK INSURANCE, OTHER BENEFITS (HRD-91-56, Mar. 1991); *Rising Use of Part-Time and Temporary Workers: Who Benefits and Who Loses? Hearing Before a Subcomm. of the House Comm. on Gov't Operations*, 100th Cong., 2d Sess. 137-38 (1988) (statement of R. Dillon).

12. *See id.* at 37 (statement of A. Freedman); RICHARD BELOUS, THE CONTINGENT ECONOMY: THE GROWTH OF THE TEMPORARY, PART-TIME AND SUBCONTRACTED WORKFORCE 31 (1989); Peter Kilborn, *Part-Time Hirings Bring Deep Change in U.S. Workplaces*, N.Y. Times, June 17, 1991, at A1, col. 6; Anthony Millican, *IRS Auditing Harbor Trucking Firms Over Status of Drivers*, L.A. Times, Aug. 30, 1991, at B3, col. 3 (NEXIS).

13. *Rising Use of Part-Time and Temporary Workers* at 20 (statement of Janet Norwood, Comm'r, U.S. Bureau of Labor Statistics). *See also* BNA PENSIONS & BENEFITS DAILY, Aug. 28, 1991 (NEXIS) (laid-off employees returning as '"consultants'" without benefits).

14. 1 KARL MARX, DAS KAPITAL, *republished in* II:5 KARL MARX [&] FRIEDRICH ENGELS, GESAMTAUSGABE (MEGA) 128 (1983 [1867]). Of "Bentham," that is, egotism, they may not have tired.

15. Although often regarded as Marxist jargon, the term *labor power* (*Arbeitskraft* or *Arbeitsvermögen*) was commonly used in legal and economic discourse in Germany in the nineteenth century. *See, e.g.*, 1 Annalen des Königl. Sächs. Oberappellationsgerichts, No. 44, 1 Apr. 1859, at 130, 132 (1860) ("Bei eintretender Entlassung und Vorenthaltung der Gegenleistung wird derselbe in der Regel genöthigt sein, seine Zeit und Arbeitskraft zu anderweitigem Erwerbe zu benutzen"). For earlier use in the same sense without a source, see 1 JACOB GRIMM & WILHELM GRIMM, DEUTSCHES WÖRTERBUCH 543 col. 2 (1854). When writing in English, Marx used the term *labouring power*. *See* Karl Marx, VALUE, PRICE AND PROFIT, in II:4, text. pt. 1 KARL MARX [&] FRIEDRICH ENGELS, GESAMTAUSGABE (MEGA) 383, 411 (1988 [1865]).

16. Dupeyroux, *Et maintenant?* at 486.

2

Methodology

Certainly there would be some advantage in clarity deriving from greater emphasis on the distinction between the self-employed and wage and salary workers. ... Occasionally, even persons quite familiar with labor force concepts seem to forget what they include.[1]

Count First and Ask Questions Later--
or, No Enumeration without Cogitation?

It is well-known that the first theoretical activity of Understanding, which still wavers halfway between sensuousness and thinking, is *counting*. Counting is the first free theoretical act of Understanding of the *child*.[2]

Enumeration demands *kinds* of things or people to count. Counting is hungry for categories. ... What could be more inevitable than the class struggle about which Marx hectored us. Yet the social classes are not something into which a society is intrinsically sorted. On the contrary, it is the early nineteenth-century counting-bureaucracies that designed the class structure in terms of which we view society. [B]ureaucrats...designed easily countable classifications into which everybody had to fall--and thenceforth did.[3]

Quantitative studies of self-employment are a case study in unself-conscious "concept-laden perception."[4] Although at times conceding that "[t]he meaning and measurement of self-employment is itself something of an enigma,"[5] the empirical literature neglects to conceptualize that puzzle.[6] Its procedures reveal no effort that even remotely resembles decoding. To the extent that the surveys generating the 'raw' data rest on the same unreflective methodology underlying the explanatory loop into which the refined numbers are fed back, the system becomes immune to disconfirmation.

To be sure, self-employment hardly represents the first instance of social scientists' counting a group that they have not bothered to define or to conceptualize. Yet empirical research founded on the assumption that everyone knows a self-employed person on sight[7] or through introspection carries with it special methodological and substantive perils. These derive from the fact that self-employment itself belongs to that class of social forms of "pseudo-objectivity (and thus pseudo-legitimacy) that agents unwittingly impose on their social relations and whose proper characterization requires a special sort of critical theory."[8] The appearance of a self-employing and self-exploiting worker-capitalist is both incongruous and reflective of reality--a false reality that is necessarily generated by the reification arising from the need to process the anomaly of the ownership and control of the means of production by the person working on them in a society in which the two are categorically assigned to two different classes.[9] The resulting "economic mysticism"[10] is both reality and a distortion of reality. Although it may be true that "[a] man who can explain mirages does not thereby cease to see them,"[11] social scientists have not even conceived of self-employment as requiring social theorizing.

Isolated voices of protest have alerted colleagues to the problematical character of this cavalier empirical methodology--if not of the concept of self-employment itself. Thus, one social scientist, then in the employ of the British Department of Employment, argued that statistics on self-employment "are not designed to serve anyone's purposes, with the self-employed category being merely the 'residual' group left over once employees were identified. [T]hey don't serve lawyers' interest in the master-servant dichotomy."[12]

Economists and sociologists interested in entrepreneurial activity and social stratification, respectively (that is, investment and ownership of the means of production), are said to be similarly ill served.[13] Hoping to overcome this tradition, this social scientist proposes as empirically operationalizable desiderata both a "refined classification of different types of self-employment" on a continuum from nominal self-employment to the entrepreneurial small business owner-manager and a reliable rule of thumb to distinguish employees, nominally self-employed labor-only subcontractors, and one-person businesses.[14]

An empiricist has attacked the assumed "identity between entrepreneurship and self-employment" because the two "are conceptually distinct and have been muddied by the lack of measures that would distinguish those who innovate from those offering labor directly rather than through an intermediary, such as an employer."[15] He, too, pleads "for empirical research to distinguish...those who simply wish to sell their labor on the best terms under the circumstances"[16]--presumably in order to eliminate them from the ranks of the self-employed.

Ironically, by way of contrast, Marxist sociologists who trivialize the conceptual defects as mere taxonomic "slippages between concepts and measurements" while conceding the need "to investigate such internal differentiation and proletarianization tendencies"[17] seem prepared to proceed with theoretical elaboration based on thoughtless enumeration. At such a juncture in the research process, it is therefore appropriate to open the black box in order to observe the chaos that prevails at the point of data collection.

The Origin of the Term *Self-Employed*

There is now a regular association of *employment* with *work*. For most people of working age, it is widely believed, to be not employed is to be not working. ... So prepotent is this idea that even those people who work on their own account, as independent craftsmen, consultant professionals, freelances, contractors, owner-occupier farmers and so on, are said to be *self-employed*. A legal

Farewell to the Self-Employed

fiction, of an employer who employs himself, is invented to conform to the predominant idea that all work is employment.[18]

If the woman on the street or the man on the Clapham omnibus were asked today to state spontaneously what *self-employed* means, the answer might be something to the effect: 'Working on your own, working for yourself.' Eliciting exactly what that means and how it differs from 'working for someone else,' would doubtless require an extended dialogue. Tracing the rise and diffusion of such terms and their incorporation into a community's lexicon may shed light on the timing, frequency, intensity, and spread of, and general familiarity with, the underlying phenomena. Socioeconomic conceptualizations such as *employment* and *self-employment*, as Marx and Raymond Williams have explained, both reflect and distort reality. Although the American *self-employment* captures the twofold character of the ideology more poignantly[19] than the preferred English term, *working on own account*,[20] it is the meaning attached to the term[21] rather than the precise lexical identification that is at issue.[22] Lexicographers, who missed the dating of the printed use of the word by at least three decades, perversely did not introduce "self-employed" until the group's decline was established and its fall forecast.[23] Yet there was a logic to this belated recognition: by delaying acceptance until the core of the independent workers was hollowed out by the consolidation of an economy dominated by oligopolistic capitals,[24] dictionaries unwittingly underscored the increasingly ideological motif of "self-employment."

Internationally, the great national census bureaucracies could not generate convergence toward a uniform terminology until they evinced an interest in the underlying phenomenon of socioeconomic class.[25] This they did not do until the end of the nineteenth century,[26] when the national governments in the three leading European capitalist countries, Germany (in 1882), England (in 1891),[27] and France (in 1896), introduced a tripartite class taxonomy--employer, employee, and "worker on own account" (*Selbständige* or *travailleurs isolés*)[28] into their censuses of population.[29] In the United States, the Bureau of the Census

(BOC) did not begin collecting usable data on class until 1940, in spite of the fact that as early as 1869, the economist Francis Walker, who was to become the superintendent of the census the next year, published an article in the popular press calling for such an enumeration:

> It is undoubtedly very interesting and amusing for gentlemen of leisure, to take down the ponderous volumes of the census, and find that there were ten submarine divers in the United States in 1860, and five chiropodists.... But it is of a great deal more consequence that the statesman and the economist be able to ascertain...how many...are working for themselves, and sharing in the profits of business, and how many are dependent upon stipulated wages. The greatest social and industrial questions of the day connect themselves with this.[30]

The U.S. Census of Population did not begin collecting data on those "Working on Own account" until 1910,[31] which, however, because of their poor quality, were never published.[32] In its "Instructions to Enumerators" that year, the BOC also delineated the group residually:

> Persons who have a gainful occupation and are neither employers nor employees are considered working on their own account. They are the independent workers. They neither pay nor receive salaries or regular wages. Examples of this class are: Farmers and owners of small establishments who do not employ helpers; professional men who work for *fees* and employ no helpers; and, generally speaking, hucksters, peddlers, newsboys, bootblacks, etc., although it not infrequently happens that persons in these pursuits are employed by others and are working for wages, and in such case should, of course, be returned as employees.[33]

The precise class focus on those whom sociologists have taken to calling the "pure petty bourgeois"[34] is remarkable. It avoids the trap of labeling as self-employed small (or even large) employers, whose livelihoods depend on the exploitation of others' labor. The emphasis on the apartness or isolation from the relationship of wage labor captures more of the essence of the socioeconomic position occupied by such persons than does the later--and ideologically more freighted--term *self-employed*. Yet its limitations become evident in the light of the BOC's insistence on a formalistic, spatially defined class framework: "[A] washerwoman or laundress who works out by the day is an *employee*, but a washerwoman or laundress who takes in washing is either *working on own account*, or, it may be, an *employer*."[35]

Although the censuses of population asked questions concerning class of worker from 1910 forward, the BOC did not publish the data until 1940.[36] The BOC had originally planned to publish separate data for employers and "own-account workers...who employed no helpers." Ultimately, however, it combined the two categories because enumerators had "failed to distinguish properly between them."[37]

The first usage of *self-employment*, according to the *Oxford English Dictionary* (OED), dates back to 1745, but the expression was not used in its current and relevant sense.[38] The OED lists as the first use of *self-employed* a question propounded by a member of Parliament in 1947 as to "why persons who would qualify otherwise for the extra cheese ration are ineligible if they are self-employed."[39] When Noah Webster published his *A Dictionary of the English Language* in 1828, he did not include an entry. Neither did the twelve-volume *The Century Dictionary and Cyclopedia* of 1911.[40] Two decades later, the second edition of *Webster's New International Dictionary of the English Language*[41] finally listed (without definition) the currently unusual "self-employer"[42] along with "self-employment."[43] By the 1960s, *Webster's Third New International Dictionary of the English Language* at last included "self-employed"[44] as "earning income directly from one's own business, trade, or profession rather than as a specified salary or wages from an employer."[45] Why other large dictionaries continued to omit the word[46] is unclear since it met the traditional criteria for inclusion.[47] By the 1970s, *The Random House Dictionary of the English Language* was tracing "self-employed" to the years 1945-50.[48] A decade later, *Webster's Ninth New Collegiate Dictionary* narrowed the origin to 1946.[49] Although unidentified,[50] that source turned out to be a brief reference in the *New Republic* to benefits to which "self-employed veterans" were entitled.[51]

Several early uses,[52] antedating those traced by lexicographers, served to define the universe of covered workers under ameliorist social legislation. The tentative draft of a health insurance act submitted by the American Association for Labor Legislation in 1916 included a provision for voluntary insurance of "[s]elf-employed persons whose earnings do not exceed $100 a month on average."[53] When California enacted its workers' compensation statute in 1917, it treated as employees working members of partnerships who received wages irrespective of profits, and then established a procedure to resolve insurance issues concerning "self-employing persons."[54] The first state unemployment compensation statute in the United States, enacted in Wisconsin in 1932, in an apparent attempt to mark off those whose attachment to the wage-earning labor force made it reasonable to expect their employers "to build up a limited reserve for unemployment,"[55] deemed ineligible for benefits any employee "[i]f he is ordinarily self-employed, but has been temporarily (for not more than five months) employed in an employment subject to this chapter and can, at the termination of such temporary employment, reasonably return to this self-employment."[56]

A landmark study in the 1920s by the National Bureau of Economic Research (NBER) of the growth of unions was confronted with an embarrassing lack of data when, in seeking to calculate the degree of organization, it discovered the absence of an appropriate denominator encompassing only wage earners. Other scholars sifting through the data of the censuses of 1900 and 1910 had applied various criteria to crystallize out what they called "independent" workers (such as farmers, entrepreneurs, and professionals).[57] Later, economists and statisticians began reserving the term "independent workers" for entrepreneurs without employees.[58] The NBER study, carrying on the tradition of making "arbitrary decisions," segregated out employers and "self-employed."[59]

A second, even more urgent, need for data on the self-employed arose in connection with the enactment of social security legislation in 1935.[60] Because old-age benefit payments were keyed to wages for "employment" performed "by an employee for an employer,"[61] those who fell into neither group had to be subtracted from the estimated number of covered workers.[62] The Committee on Social Security of the Social Science Research Council commissioned Wladimir Woytinksy to work up such data. Woytinksy, who in the 1920s had compiled a massive international comparative statistical work from a socialist class perspective,[63] pointed to the need to collect data "on the shiftings of workers from wage or salaried work, i.e. from *dependent* work, to proprietary or *independent* pursuits."[64] Like his predecessors, Woytinsky was unable to disentangle within the "independent workers" employers on the one hand and those "working on their own account without employees," that is, "self-employed persons,"[65] on the other.

Continued dissatisfaction with the lack of census data on "the so-called self-employed,"[66] especially in connection with efforts during the Great Depression to create macroeconomic national accounts that lent themselves to Keynesian policies to overcome mass unemployment,[67] led the BOC to initiate monthly household surveys in 1940 that finally collected data on "the self-employed class."[68] The popularization of the expression *self-employed* in the immediate post-World War II period may have been associated with the inception of BOC's Current Population Survey (CPS) in 1947[69] and especially with the so-called GI Bill of Rights. That statute was well known for providing loan guarantees to veterans for investments in businesses.[70] More remarkably, the act conferred readjustment allowances on unemployed and underemployed self-employed veterans of World War II. Thus, any veteran who was "self-employed for profit in an independent establishment, trade, business, profession or other vocation" and showed net monthly earnings of less than $100 when "fully engaged in such self-employment," was entitled to receive a subsidy up to $100 per month.[71] In explaining this provision, which was absent from the Senate bill, the House report justified the "equality" of treatment as between employees and "persons not employed by any one other than themselves" by reference to "pursuits which require a period of waiting before any considerable returns may be expected."[72] Undercutting all objections to inclusion of the self-employed in the unemployment insurance system before[73] and since, Congress found that the administrative difficulties could be overcome.[74]

What is most remarkable about this congressionally mandated sponsorship of the vocabulary and substance of self-employment[75] is that it firmly operated with the notion of the self-employed as a dependent class of workers subject to the same vicissitudes of a dynamic postwar economy[76] and as deserving of state intervention as employees.[77] That this subversive sense did not catch on in popular rhetoric may be explained by the contemporaneous campaign on the right to prevent the self-employed from being "scoop[ed]...into the voracious maw of Social Security"[78] and to prohibit unions from "forcing or requiring any...self-employed person to join any labor or employer organization."[79]

The BOC retained the "working on own account" language through the 1940 census,[80] modifying it to "In OWN Business" in 1950.[81] The gradualness of the linguistic transition to *self-employment* is shown by the curious fact that the data collection (input) and result (output) terms were disjointed in 1950: while the schedule did not ask respondents whether they were "self-employed" but rather whether they were "in OWN business," the answers were published as referring to "Self-employed workers."[82] Whether this terminological conflation served to identify in the public mind operating a business with "employing" oneself is unclear. In any event, not until the 1960 census were respondents themselves directly asked whether they were "self-employed in own business, professional practice or farm."[83] By the time of the following censuses, *self-employed* finally achieved the status of the hegemonic public term.[84]

What You See Is What You Conceived:
The Current Population Survey

> There is a sense in which many of the facts presented by the
> bureaucracies did not even exist ahead of time. Categories had to
> be invented into which people could conveniently fall in order to
> be counted.[85]

> [F]acts do not owe their origin to an act of authorship. [T]he first
> person to find and report a particular fact has not created the fact;
> he or she has merely discovered its existence. ... Census-takers, for
> example, do not "create" the population figures that emerge from
> their efforts; in a sense, they copy these figures from the world
> around them.[86]

Since virtually all analyses of self-employment are based
on the data generated by the CPS, it is crucial to examine
the specific question that is supposed to elicit that
information.   When the BOC gathers data on the self-
employed, it does so from the perspective of class--that is,
"class of worker."[87] How similar is the BOC approach to
those prevailing in academic sociological circles? According
to two influential Marxist sociologists, "[a] self-employed
person...earns an income at least in part through his or her
own labor but not by selling his or her labor power to an
employer for a wage."[88] One problem in operationalizing this
class-based definition is that although the BOC defines
"[s]elf-employed persons" as "those who work for profit or
fees in their own business, profession or trade, or operate a
farm,"[89] it does not screen responses to sort out active
owner-managers from the passive drawers of profit. In fact,
apart from obvious and gross inconsistencies such as a self-
identified government employee's responding that he is self-
employed, neither the interviewer on the spot nor the BOC
after the fact probes into or challenges respondents' replies
to the question relating to "class of worker."
      The question as to class of worker that is put to
approximately 70,000 households monthly[90] is the last part of
a five-part question labeled: "23. DESCRIPTION OF JOB
OR BUSINESS."[91] The first part of the question that the
interviewer propounds to the respondent[92] reads: "23A. For

whom did...work? *(Name of company, business, organization or other employer.)*"[93] Following three further parts directed at the nature of the business or industry, the kind of work, and the activities or duties of the job, the interviewer asks the class-of-worker question:

23E. Was this person

An employee of a PRIVATE Co, bus., or individual for wages, salary or comm[ission].

A FEDERAL government employee

A STATE government employee

A LOCAL government employee

Self-empl. in OWN bus., prof. practice, or farm

Is the business incorporated? {Yes
{No

Working WITHOUT PAY in fam. bus. or farm[94]

Although these questions appear straightforward enough, the empirical world is full of surprises and oddities, so the BOC equips its fieldworkers with a thick manual, a number of pages of which are devoted to the question at hand, to help them deal with the unusual and unexpected. But before it proceeds to the convolutions of reality, the *Interviewer's Manual* seeks to make the interviewer's work easier by means of the following instruction:

Item 23E can frequently be filled from information already given for items 23A-D. However, if there is any doubt at all, ask the necessary questions to ascertain the facts. Utilize the "Who Pays" criteria, that is, record the class of worker category according to who pays the person's wages or salary. For persons paid by check, the employer's name will usually be entered on the check.[95]

The instruction seems to suggest that the preferred or presumptive or at least a common method of identifying the self-employed is not based on self-reporting at all; instead, interviewers are encouraged to use their powers of deduction. Precisely how an interviewer could conclude that a respondent is self-employed based on the name and kind of business, kind of work, and nature of job is unclear--unless the respondent specifically stated in answer to question 23A that she worked for "herself."[96] It is instructive to examine the possible results of a response that she worked as a cosmetologist at a business called The Herr Doctor.

First, the BOC defines "business" very generously:

> A business exists when one or more of the following conditions is met:
>
> • Machinery or equipment of substantial value in which the person has invested capital is used by him/her in conducting the business. Hand rakes, manual lawnmowers, hand shears, etc., would not meet the criterion of substantial value; however, if a business or service is publicly advertised...consider it a business even if the invested capital is not of substantial value.
>
> • An office, store, or other place of business is maintained.
>
> • There is some advertisement of the business or profession by:
>
>> --listing it in the classified section of the telephone book
>>
>> --displaying a sign
>>
>> --distributing cards or leaflets or otherwise publicizing that a particular kind of work or service is being offered to the general public.[97]

Within this capacious framework, it comes as no surprise that even if he or she is a sixteen-year-old full-time school child working only a few hours per week, "a paperboy/girl has his/her own business"[98] and will be reported as a full-fledged self-employed person--provided that the publisher imposes the risk of nonpayment (by the subscriber) on the child.[99]

Given this extensive latitude, no inference could logically be drawn as to whether the cosmetologist (1) owned the business and worked there alone or with employees, (2) really worked there at all or merely lived on the profits created by the employees, (3) was an employee of the business, or (4) 'rented a chair' there, being treated by the owner as self-employed regardless of how she viewed herself.[100] The "'Who Pays'" criterion, finally, appears calculated not only to befog the distinction between employees and self-employees but also to mislead as to which of two entities might be the real employer of an uncontroverted employee.[101]

After this interlude, the *Manual* continues with "Cautions regarding class-of-worker entries":

> Report employees of a corporation as employees of a <u>private</u> employer.... Do <u>not</u> report corporation employees as owning their own business even though they may own part or all of the stock of the incorporated business. If a respondent says that a person is self-employed, and you find that the business is incorporated, mark "I" for the "Is the business incorporated?" circle.[102]

A literal reading of this instruction suggests that no one would ever be classified as an incorporated self-employed unless the respondent intoned the talismanic word, *self-employed*. The intent of this instruction may have been to prevent the classification of people such as the president of General Motors (and of smaller corporations) as self-employed,[103] as well as to avoid involving the interviewers in complicated issues of corporation and securities law. Yet even on its face, it is a singularly inept and perverse method of identifying the incorporated self-employed.[104]

The directive issued as to partners is similarly puzzling. First, a blanket rule is set forth that "two or more persons who operate a business in partnership should be reported as self-employed in own business."[105] Thus, even if the respondent is one among hundreds of partners in a rigidly hierarchically managed firm, she would automatically be listed as self-employed without having to utter the magic word. Then the interviewer is required to ask whether the business is incorporated.[106] How the interviewer would know an 'incorporated partnership' when she saw one, the *Manual* does not explain.

The instructions relating to several specific occupations also raise questions as to the meaningfulness of the survey results. That housecleaners, launderers, cooks, cleaning persons, and baby-sitters employed in other people's households are peremptorily excluded from the class of self-employed[107] is a surprising stroke of substantive economic realism.[108] Yet by virtue of answering "herself" to question 23A, a respondent could evade this restriction--and join the tens of thousands of self-employed reported for these occupations. Another substantive intervention involves the directive to record as self-employed "persons who own a sales franchise and are responsible for their own merchandise and personnel."[109] Because the *Manual* does not spell out what such responsibility entails, it is difficult to imagine either that the interviewer knows on her own or that nationally uniform reporting can result. In any event, the directive suggests that sales franchisees may be recorded as self-employed without their direct self-identification or any probing into the details of their relationship with the franchiser.

Finally, the *Manual* expressly instructs the interviewers that "[p]eople who sell Avon and Tupperware products...because they are not considered employees of those companies...are self-employed."[110] The elusive passive voice of the directive appears to suggest that the sellers are not considered employees *by those companies*. By this substantive intervention the Bureau of Labor Statistics (BLS) and BOC are, without justification, helping to consolidate the public relations gains secured by these companies in their efforts to evade payment of employment taxes for their low paid workers.[111] This hands-off attitude toward self-identification stands in sharp contrast to an instruction to enumerators at the 1910 Census of Population. Then even lawyers and doctors were excluded from the "employee" category only if they "in their work, are not subject to the control and direction of those whom they serve."[112]

Against the background of all these defects, it is hardly surprising that when questions were raised as to whether the CPS questionnaire was adequately designed to elicit accurate responses to the class-of-worker questions, one of the managers of the CPS conceded that the question might be conceptually flawed.[113]

NOTES

1. JOSEPH PHILLIPS, THE SELF-EMPLOYED IN THE UNITED STATES 8 (1962).

2. Karl Marx, *Die Verhandlungen des 6. rheinischen Landtags. Erster Artikel: Debatten über Preßfreiheit und Publikation der Landständischen Verhandlungen*, Rheinische Zeitung, May 5, 1842, Beiblatt, at 1, col. 1; *reprinted in* I:1 KARL MARX [&] FRIEDRICH ENGELS, GESAMTAUSGABE (MEGA) 121, 122 (1975).

3. Ian Hacking, *Biopower and the Avalanche of Printed Numbers*, 5 HUMANITIES IN SOCIETY 279, 280 (1982).

4. HAROLD BROWN, PERCEPTION, THEORY AND COMMITMENT: THE NEW PHILOSOPHY OF SCIENCE 85 (1979 [1977]).

5. ARONSON, SELF-EMPLOYMENT at xi.

6. Although Aronson completes this sentence with the phrase, "as readers of this study will discover," he never explores the subject--notwithstanding references to "[q]uestions about the degree of independence of some individuals reported...as self-employed." *Id*. at 140.

7. Unjustifiably so since thirty-eight per cent of employers from any one of which workers received all their income (amounting to at least $10,000 reported on Form 1099-MISC) misclassified their workers as independent contractors. *See* U.S. GENERAL ACCOUNTING OFFICE, TAX ADMINISTRATION: INFORMATION RETURNS CAN BE USED TO IDENTIFY EMPLOYERS WHO MISCLASSIFY WORKERS 4-5 (GGD-89-107, Sept. 25, 1989). In light of the significant cost reductions accruing to employers who succeed in converting their employees into self-employees, it is plausible that many such employers know full well that their workers are not self-employed. A simpler strategy still is not to report such transactions at all. *See idem*, TAX ADMINISTRATION: MISSING INDEPENDENT CONTRACTORS' INFORMATION RETURNS NOT ALWAYS DETECTED (GGD-89-110, Sept. 1989).

8. Julius Sensat, Reification as Dependence on Extrinsic Information 3 (unpub. MS, 1991).

9. *See infra* ch. 3.

10. Julius Sensat, *Methodological Individualism and Marxism*, 4 ECON. & PHIL. 189, 203-207 (1988).

11. G. Cohen, *Karl Marx and the Withering Away of Social Science*, in MARX, JUSTICE, AND HISTORY 288, 294 (Marshall Cohen et al. ed. 1980 [1972]).

12. Catherine Hakim, *Self-Employment in Britain: Recent Trends and Current Issues:* 2 WORK, EMPLOYMENT & SOCIETY 421, 424 (1988).

13. *Id.*

14. *Id.* at 445.

15. ARONSON, SELF-EMPLOYMENT at 21 n.3.

16. *Id.* at 28.

17. George Steinmetz & Erik Wright, *Reply to Linder and Houghton*, 96 AM. J. SOC. 736, 738, 739 (1990).

18. RAYMOND WILLIAMS, THE YEAR 2000, at 85 (1983).

19. As do the German *Arbeitgeber* and *Arbeitnehmer* vis-à-vis *employer* and *employee*. For positive valuation of the German terms as opposed to *capital* and *labor*, see ARTHUR PERRY, PRINCIPLES OF POLITICAL ECONOMY 183 (1891).

20. Even as late as World War II, Beveridge, in his report that crucially contributed to the expansion of the social insurance system in Britain under the Labour government, used the terms "persons working on their own account" and "independent workers" rather than *self-employed*. WILLIAM BEVERIDGE, SOCIAL INSURANCE AND ALLIED SERVICES 126, 53 (Cmd. 6404, 1942).   The expression was also current in the United States in the nineteenth century: "[T]he laboring class here...have a small capital, which, if they saw fit, they might employ in establishing themselves in business on their own account...thus ceasing to work for Wages." FRANCIS BOWEN, AMERICAN POLITICAL ECONOMY 179-80 (1969 [1870]). French economists also used it: "[L]es travailleurs industriels se divisent en deux classes, celle de *entrepreneurs* qui travaillent pour leur propre compte, et celle de ouvriers qui louent leur travail aux entrepreneurs." 1 HENRI STORCH, COURS D'ÉCONOMIE POLITIQUE 277 (J. B. Say ed. 1823 [1815]).   The French translation of *Das Kapital*, which, according to Marx, possessed a scientific value independent of the German original, contains a passage--without a parallel in the German--referring to "petits producteurs indépendents, travaillant à leur compte." KARL MARX, LE CAPITAL, *republished in* II:7 KARL MARX [&] FRIEDRICH ENGELS, GESAMTAUSGABE (MEGA) 678 (1989 [1875]).

21. The only major American dictionary to capture even part of the socioeconomic essence of "self-employed" defines it as "[e]arning and directing one's own livelihood, working for oneself, rather than an employer." AMERICAN HERITAGE DICTIONARY OF THE ENGLISH LANGUAGE 1176 (1969).   One modern British dictionary defines "self-employed" with the emphasis on independence: "working independently in one's own business." CHAMBERS 20TH CENTURY DICTIONARY 1177 (1987).

22. On the evolution of the underlying concept in economic theory before the use of the term *self-employment*, see *infra* ch. 3.

23. *See* LEWIS COREY, THE CRISIS OF THE MIDDLE CLASS 112-50 (1935); SUMNER SLICHTER, THE CHALLENGE OF INDUSTRIAL RELATIONS: TRADE UNIONS, MANAGEMENT, AND THE PUBLIC INTEREST 1 (1947); FRANÇOISE BOURIEZ-GREGG, LES CLASSES SOCIALES AUX ÉTATS-UNIS 28-29 (1954); JOSEPH PHILLIPS, THE SELF-EMPLOYED IN THE UNITED STATES 1, 3 (1962).

24. On the ideology of independence in the nineteenth century, see DANIEL RODGERS, THE WORK ETHIC IN INDUSTRIAL AMERICA, 1850-1920, at 30-43 (1978).

25. IAN HACKING, THE TAMING OF CHANCE 3 (1990), fails to reflect on the possibility that bureaucrats became interested in collecting data on classes because the latter's objective existence had turned into a subjective problem for the state or that classes became self-conscious without the prior intercession of national census bureaus: "Marx read the minutiae of official statistics.... One can ask: who had more effect on class consciousness, Marx or the authors of the official reports which created the classification into which people came to recognize themselves?" As an example of how "counting...creates new ways for people to be," Hacking argues that after factory inspectors had finished their reports, "the owner had a clear set of concepts about how to employ workers according to the ways in which he was obliged to classify them." Ian Hacking, *Making Up People*, RECONSTRUCTING INDIVIDUALISM: AUTONOMY, INDIVIDUALISTS, AND THE SELF IN WESTERN THOUGHT, 222, 223 (T. Heller ed. 1986). At one point, however, Hacking does differentiate himself from the static nominalist (such as Hobbes), who "thinks that all categories, classes, and taxonomies are given by human beings rather than by nature and that these categories are essentially fixed throughout the several eras of humankind." Instead he aligns himself with a more plausible "dynamic nominalism," which claims "not that there was a kind of person who came increasingly to be recognized by bureaucrats or by students of human nature but rather that a kind of person came into being at the same time as the kind itself was being invented. In some cases...our classification and our classes conspire to emerge hand in hand, each egging the other on." *Id*. at 228. He envisions two vectors: (1) "labeling from above, from a community of experts who create a 'reality' that some people make their own" and (2) "autonomous behavior of the person so labeled, which presses from below, creating a reality every expert must face." *Id*. at 234. As a result, "numerous kinds of human beings and human acts come into being hand in hand with our invention of the categories labeling them." *Id*. at 236.

26. In 1831, the British census for the first time divided "[t]he agricultural class" into "families of Occupiers of land who employ labourers," "of Occupiers who do not employ Labourers," "and of Agricultural Labourers," "the two first of these distinctions being deemed more generally illustrative of the grade and condition of those under whose care the soil is cultivated, than the number of acres occupied, or the amount of rental." 1 ABSTRACT OF THE ANSWERS AND RETURNS: ENUMERATION ABSTRACT ix (1831). "Masters" and "Workmen" outside of agriculture were returned together. *Id*.

at xiii. Although the census of 1841 discontinued the collection of data on agricultural employers and nonemployers, the practice was resumed in 1851, at which time an "imperfect" return of masters in trades was also published: "Many persons, who have no men in their employ, work on their own account in a small way, and call themselves masters. To this head 41,732 masters in the return apparently belong; which includes, however, probably a certain number of masters who employ men, but did not state their numbers." II:I CENSUS OF GREAT BRITAIN, 1851. POPULATION TABLES: AGES, CIVIL CONDITION, OCCUPATIONS, AND BIRTH-PLACE OF THE PEOPLE lxxviii (1854). The data are at *id.*, tab. 31 at lxxvii. The imperfection of these data was emphasized at the next census as well. *See* 3 CENSUS OF ENGLAND AND WALES FOR THE YEAR 1861: GENERAL REPORT 29 (1863). For analysis of these data, see J. Banks, *The Social Structure of Nineteenth Century England as seen through the Census*, in THE CENSUS AND SOCIAL STRUCTURE: AN INTERPRETATIVE GUIDE TO NINETEENTH CENTURY CENSUSES FOR ENGLAND AND WALES 179, 186-91 (Richard Lawton ed. 1978) On partial censuses already in the 1840s in some German states, see 2 QUELLEN ZUR BEVÖLKERUNGS-, SOZIAL- UND WIRTSCHAFTSSTATISTIK DEUTSCHLANDS 1815-1875. QUELLEN ZUR BERUFS- UND GEWERBESTATISTIK DEUTSCHLANDS 1816-1875: PREUßISCHE PROVINZEN (Antje Kraus ed. 1989).

27. The relevant questions on the British census schedule (cols. 7-9) referred to "Employer," "Employed," "Neither Employer, nor Employed, but worker on own account," with the last named further defined as "independent workers or dealers." 4 CENSUS OF ENGLAND AND WALES, 1891: GENERAL REPORT 139, 36 (C.--7222, 1893). So many returns were marred by intentional and unintentional mistakes--in part "dictated by the foolish...desire of persons to magnify the importance of their occupational condition"--however, as to make the data "excessively untrustworthy." *Id.* at 36. In his otherwise interesting account of these censuses, ARTHUR MARWICK, CLASS: IMAGE AND REALITY IN BRITAIN, FRANCE AND THE USA SINCE 1930, at 59-63 (1980), missed the tripartite class taxonomy, confusing it with occupational classifications.

28. The French census category included "petits patrons travaillant seuls," "ouvriers à domicile," and "ouvriers ou des employés occupés irrégulièrement dans des maisons différentes." RÉPUBLIQUE FRANÇAISE, MINISTÈRE DU COMMERCE, DIRECTION DU TRAVAIL, SERVICE DU RECENSEMENT PROFESSIONNEL, 4 RÉSULTATS STATISTIQUES DU RECENSEMENT GÉNÉRALE DE LA POPULATION EFFECTUÉ LE 24 MARS 1901: POPULATION PRÉSENTE. RÉSULTATS GÉNÉRAUX 230 (1906). W. WOYTINSKY, DIE WELT IN ZAHLEN: DIE ARBEIT 24 n.1 (1926), notes that this category may include "proletarian elements."

29. For an analysis of the data and identification of the sources, see MARC LINDER, EUROPEAN LABOR ARISTOCRACIES: TRADE UNIONISM, THE HIERARCHY OF SKILL, AND THE STRATIFICATION OF THE MANUAL WORKING CLASS BEFORE THE FIRST WORLD WAR 68, 220, 269 n.155, 332-33 nn. 44-46 (1985).

30. Francis Walker, *American Industry in the Census*, 24 ATL. MONTHLY, 689, 700 (1869).

31. The Twelfth Census expressly refrained from distinguishing employers from employees by means of special returns on the schedule. U.S. BUREAU OF THE CENSUS, SPECIAL REPORTS: OCCUPATIONS AT THE TWELFTH CENSUS xix (1904).

32. *See* U.S. BUREAU OF THE CENSUS, THIRTEENTH CENSUS OF THE UNITED STATES TAKEN IN THE YEAR 1910, 4 POPULATION: OCCUPATIONAL STATISTICS 15 (1914).

33. U.S. BUREAU OF THE CENSUS, 200 YEARS OF U.S. CENSUS TAKING: POPULATION AND HOUSING QUESTIONS, 1790-1990, at 53 (1989).

34. *See, e.g.*, George Steinmetz & Erik Wright, *The Fall and Rise of the Petty Bourgeoisie: Changing Patterns of Self-Employment in the Postwar United States*, 94 AM. J. SOC. 973 980 n.8 (1989).

35. U.S. BUREAU OF THE CENSUS, 200 YEARS at 53. For a more coherent reconceptualization of this spatial framework, which divides the group into two sectors--the substantively independent (such as doctors and lawyers) and the isolated quasi-employees--see *infra* ch. 7.

36. *See* U.S. BUREAU OF THE CENSUS, SIXTEENTH CENSUS OF THE UNITED STATES: 1940, 2 POPULATION: CHARACTERISTICS OF THE POPULATION, part 1: UNITED STATES SUMMARY 14 (1943); ROBERT JENKINS, PROCEDURAL HISTORY OF THE 1940 CENSUS OF POPULATION AND HOUSING 63 (1985).

37. U.S. BUREAU OF THE CENSUS, SIXTEENTH CENSUS, 2 POPULATION, pt. 1 at 14.

38. 9 OXFORD ENGLISH DICTIONARY 411 (1933); 14 OXFORD ENGLISH DICTIONARY 908 (2d ed. 1989), citing JOHN MASON, SELF-KNOWLEDGE: A TREATISE 60 (1853 [1745]). An American edition reveals that Mason did not use the term in an economic or occupational sense. JOHN MASON, SELF-KNOWLEDGE: A TREATISE 76 (Philadelphia 1801).

39. 14 OED at 911 (citing 445 PARL. DEB., H.C. (5th ser.) 1441 (1947)). In fact, the previous year, the Minister of National Insurance and a member of Parliament both spoke of "self-employed persons" in connection with coverage under the national insurance bill. 419 PARL. DEB., H.C. (5th ser.) 537 (1946). From the context, they do not appear to have been coining the term.

40. SIDNEY LANDAU, DICTIONARIES: THE ART AND CRAFT OF LEXICOGRAPHY 336 (1989 [1984]), calls it "[t]he finest American historical dictionary."

41. Which, according to Landau, "takes the prize as the largest lexicon in English." *Id.* at 64.

42. Although the dictionary did not offer a citation, a slip bearing this entry is in the citation file of Merriam-Webster, which Roger Pease made available on April 22, 1991. The left-wing authors of a tripartite ("employee, self-employer, or employer") class analysis of the 1920 census of population included tenant farmers "among the self-employers, along with small shopkeepers, although the economic condition of many in both groups is worse than the condition of many wage-earners." 6 RAND SCHOOL OF SOCIAL SCIENCE, THE AMERICAN LABOR YEAR BOOK 20-21 (1925).

43. WEBSTER'S NEW INTERNATIONAL DICTIONARY OF THE ENGLISH LANGUAGE 2269 (2d unabridged ed. 1947 [1934]).

44. Lexicographers appear to have acknowledged *self-employed* only as an adjective, although it is used as a noun. Merriam-Webster has in its citation file a source from the 1930s using the word as a substantive: "Its [social security's] technique cannot be readily adjusted to the problems of insecurity confronting such large sectors of the population as the farmers, the business men, the professional classes, and the self-employed." Abraham Epstein, *The Future of Social Security: Needed Amendments in the Present Law,* NEW REPUBLIC, Jan. 27, 1937, at 373, 373. This citation was omitted from the dictionary apparently because of a corrupt entry on the slip. Telephone interview with Roger Pease, Apr. 22, 1991.

45. WEBSTER'S THIRD NEW INTERNATIONAL DICTIONARY OF THE ENGLISH LANGUAGE 2060 (unabridged ed. 1969 [1961]).

46. *See, e.g.,* AMERICAN COLLEGE DICTIONARY (1963); FUNK AND WAGNALL'S NEW STANDARD DICTIONARY OF THE ENGLISH LANGUAGE (1963); WEBSTER'S NEW TWENTIETH CENTURY DICTIONARY (unabridged ed. 1962); WEBSTER'S NEW COLLEGIATE DICTIONARY (1961). "Self-employed" finally was adopted in WEBSTER'S SEVENTH NEW COLLEGIATE DICTIONARY 784 (1965), which was based on WEBSTER'S THIRD NEW INTERNATIONAL DICTIONARY.

47. These include frequency, duration, and diversity. *See* LANDAU, DICTIONARIES at 162. A possible reason for exclusion was the apparent bias some dictionaries exhibited against overloading with *self-* words.

48. THE RANDOM HOUSE DICTIONARY OF THE ENGLISH LANGUAGE 1736 (2d ed. 1987). Although the source is not identified, the citation file is based on the OED source for 1947. Telephone interview with Charles Steinmetz (an editor of RANDOM HOUSE DICTIONARY), Apr. 22, 1991. In the first edition, this dictionary defined "self-employed" as "earning one's living directly from one's own profession or business, as a free-lance writer or artist, rather than as an employee earning salary or commission from another." THE RANDOM HOUSE DICTIONARY OF THE ENGLISH LANGUAGE 1294 (1969 [1966]). The hired-gun imagery is noteworthy, as is the focus on occupations largely occupied by self-employed.

49. WEBSTER'S NINTH NEW COLLEGIATE DICTIONARY 1066 (1983).

50. Roger Pease of Merriam-Webster identified it from the citation file. Telephone interview, Apr. 22, 1991.

51. NEW REPUBLIC, Aug. 26, 1946, at 218.

52. One of the standard economics textbooks around World War I used the term in a straightforward fashion, suggesting that it was not a neologism. *See* THOMAS CARVER, PRINCIPLES OF POLITICAL ECONOMY 216-17 (1919). The most widely used English translations of DAS KAPITAL have Marx writing (in the 1860s) of "the self-employed worker," "self-employment of producers" and "self-employed producers." 1 KARL MARX, CAPITAL 928 (Ben Fowkes tr. 1976); 2 KARL MARX, CAPITAL 34 (1974 [1967]); 3 KARL MARX, CAPITAL 600 (1974 [1967]). The originals (some of which have not been published yet) and the manuscript that Engels published after Marx's death use the expressions "selbstwirtschaftende Arbeiter," "Selbstarbeit der Produzenten," and "selbst arbeitenden Produzenten." 23 MARX-ENGELS WERKE 790 (1962); 24 MARX-ENGELS WERKE 41 (1963); 25 MARX-ENGELS WERKE 614 (1964). They can more accurately be rendered as "self-laboring," "self-labor," or "self-working producers" (or "producers who themselves work"). The English translation of the first volume, which was prepared under Engels' supervision, comes closer by translating the term as "the labourer working for himself." KARL MARX, CAPITAL: A CRITICAL ANALYSIS OF CAPITALIST PRODUCTION, in II:9 KARL MARX [AND] FRIEDRICH ENGELS, GESAMTAUSGABE (MEGA) 661 (1990 [1887]). Ironically, Marx may nevertheless have coined the term in English. In his notebooks from the 1860s he characterized absolute surplus value production as the formal subsumption of labor under capital "weil sie sich nur *formell* von den frühren Productionsweisen unterscheidet, auf deren Grundlage sie unmittelbar entspringt..., sei es nun daß darin die Producer selfemploying, sei es daß die unmittelbaren Producenten Surplusarbeit für andre liefern müssen." Karl Marx, *Das Kapital (Ökonomische Manuskripte 1863-1865)*, in II:4, text pt. 1 KARL MARX [AND] FRIEDRICH ENGELS, GESAMTAUSGABE (MEGA) 96 (1988).

53. Comm. on Soc. Insur. of the Am. Ass'n for Lab. Legis., *Health Insurance: Tentative Draft of an Act*, 6 AM. LAB. LEGIS. REV. 239, 242 (1916). The draft was printed and circulated in December 1915. *See* HACE TISHLER, SELF-RELIANCE AND SOCIAL SECURITY, 1870-1917, at 169 (1971). I. M. Rubinow, one of the leading advocates of universal sickness insurance at the time, referred, in the period immediately preceding the publication of the aforementioned draft on health insurance, not to the self-employed but to "the small independent producer or shopkeeper," such as a cobbler, tailor, or bicycle repairer, "who often is forced to remain independent because he is unable to obtain remunerative employment." I. Rubinow, *Standards of Sickness Insurance. I*, 23 J. POL. ECON. 221, 233 (1915). *See also* I. Rubinow, *Compulsory Old-Age Insurance in France*, 26 POL. SCI. Q. 500, 515 (1911) ("small independent farmers and merchants employing no hired help"). The fact that a contemporaneous massive government compilation regarding various social security systems in Europe consistently used terms like "independent persons" rather than *self-employed* to describe those excluded

from coverage suggests that the term may not have been coined before World War I. *See* 1 TWENTY-FOURTH ANNUAL REPORT OF THE COMMISSIONER OF LABOR: WORKMEN'S INSURANCE AND COMPENSATION SYSTEMS IN EUROPE 1363 (1911).

54. 1917 Cal. Stat. ch. 586, §§ 8(b) and 57(b); Employers' Liability Assur. Corp. v. Industrial Accident Comm'n, 187 Cal. 615, 203 P. 95 (1921).

55. 1931 Wis. Laws ch. 20, § 108.01(1) (Spec. Sess.).

56. *Id.* § 108.04(5)(f).

57. *See, e.g.*, Isaac Hourwich, *The Social-Economic Classes of the Population of the United States. II*, 19 J. POL. ECON. 309, 314 (1911); Carl Hookstadt, *Reclassification of the United States 1920 Occupation Census, by Industry*, MONTHLY LAB. REV., July 1923, at 1.

58. *See, e.g.*, WILLFORD KING, THE NATIONAL INCOME AND ITS PURCHASING POWER 48 (1930). DAVID MONTGOMERY, BEYOND EQUALITY: LABOR AND THE RADICAL REPUBLICANS 1862-1872, at 449 (1967), in analyzing the census of 1870, includes employers, company officials, and self-employed under the rubric "independent." By way of contrast, the British census of 1841 restricted the term "independent" to those who did not work at all but "who support themselves upon their own means without any occupation." ABSTRACT OF THE ANSWERS AND RETURNS: OCCUPATION ABSTRACT, M.DCCC.XLI, Pt. 1: ENGLAND AND WALES 8 (1844).

59. LEO WOLMAN, THE GROWTH OF AMERICAN TRADE UNIONS 1880-1923, at 75 (1924). The two were lumped together since the census offered no way to separate them. Since Wolman uses "self-employed" in a very unself-conscious manner, it seems unlikely that he was coining the term. ABRAHAM EPSTEIN, INSECURITY: A CHALLENGE TO AMERICA 5 (1933), referred to "the total number of employers and self-employed."

60. *See* Laura Wendt, *Census Classifications and Social Security Categories*, SOC. SEC. BULL., April 1938, at 3.

61. Ch. 531, §§ 202(a)(1) and 210(a) and (b), 49 Stat. 620, 623, 625 (1935).

62. The original exclusion of the self-employed from the old-age insurance system appears to have been based on perceived administrative difficulties. *See* U.S. ADVISORY COUNCIL ON SOCIAL SECURITY, FINAL REPORT: DECEMBER 10, 1938, S. DOC. NO. 4, 76th Cong., 1st Sess. 23 (1939); *idem*, RECOMMENDATIONS FOR SOCIAL SECURITY LEGISLATION, S. DOC. NO. 208, 80th Cong., 2d Sess. 15 (1949); *Social Security Revision: Hearings Before the Sen. Comm. on Finance*, 81st Cong., 2d Sess. 2138-39 (1950) (testimony of J. Brown).

63. *See, e.g.*, W. WOYTINSKY, DIE WELT IN ZAHLEN: DIE ARBEIT 1-68 (1926).

64. W. Woytinsky, The Labor Supply of the United States: Occupational Statistics of the 1930 Census Tabulated by Class of Worker and Industry, As Well As by Sex, Race, and Age Groups 8 (1936).

65. W. Woytinsky, Labor in the United States: Basic Statistics for Social Security 16, 24, 240 (1938).

66. Spurgeon Bell, Productivity, Wages, and National Income 210 (1940). Bell's computations were made difficult by the fact that many census occupational classifications, including barbers, lawyers, and retail dealers, undifferentiatedly included wage earners and self-employed. *Id*. at 212-13. His own criteria for resolving borderline workers--single versus numerous employers, payment according to time versus piece, and provision of no versus some productive capital, whereby the presence of two of the three was dispositive; *id*. at 214--are not persuasive. *See* Marc Linder, *Employees, Not-So-Independent Contractors, and the Case of Migrant Farmworkers: A Challenge to the "Law and Economics" Agency Doctrine*, 15 N.Y.U. Rev. L. & Soc. Change 435 (1986-87).

67. Without using the term *self-employed*, Simon Kuznets was attempting to bring some functional order into national income accounting. The distinctions that he drew between labor income and entrepreneurial income as based on whether the participant "himself engages in the production process or participates solely through his property" and whether he shares in the management and disposition are, to be sure, plausible. Simon Kuznets, National Income and Its Composition, 1919-1938, at 80-81 (1941). Nevertheless, as Kuznets realized, the problem remains that "frequently one who may appear to be an entrepreneur is really an employee." *Id*. at 405. And if employees are defined as those "who have little voice in the decisions an enterprise makes and can be easily separated from it," *id*. at 81, workers in one-person entities, no matter how dependent they were substantively, would be classified as entrepreneurs.

68. U.S. Bureau of the Census, Current Population Reports: Labor Force 3 (Ser. P-50, No. 1, July 11, 1947). The self-employed were defined as "working on their own farm or in their own business, profession, or trade for profit or fees." *Id*. at 4.

69. *See* U.S. Bureau of the Census, Supplement to the Monthly Report on the Labor Force, No. 58-S, May 12, 1947, at 1, 3; *idem*, Current Population Reports: Monthly Report on the Labor Force: August, 1947, at 5, 8 (Ser. P-57, No. 63, Sept. 4, 1947); Joseph Duncan & William Shelton, Revolution in United States Government Statistics, 1926-1976, at 54-55 (U.S. Dep't of Commerce, 1978); Margo Anderson, The American Census: A Social History 159-90 (1988).

70. Servicemen's Readjustment Act of 1944, ch. 268, § 503, 58 Stat. 284, 292 (1944).

71. *Id*. § 902(a) and (b), 58 Stat. at 297-98.

72. H. REP. NO. 1418: PROVIDING FEDERAL GOVERNMENT AID FOR THE READJUSTMENT IN CIVILIAN LIFE OF RETURNING WORLD WAR II VETERANS, 78th Cong., 2d Sess. 13, 14 (1944). In conference the wording of the House version was modified; for the original House provision, see 90 CONG. REC. 4336 (1944).

73. On the unprecedented nature of this inclusion, see National Comm. on Soc. Legis., Nat'l Lawyers Guild, *The Servicemen's Readjustment Act of 1944: "The G.I. Bill of Rights,"* 5 LAWYERS GUILD REV. 90, 98 (1945).

74. H. REP. 1418 at 14. The straightforward administrative procedures are set out at 38 C.F.R. § 36.514 and §§ 36.525-.532 (Supp. 1944). WILLIAM HABER & MERRILL MURRAY, UNEMPLOYMENT INSURANCE IN THE AMERICAN ECONOMY: AN HISTORICAL REVIEW AND ANALYSIS 147 n.6 (1966), assert without sources that "[a] number of self-employed, especially farmers, drew benefits under conditions that brought criticism of the program." A review of state administrative agency decisions, many of which turned on whether workers met the requirement of being "fully engaged," does not reveal outrageous facts. *See* 8-10 Fed. Security Agency, Unempl. Compensation Interpretation Serv.: Benefit Series (1945-1947).

75. "Congress obviously thought it desirable to encourage discharged veterans to go into self-employment, or at least to assist those who wished to do so." 8 Fed. Security Agency, Unemployment Compensation Interpretation Service: Benefit Series 166, 167 (10159-Kans. V, Decision of App. Referee, June 20, 1945).

76. *See* Employment Act of 1946, ch. 33, § 2, 60 Stat. 23 (1946) (including self-employment). In an interesting postwar labor dispute, picketers described themselves as "self-employed veterans." Miller v. Tobin, 70 N.Y.S.2d 36, 37 (1947). The number of reported nonagricultural self-employed and the rate of self-employment rose sharply during the first two postwar years. *See* PHILLIPS, THE SELF-EMPLOYED IN THE UNITED STATES at 15-20.

77. After World War II, the Social Security Bd. renewed its advocacy of the incorporation of the self-employed into the social security system. *See, e.g.,* A. Altmeyer, *Improving Old-Age and Survivors Insurance*, SOC. SEC. BULL., March 1946, at 3 (Chairman of Social Security Bd.); Wilbur Cohen, *Coverage of the Self-Employed under Old-Age and Survivors Insurance: Foreign Experience, id.*, Aug. 1949, at 11 (advisor to Social Security Comm'r).

78. 94 CONG. REC. 2143 (1948) (statement of Rep. Gearhart). On the background to this campaign in the 1940s, see Marc Linder, *From Street Urchins to Little Merchants: The Juridical Transvaluation of Child Newspaper Carriers*, 63 TEMPLE L. REV. 829, 840-45 (1990).

79. Labor Management Relations Act, ch. 120, § 101, 61 Stat. 140 (1947) (codified at 29 U.S.C. § 158(b)(4)(i)(A) (1973).

80. U.S. Bureau of the Census, 200 Years at 59, 65. It was in 1940 that the BOC began referring to this question as "class of worker." *Id.* at 65. Only persons, including peddlers, "operating their own unincorporated business enterprises" were classified as employers or own-account workers. U.S. Bureau of the Census, Sixteenth Census, 2 Population, pt. 1 at 14; U.S. Bureau of the Census, Sixteenth Census of the United States: 1940, 3 Population: The Labor Force, part 1: United States Summary 299 (1943).

81. U.S. Bureau of the Census, 200 Years at 74.

82. 2 U.S. Bureau of the Census, Census of Population: 1950: Characteristics of the Population, part 1: United States Summary 61, tab. 53 at 1-101, 1-461, 1-475 (1953). Enumerators were instructed not to report employees of incorporated businesses as being in their own business "even though they own part or all of the stock of the incorporated business." *Id.* at 1-476. A similar transition occurred earlier in the household surveys: when the BOC began publishing data on the "self-employed," the question on the schedule actually referred to "own-account worker." U.S. Bureau of the Census, Current Population Reports: Labor Force Bulletin: Labor Force, Employment, and Unemployment in the United States, 1940 to 1946, at 5, tab. 2 at 18 (Ser. P-50, No. 2, Sept. 11, 1947).

83. U.S. Bureau of the Census, 200 Years at 79.

84. *Id.* at 85, 92, 102 (1970, 1980, and 1990 censuses included an additional subquestion as to whether the business was not incorporated or incorporated).

85. Hacking, The Taming of Chance at 3.

86. Feist Publications, Inc. v. Rural Telephone Service Co., 59 U.S.L.W. 4251, 4253 (No. 89-1909, Mar. 27, 1991). Telephone subscribers' names and telephone numbers "are uncopyrightable facts; they existed before Rural reported them and would have continued to exist if Rural had never published a telephone directory." *Id.* at 4257. The U.S. Supreme Court here adopts a naive epistemology. Its application to the self-employed would make it impossible to recognize that if "employees" are socially constructed, then dependent "self-employed" are second-order constructions.

87. U.S. Bureau of the Census, Interviewer's Manual: Current Population Survey D6-21 (CPS-250, rev. July 1989) (hereinafter "Manual"). The BOC made available a copy of this internal document, which is not published by the Government Printing Office.

88. Steinmetz & Wright, *The Fall and Rise of the Petty Bourgeoisie* at 979.

89. Employment and Earnings, Mar. 1989, at 120.

90. A facsimile of CPS-1--Basic Questionnaire (Form CPS-1) for March 1988 is reproduced in U.S. BUREAU OF THE CENSUS, MONEY INCOME OF HOUSEHOLDS, FAMILIES, AND PERSONS IN THE UNITED STATES: 1987, at 197-201 (Curr. Pop. Rep., Ser. P-60, No. 162, 1989).

91. *Id.* at 200.

92. The respondent--who may be as young as fourteen--may be answering on behalf of all other members of the household. One possible source of error in the CPS is the fact that proxies respond on behalf of eighty per cent of all male household members. *See* NATIONAL COMMISSION ON EMPLOYMENT AND UNEMPLOYMENT STATISTICS, COUNTING THE LABOR FORCE 143 (1979). The BOC believes that the data on self-employment are not significantly affected by reliance on proxy respondents. *See* PHILIP MCCARTHY, SOME SOURCES OF ERROR IN LABOR FORCE ESTIMATES FROM THE CURRENT POPULATION SURVEY 31-37 (Nat'l Comm'n on Employment and Unemployment Statistics Background Paper No. 15, 1978). *See generally,* U.S. BUREAU OF LABOR STATISTICS, CONCEPTS AND METHODS USED IN LABOR FORCE STATISTICS DERIVED FROM THE CURRENT POPULATION SURVEY (Rep. No. 463, 1976); U.S. BUREAU OF THE CENSUS, THE CURRENT POPULATION SURVEY: DESIGN AND METHODOLOGY (Technical Paper 40, 1978); U.S. DEP'T OF COMMERCE, OFFICE OF FEDERAL STATISTICAL POLICY AND STANDARDS, AN ERROR PROFILE: EMPLOYMENT AS MEASURED BY THE CURRENT POPULATION SURVEY (Statistical Working Paper 3, 1978).

93. MONEY INCOME OF HOUSEHOLDS, FAMILIES, AND PERSONS IN THE UNITED STATES: 1987 at 200.

94. *Id.*

95. MANUAL at D6-22.

96. That this response is not uncommon becomes clear from the instruction relating to consultants who state that they do not have a business: they are to be reported as self-employed under 23A and 23E. *See Id.* at D6-27.

97. *Id.* at D5-8-9.

98. For belated judicial recognition of the absurdity of this position, see Hearst v. Iowa Dep't of Revenue & Fin., 461 N.W.2d 295, 306 (Iowa 1990) ("To expect these child carriers, the majority of whom are between the ages of ten and twelve, to correctly figure, collect, and remit the proper amount of tax due is ludicrous") (dictum). Or as the chairman of a congressional subcommittee, confronting an employer of child newspaper subscription solicitors who had treated them as independent contractors, put it: "How do you visualize a 10 year old being an independent contractor? ... We can call him a rear admiral but that doesn't make him a rear admiral." *Children at Risk in the Workplace: Hearings Before the Employment and Housing Subcomm. of the Comm. on Government Operations,* 101st Cong., 2d Sess. 295 (1990) (Rep. Lantos).

99. MANUAL at D5-10. Although the CPS collects data on fifteen year olds, the BLS currently reports labor force data only on those sixteen and older. On school children, see *id*. at D-5-1, 5-14, 5-17. For an explanation of why such imposition of risk does not convert an employee into independent businessboy/girl, see Linder, *From Street Urchins to Little Merchants*. The number of self-employed sixteen and seventeen year olds rose from 36,000 in 1969 to 51,000 in 1975, falling off to 24,000 by 1990. Before BOC/BLS stopped collecting data on fourteen-and-fifteen-years-olds (in 1982), the self-employed among them peaked at 100,000 in 1972 and 1975. *See* EMPLOYMENT AND EARNINGS, Jan. 1970, tab. A-18 at 116, A-26 at 130; *id*., Jan. 1973, tab. 26 at 142; *id*., Jan. 1976, tab. 20 at 148, tab. 28 at 155; *id*., Jan. 1991, tab. 23 at 191. That twice as many of the younger cohort were reported as self-employed despite the fact that more than twice as many of the older cohort were in the labor force may largely be accounted for by the dearth of lawful employment opportunities available to the younger children other than newspaper delivery; sixteen and seventeen year olds have predominantly found employment in stores and fast-food restaurants. *See* ELLEN GREENBERGER & LAURENCE STEINBERG, WHEN TEENAGERS WORK: THE PSYCHOLOGICAL AND SOCIAL COSTS OF ADOLESCENT EMPLOYMENT 10-89 (1986).

100. On the extent of self-employment in beauty and barber shops, see Horst Brand & Ziaul Ahmed, *Beauty and Barber Shops: The Trend of Labor Productivity*, MONTHLY LAB. REV., Mar. 1986, at 21, 23.

101. Thus, for example, crewleaders, fronting for farmers, often pay migrant farmworkers with checks drawn on accounts that are in economic reality the farmers'. *See generally*, Marc Linder, *The Joint Employment Doctrine: Clarifying Joint Legislative-Judicial Confusion*, 10 HAMLINE J. PUB. L. & POL. 321 (1989). Interestingly, in its Instructions to Enumerators at the 1910 Census of Population, the BOC stated that "the boss of a gang" should not be returned as an employer because "while any one of these may employ persons, none of them does so in transacting his *own* business." U.S. BUREAU OF THE CENSUS, 200 YEARS at 53.

102. MANUAL at D6-24. How interviewers are supposed to "find" the business to be incorporated, the *Manual* does not explain. It seems implausible that they would demand to see the articles of incorporation. Not much more plausible is the notion that all the respondents answering on behalf of the eighty per cent of men not at home at the time of the interview really know whether that household member's business is incorporated.

103. In a previous section devoted to "Definition of class-of-worker entries," the MANUAL instructs the interviewer not to ask "foremen, superintendents, managers, or other executives hired to manage a business or farm, salesmen working on commission or officers of corporations" "who report themselves as working for profit or fees in OWN business" whether the business is incorporated. Instead, these persons are to be entered directly as private employees. *Id*. at D6-23. This injunction was first adopted for the 1910 Census of Population. *See* U.S. BUREAU OF THE CENSUS, 200 YEARS at 53.

104. Ronald Tucker of the Demographic Surveys Div. of the BOC expressed the fear that the incorporated self-employed might be undercounted because interviewers, upon hearing the response that the respondent worked for a corporation, might never proceed to ask whether the respondent was self-employed. Telephone interview Ronald Tucker, Apr. 18, 19, 1991.

105. MANUAL at D6-24.

106. *Id.*

107. *Id.* at D6-24-25. Although the CPS records hardly any household self-employed in these occupations, many are recorded for nonpersonal services. Already at the time of the 1910 Census of Population, enumerators were instructed to return domestic servants "always" as employees although "the person employing a domestic servant is not always returned as an employer." U.S. BUREAU OF THE CENSUS, 200 YEARS at 53.

108. Real estate agents are deemed mandatory employees "because they must work for a licensed broker." MANUAL at D6-26. It is unclear how the BOC knows that registered and practical nurses who report "'private duty'" as their business are self-employed rather than employees of a nurses' registry. *See id.* at D6-25. These comments were absent from the July 1985 revision of the *Manual*. For a contrary classification, see SPURGEON BELL, PRODUCTIVITY, WAGES, AND NATIONAL INCOME 214-15 (1940); SPEC. COMM. TO STUDY PROBLEMS OF AMERICAN SMALL BUSINESS, SMALL BUSINESS PROBLEMS: SMALL BUSINESS WANTS OLD-AGE SECURITY, 78TH CONG., 1ST SESS. 14 (Sen. Comm. Print No. 17, 1943). Even an author who laments the transformation of self-employed private duty nurses into employees concedes that even in their heyday their status was "contradictory" because of their "use by patrons as servant, maid, cook, and housemother." This position was reflected in the fact that they commonly received compensation in the form of room and board, which depressed their wage levels. David Wagner, *The Proletarianization of Nursing in the United States, 1932-1946*, 10 INT'L J. HEALTH SERVICES 271, 273 (1980). *See also* BARBARA MELOSH, "THE PHYSICIAN'S HAND": WORK CULTURE AND CONFLICT IN AMERICAN NURSING 77-111 (1982); SUSAN REVERBY, ORDERED TO CARE: THE DILEMMA OF AMERICAN NURSING, 1850-1945, at 95-105, 176-79 (1987).

109. MANUAL at D6-26.

110. *Id.* at D6-26. This reference to Avon and Tupperware was not in the *Manual* at the time of the July 1985 revision.

111. *See* Marc Linder, *The Involuntary Conversion of Employees into Self-Employed: The Internal Revenue Service and Section 530*, 22 CLEARINGHOUSE REV. 14, 20 n.77, 21 (1988).

112. U.S. BUREAU OF THE CENSUS, 200 YEARS at 53.

113. Ronald Tucker also expressed surprise and concern to the BLS that BLS was tabulating data on the incorporated self-employed at all.

3

Class: Exploitation, Dependence, Risk, and Insecurity

[U]ne question aussi controversée que celle de la petite bourgeoisie, et aussi génératrice de bla-bla-bla.[1]

The Hybrid Character of the Self-Employed: Extraterritorial Tertium Quid

The *separation* [of labor and the ownership of the means of production] appears as the normal relationship in this society. Where it therefore in fact does not occur, it is presumed and...so far correctly; for (in contrast to ancient Roman or Norwegian conditions) (or American conditions in the Northwest of the United States) here the *union* appears as accidental, the *separation* as normal, and therefore the separation is seized on as the relationship even if the person unites the various functions. It stands out here very strikingly that the capitalist as such is only [a] function of the capital, the worker [a] function of the capacity to work.[2]

Among the preclassical and classical economists of the eighteenth and nineteenth centuries the figure of those who today would be called self-employed was a common trope in the context of a theory of value and the distribution of income.[3] Writing almost a half-century before Adam Smith, Richard Cantillon discussed capitalless, labor-only independent workers--"les Entrepreneurs dans leurs propre travail...qui n'ont pas besoin de fonds pour s'établir"--such as coppersmiths, needle women, chimney sweeps, water carriers, painters, doctors, and lawyers.[4]   These--together with "beggars" and "robbers"--he classified with entrepreneurial merchants, manufacturers, and employers as receiving "gages uncertains" in contradistinction to those who received "gages certains."[5]   Interestingly, Cantillon subtly relativized the degree of uncertainty distinguishing the "two classes" by adding that the wages of the hired class were certain only "pour le tems [sic] qu'ils en jouissent."[6]   Widespread unemployment among employees would then have tended to undermine any categorical divide between the two groups.

The classical economists, writing as the capitalist mode of production began to create a categorical class division between those who owned only their labor and those who owned capital and employed the former, regarded the independent worker as an anomaly.[7]   Adam Smith, for example, alluded to the unusual hybrid character of workers who still possessed capital or of capitalists who still worked:

> It sometimes happens...that a single independent workman has stock sufficient both to purchase the materials of his work, and to maintain himself till it be compleated. He is both master and workman, and enjoys the whole produce of his own labour.... It includes what are usually two distinct revenues, belonging to two distinct persons, the profits of stock, and the wages of labour.
>
> Such cases, however, are not very frequent, and in every part of Europe, twenty workmen serve under a master for one that is independent.[8]

By the middle of the nineteenth century, John Stuart Mill adopted a much more radical position, relegating the independents to the role of atavists. While recognizing that only in England, Scotland, and parts of Belgium and Holland were land, capital, and labor "the property of separate owners" in agriculture,[9] Mill observed a definitive class divide in industry:

> In the case of manufacturing industry there never are more than two classes, the labourers and the capitalists. The...system in which capital was owned by the labourer, was coeval with free labour.... The artisan owned the loom or the few tools he used, and worked

on his own account.... In country villages, where a carpenter or a blacksmith cannot live and support hired labourers on the returns of his business, he is even now his own workman; and shopkeepers are their own shopmen or shopwomen. But wherever the extent of the market admits of it, the distinction is now fully established between the class of capitalists, or employers of labour, and the class of labourers; the capitalists, in general, contributing no other labour than that of direction and superintendence.[10]

The question of the laborer's dependence on capital was raised in a more self-consciously theoretical form in connection with the late nineteenth-century economists' debate over the so-called wage-fund doctrine. One of the leading American political economists of the period, Frank Taussig, objectively synthesizing the themes raised by Cantillon and Smith, stated that whereas "hired laborers...get stipulated money shares [and] take no chances," "independent laborers," who "have some capital," are "residual sharers" "because they are independent producers. They are owners of part of the gross output of society. They sell what they turn out and so become holders in the first instance of part of the money income of society."[11] Ironically, as in present-day sociological and economic discussions of self-employment, this economists' debate also appeared to turn on legal formalisms:[12]

[W]e should not be consistent if we drew the line between wages and not wages according to the bare independence of the workman. The cobbler who works alone in his petty shop gets, in the main, a return for labor as much as the workman in the shoe factory; the peddler and the shopkeeper's assistant...all earn an income by labor. ... But in one important respect the receipts of the independent laborer...are to be put in the same class as those of well-to-do capitalists.... The independent workman gets a primary and not a derivative share of the total income of society. ... He becomes legal and absolute owner of a part of the output of society, and so comes into control of part of the gross money income. He may be fettered by debt...but he is dependent on no fixed bargain for the money income. Herein his situation differs essentially from that of the hired laborer [who] gets his money income as a result of a bargain by which he sells his working power for a space. The independent workman gets his income directly from the sale of what he makes. The situation is not always advantageous to the latter. ... But the hired workman is directly dependent for his money income on an employing capitalist; the independent workman is not.[13]

Reduced to its conceptual core, Taussig's point is that so-called independent workers are subject to greater risk than are wage workers.[14] This distinction appears more plausible with regard to artisans than with regard to those selling services. There does seem to be a tangible difference between a cobbler's selling shoes to the public and a factory worker's selling his labor power to a capitalist, who controls every aspect of the production and investment process. But what happens to this difference as applied, for example, to workers, such as taxi drivers, whose physical distance from their employers and direct cash contact with final consumers render the conventional indicia of control ambiguous and therefore amenable to contractual manipulation by employers?[15] Even bracketing the puzzles created by the materiality or corporeality of the services rendered, an issue subsists regarding the quality of risk. Unless the 'independent worker' has invested considerable capital (including human capital), the loss of which would impose a telling economic injury on him,[16] it is unclear how the risks differ. Thus, a service provider with few or no means of production is as economically "mobile" as a wage laborer. Although the hired worker may be guaranteed his wages for all the work he has performed, that guarantee lasts only as long as his pay period. Beyond that, he assumes all the risks of insecurity associated with unemployment.[17] How a buffer of one day's or one week's wages (which the employee has effectively 'lent' to the employer)[18] can qualitatively distinguish the employee from the self-employee is unclear.[19]

A rough analogy, then, obtains between the situation of an at-will employee and that of a tailor who produces only for the bespoke trade (rather than for inventory for an anonymous market). The further removed the employee becomes from the pure at-will regime and the more protected she is by agreements secured by unions and state intervention, and the more means of production in which the "independent worker" has invested and the more she produces ex ante for the market, the more plausible the distinction becomes. But with regard to the capitalless service provider, the distinction is legal and circular: she is excluded from labor unions and unemployment insurance programs because she is independent--that is, because the customer pays the employee rather than the employer; yet that independence--that is, assumption of risk--may, on closer scrutiny, consist of little else than the modicum of income security that she is denied by virtue of those very legal exclusions.

In conceptualizing the self-employed, it is crucial to focus on the proposition, which existed in inchoate form among the classical economists, that the self-employed are a *tertium quid* enjoying a kind of extraterritorial status within capitalism and yet crucially informed by it.[20] Whether they were regarded as a vestigial curiosity or as having a future niche as well,[21] independent workers came to be seen as an exception to a binary world who were of neither class and yet of both. This framework posits that the independent, "so-called old middle class [*Mittelstand*]" does not represent a nominal category arbitrarily created by considerations of expediency but rather a group the members of which "even on the basis of *economic* logic are neither proletarians nor capitalists, but rather some third entity...labor citizens [*Arbeitsbürger*]."[22]

The theoretically most sophisticated formulation of this conceptualization of independent producers as a hybrid form is to be found in one of the complex of manuscripts Marx prepared in the early 1860s for use in his unfinished magnum opus:

> It is possible that these producers, who work with their own means of production, not only reproduce their laboring capacity, but also create surplus value inasmuch as their position permits them to appropriate their own surplus labor or a part of the same.... The independent peasant or artisan is cut up into two persons. ... As owner of the means of production he is a capitalist, as worker he is his own wage laborer. Thus he pays himself his salary as capitalist and draws his profit from his capital, i.e., he exploits himself as wage laborer and pays himself in the surplus value the tribute that labor owes capital. ... The *social determinateness* of the means of production in capitalist production--so that they express a certain relation of production--has so coalesced with, and in the

> mode of representation of bourgeois society is so inseparable from the material existence of these means of production as means of production that that determinateness (categorical determinateness) is applied even where the relationship directly contradicts it. The means of production become capital only so far as they become autonomous as an autonomous power over against the labor. In the stated case the producer--the worker--is owner, proprietor of his means of production. They are therefore not capital, as little as he is a wage laborer vis-à-vis them. Nevertheless they are conceived of as capital and he himself is sundered in himself, so that *he* as capitalist employs himself as wage laborer. ... That he however can appropriate the whole product of his own labor *for himself*, and the surplus of the value of his product over the average price is not appropriated by a third *master*...he owes not to his labor--which does not distinguish him from other workers--but rather to the ownership of the means of production.[23]

A crucial implication of this analysis is the subversion of the notion that a worker who is "his own employer"[24] moves within a solipsistic world. The very subsumption of this self-exploiter under capitalistically determined forms of production means that he can appropriate his surplus labor only in the manner that all capitalists do: by participating in the competitively induced redistribution of societally created surplus value effected by the equalization of the rate of profit in accordance with the total capital of each capitalist.

Unconcerned with operationalizing these criteria, Marx offered no practical guidelines as to the threshold volume of means of production in any particular branch of production that would enable solo owner-workers to ward off interloping surplus-value snatchers.[25] Marx's overarching conception of the tendencies of capitalist accumulation, which would, by raising the capital requirements for competitiveness, undermine the tenability of niches for small producers, presumably subordinated this phenomenon to the main lines of societal development. To the extent that such interstices are constantly being reproduced within capitalism, Marx posed a methodological puzzle. For if Joan Robinson, adapting Oscar Wilde's bon mot, was right that from a Marxist perspective the only thing worse than being exploited is not being exploited (that is, being unemployed), then with regard to independent workers the predicament becomes:

The only thing worse than being successfully self-exploiting is being unsuccessfully self-exploiting. In other words, the would-be or pseudo-independent who exploits herself but only for the benefit of her real but informal employer has worse than the worst of both worlds because the conditions (including the length of the workday, the intensity of work, and the exploitation of family members) to which she subjects herself often are worse than those of the factory. The problem is separating out the successes from the failures.

That this is no easy analytic undertaking can be seen from the case of so-called contract farmers with significant capital investment whose relationships with the processing industry have led some to characterize them as "'semi-proletarians.'"[26] Identifying those who own and control enough means of production to be in a position to capture some part of the surplus they produce is also exacerbated by the fact that many run-of-the-mill workers--for example, skilled tradespeople in construction, whose employee status is uncontested--may derive some portion of their income from their ownership of their tools.[27] The need to ferret out and to understand myriad complex, intricate, and subtle details of alleged self-employees' work situations therefore precludes the use of individualized census surveys alone because of the cost.

The reason that economists are currently engaged in a dispute as to whether the self-employed should be studied from the perspective of entrepreneurship or as a labor market phenomenon is that they fail to appreciate the hybrid character of capital-owning workers. The most recent monograph devoted to self-employment in the United States does recognize that the self-employed combine the functions of employer and employee in a single individual.[28] That Aronson's analysis is nevertheless marred by confusion is all the more remarkable because he states programmatically that "self-employment is basically an alternative means of earning a living by the sale of one's labor."[29] Ironically, Aronson's critical insight becomes submerged because he extinguishes the categorical distinction between the self-employed and employees by erring in an unusual direction--by implying that even the most independent of the self-employed are merely selling their labor: "Self-employment is the oldest way by which individuals offer and sell their labor in a market economy."[30] Ultimately, then, all Aronson means is that "most self-employed workers are not entrepreneurs in the classic sense, that is, individuals with a unique mission of breaking new ground in the production and/or distribution of goods and services."[31]

Aronson's inability to adhere consistently to this program emerges clearly in his explanation of his decision to use a narrow definition of self-employment that excludes unpaid family workers and partners: "These more inclusive definitions raise questions...about the degree of autonomy and control these workers have over their labor, which, in my view, theoretically distinguishes self-employment from wage and salary employment."[32] The presence of patriarchal domination may be an excellent reason to withhold self-employed status from unpaid wives and children,[33] and subordination to the decision-making process of a bureaucracy controlled by hundreds of co-equals may also justify the refusal to classify partners as self-employed.[34] But what Aronson fails to recognize is that even the most exclusive definition raises exactly the same question as to adequate criteria of class membership,[35] which he neglects in his substantive discussions.

The way out of this analytic morass leads through a discussion of the touchstone of the microeconomics of self-employment: dependence.

Heteronomy

Others, who may be counted as and may consider themselves as self-employed, perhaps working at home, are essentially disguised employees, receiving inputs and delivering outputs to a single "employer". While the "employers" may reduce their exposure in the sense that they are given some paid work, these "nominal" or "pseudo" self-employed workers may be in an especially precarious situation, as they are atomised, have little market (or bargaining) power and are generally unprotected by labour legislation. Other dependent workers who may be counted statistically as self-employed include artisans or street vendors who are dependent on others for their premises and whose work may be controlled by the owners of such premises or by suppliers of credit or inputs.[36]

[T]he illusion of autonomy is grasped tightly precisely because it helps to compensate for and legitimate the practical realities of being even more tied to their work, and dependent on bank managers etc., than they had been as employees.[37]

In connection with their attempt to document the rise in self-employment in the late 1970s and early 1980s, sociologists Steinmetz and Wright believe they are merely stating an obvious tautology when they assert that "[s]elf-employment means, literally, being employed by oneself."[38] Given the specific meaning of *employment* within capitalist relations of production, however, what it means to employ oneself is not quite so self-explanatory. The ideological inversion that occurs "when an independent worker...[who] works for himself and sells his own product...is viewed as his own employer (capitalist), who employs himself as worker"[39] leaves in its wake a very material consequence: his ability to appropriate his own surplus labor[40] entails a level of self-exploitation that replicates that prevailing in the canonical dichotomized capitalist-wage labor sector.[41]

Steinmetz and Wright's further specification that the nonemploying self-employed (or pure petty bourgeois) "own their own means of production and do not sell their labor power on the labor market"[42] is still not sufficient. Although guidelines may be unobjectionable as abstract principles, they are not self-executing; to identify--rather than merely to define--employment that is disassociated from the sale of labor power is precisely the complex task at hand.[43]

The socioeconomic conceptualization of what constitutes the peculiar autonomy or independence[44] of the "motley collection of occupations" embracing the self-employed centers on the fact that the latter are distinguished from employees by obtaining their income in part from the ownership of the necessary means of production ("albeit in small measure").[45] Thus, a class that stands between capital and the proletariat must be further characterized "by ownership of capital...that is large enough to give its owner...independence and autonomy vis-à-vis capital, but not large enough to afford pure surplus-value income."[46] A self-employed person who owned large amounts of physical capital presumably could not employ it alone and would almost definitionally require employees to valorize it. This conceptual link between the smallness of the capital and the ability to set it in motion alone supports the prima facie plausibility of confining the category of the self-employed to those without employees.[47] Just how complicated the process of identifying the self-employed among capital-owning workers is[48] can be gauged by the methodological shortcut to eliciting the requisite information that Steinmetz and Wright propose concerning nominally self-employed service workers with no capital and little income. They argue that the basic issue in situating such workers in the class structure is to locate them within the social relations of production:

> If they sell their labor services to individuals who buy those services directly for their use-value, then these providers would be characterized as petty bourgeois, even if their income was low. But if those services are sold to capitalists, so that after selling their labor power the providers' work is performed within capitalist production under the control of the firm, then they would be workers, even if they still had the legal status of "self-employment." The relational properties are entirely different for someone taking children into her or his own home on a fee-for-service basis and for an employee of a child-care firm.... A similar point could be made concerning the contrast between a self-employed carpenter who sells carpentry services to individuals for home repairs and a nominally self-employed carpenter who actually works for a capitalist construction firm.[49]

Steinmetz and Wright appear to have confused different levels of analysis. That a house cleaner performs so-called unproductive labor--so that her 'master' does not appropriate surplus value--in no way means that she is not an employee. Indeed, even if she cleaned house for a different family every day of the year,[50] classifying her as self-employed would be whimsical at best. And in fact the law (in the United States) deems her an employee of each and every such family.[51] The reason that an independent carpenter is not considered the employee of each and every customer for whom he builds a garage or bookshelves is presumably that the nonfirm consumer cannot control him because he is far more skilled and knowledgeable than the customer. But this relationship of nondomination at the point of production is not per se a function of the fact that the customer is using the products as use-values, for a similar relationship may arise vis-à-vis a capitalist firm that cannot control the carpenter because, being in a different product market, it knows just as little about carpentry as the house owner and cannot integrate the carpenter into its organization.[52]

The real difficulty arises in connection with an independent worker who, for example, produces commodities which he sells directly to consumers.[53] Even Wright concedes that the autonomy of such "independent direct producers characterized by a 'unity of conception and execution'" "may be a rather romantic image of the petty bourgeoisie":

> The contrast between independent producers (self-employed artisans, craftspersons, shop-keepers, farmers, etc.) with such autonomy and proletarian wage-labourers without such autonomy may simply be incorrect. [S]elf-employed petty-bourgeois producers may have little choice over how they produce or, in some circumstances, even over what they produce. Their options are constrained by markets, by credit institutions, by long-term contracts with capitalist enterprises, and so on.[54]

Indeed, Wright must also concede that even in the absence of any direct capital-labor relationship, "*some* petty bourgeois...will actually be exploited by capital (through unequal exchange on the market) because they own such minimal means of production.... Exploitation status, therefore, cannot strictly be equated with self-employment/wage-earner status."[55] But if, with regard to such controlling dimensions of class as exploitation, domination, dependence, alienation, income, and insecurity, the "semi-proletarianized self-employed (proletarian subordination within petty-bourgeois production)"[56] are virtually indistinguishable from employees,[57] the chief impediment to assimilation of the two must lie in the isolation and atomization of the self-employed. This socioeconomic location entails the absence of both a tangible exploiter[58] and co-exploited workers whom it is feasible to join in confronting the common source of exploitation.[59] To the extent, however, that the current trend toward casualization of the labor force is more than a cyclical phenomenon, even this distinguishing feature of self-employment may become muted and blurred.

One recent approach to demarcating the status of the self-employed seeks to cut the Gordian knot of class analysis. Taking as its point of departure a Weberian market position perspective, it argues that the supply and demand for anyone's services are much more determinative than ownership of the means of production:

> Owning property, whether a professional practice or a shop, owning the means of production, can hardly be important in and of itself in assuring one control over one's economic fate and one's work. Surely the more critical matter is the relationship one has to the market, capitalist or otherwise. When one's goods or services are so valuable on the market as to make consumers supplicants, then one can exercise considerable control over the terms, conditions, content, and goals of one's work. But when one's goods or services are not in heavy demand, then one can only be a desperate supplicant of indifferent consumers or employers. If one concedes the critical significance of position in the market, then whether one is employed or self-employed ceases to be a serious issue. ... Given a strong position in the market, one can be employed and nonetheless "write one's own ticket." [T]he very concept of self-employment is misleading in a market economy. In a market economy one's labor is a commodity whether one sells it to an employer or to a customer. [I]t might be well to make the assumption that, when one is self-employed, one is not independent but rather operating a franchised trade, the terms of the franchise varying with the institutions that structure one's place in the market.[60]

Although this approach purports to lead to the express dissolution of the distinction between employees and self-employees at the end of the spectrum where all manner of workers with the greatest bargaining power become independent, it also implies the breakdown of the categorical divide where self-employed and employees are powerless. But this "monetary exchange asymmetries" approach[61] tends to blur the distinction between market relations and capitalist-labor domination.[62] At some points during the business cycle and in some places it may be true that "[t]he indispensable man, like the indispensable commodity, commands the high price," in which case "the employee is very independent and must be placated by an almost obsequious attitude on the part of the employer."[63] The question, however, is whether the extraordinary character of such a constellation of market forces among employees makes this analysis fruitful.[64]

An important empirical-historical task is sorting out those among the formally self-employed who were evicted by an "economy of 'poverty'" from a wage-labor market on which they could no longer successfully compete.[65] In an "act of desperation,"[66] such "'workers have had to buy their jobs.'"[67] And the jobs that they "buy" are largely substandard, which may account for the gap in incomes in nonprofessional occupations[68] as between the self-employed and their employee counterparts.[69] Because a significant component of nominal self-employment consists of such refugees and expellees from the traditional employment relationship,[70] the self-employment rate among persons in poverty working fulltime and yearround is twice as high (13.0 per cent) as the overall self-employment rate among the full-time working population (6.25 per cent).[71]

To this group in particular the claim applies that "one of the major attractions of self-employment is that its duration is not dependent upon the will of an employer."[72] Yet the question must still be answered as to why employers are not willing to sustain the underemployment that the self-employed accept. The answer may run as follows: employers might be willing to do so if they had no capital to amortize and could pay their employees on a share basis--that is, if they had no fixed costs.[73] Steinmetz and Wright misstate this question when they argue that acceptance of the claim that the income of the self-employed is lower than that of employees is incompatible with the view of self-employment as a flight from low-wage employment.[74]

The crucial missing link is that because of institutional wage rigidity, it is not possible for employees, beyond certain narrow limits, to bid down wages in an effort to retain employment.[75] For this reason it frequently is the case that "the unemployed can drive down wage rates and secure employment only by setting up as independent entrepreneurs."[76] The real significance of this highly touted countercyclical role of self-employment[77] can be gauged by the fact that it is functionally equivalent to suspending minimum wage and maximum hours laws during depressions. After ejection from the formal wage-labor sector, such workers might, to the extent that they are perceived as selling a product rather than their labor, be able to avoid the social opprobrium associated with wage-cutting:

> It does not require any romanticism about solidarity to suggest that competing for an existing job by undercutting the wage might be seen as demeaning, whereas selling off your full load of halibut at the market-clearing price, whatever it may be, would carry no corresponding overtone of betrayal or self-abnegation.[78]

Unions, however, have traditionally not found the transmogrification persuasive.[79] In this disbelief they are supported by the so-called backward-bending supply curve of labor. Although this model is generally used to explain why an increase in wages may reduce the supply of labor,[80] it is also available to explain why during depressions a decline in wages may call forth an increase in supply.[81] At those times of distress, two phenomena that are otherwise occluded or deemed special cases emerge more clearly. One is that the labor market may be honeycombed with "forced sales."[82] The other is that those who respond 'perversely' to falling prices by offering still more should be assimilated to the class of laborers. No fruitful reconceptualization of self-employment can result from an analysis that, by failing to crystallize out what is essential to self-employment, makes it impossible to distinguish the real from the pseudo-self-employed. One such prototypically neoclassical approach[83] argues:

> Conceptually, self-employment can be considered as disintermediation in the labor market. Firms function as intermediaries and receive profit by taking the differential between what a customer pays for the service or good and what the firm pays for its labor and other costs. By selling labor directly to the customer (i.e., self-employment), they can reap part of the profit. Thus, labor increases its income.[84]

Disintermediation would make sense only where the employer serves merely as a kind of employment agency, somehow creating a market niche that secures it arbitrage profits. Temporary agencies and "employee leasing" may be contemporary examples of such arbitrage.[85] If the employees being shunted back and forth between these lessor and lessee entities could acquire the information required to break through the arbitragers' monopoly, they could presumably capture part of "the differential." But in the typical case, where the employer owns the means of production, self-employment would be of no use to a would-be former employee unless he had accumulated enough savings to replicate the employer's capital stock. Absent such means of production, the newly minted self-employed would, ceteris paribus, be working at a much lower level of productivity, which would, in turn, generate a much lower income for her. Alternatively, such a pseudo-self-employed worker would find the conditions of heteronomy reproduced in a different form.

Questionable, by way of contrast, is whether, at least in the context of the debate concerning class position, any important economic or sociological insight is gained by explaining why some highly compensated self-investors in concentrated human capital such as physicians or lawyers may be in practice by themselves or employed by or associated with a hospital or firm.[86] It seems doubtful--however these professions are classified--whether such locations have much in common with the historical controversies over class structure and the position of a petty bourgeoisie as a third force.

NOTES

1. CHRISTIAN BAUDELOT, ROGER ESTABLET, & JACQUES MALEMORT, LA PETITE BOURGEOISIE EN FRANCE 231 (1981 [1974]).

2. KARL MARX, ZUR KRITIK DER POLITISCHEN ÖKONOMIE (MANUSKRIPT 1861-1863), in II:3, text pt. 6 KARL MARX [&] FRIEDRICH ENGELS, GESAMTAUSGABE (MEGA) 2181 (1982). This manuscript used to be known as THEORIES OF SURPLUS VALUE.

3. *See, e.g.*, 1 HENRI STORCH, COURS D'ECONOMIE POLITIQUE 279 (J. B. Say ed. 1823 [1815]): "Souvent un ouvrier possède un petit capital suffisant pour acheter des outils et des matières, et pour subsister jusqu'à ce qu'il puisse porter son ouvrage au marché. Quand un pareil ouvrier travaille pour son propre compte, il est à la fois entrepreneur, capitaliste et ouvrier." *See also* JAMES MILL, ELEMENTS OF POLITICAL ECONOMY (3d ed. 1826 [1821]), *reprinted in* JAMES MILL, SELECTED ECONOMIC WRITINGS 203, 228 (Donald Winch ed. 1966): "The labourer is sometimes the owner of all the capital which his labour requires. ... In the greater number of cases...the labourer is one person, the owner of the capital another. [T]he commodity, which was produced by the shoemaker, when the capital was his own, belonged wholly to himself, and constituted the whole of his reward, both as labourer and capitalist."

4. RICHARD CANTILLON, ESSAI SUR LA NATURE DU COMMERCE EN GÉNÉRAL 52 (Henry Higgs ed. 1931 [1755]) (written between 1730 and 1734).

5. *Id.* at 54.

6. *Id.*

7. Ricardo, whose austere modeling of capitalism included the three mutually exclusive classes of laborers, capitalists, and landowners, was the most radical. On Marx's methodological abstractions in this regard, see 3 KARL MARX, DAS KAPITAL, in 25 MARX-ENGELS WERKE ch. 52 (1964 [1894]); Abram Harris, *Pure Capitalism and the Disappearance of the Middle Class*, 47 J. POL. ECON. 328 (1939).

8. ADAM SMITH, AN INQUIRY INTO THE NATURE AND CAUSES OF THE WEALTH OF NATIONS 65-66 (Edwin Cannan ed. 1937 [1776]).

9. JOHN STUART MILL, PRINCIPLES OF POLITICAL ECONOMY 238-39 (W. Ashley ed. 1921 [1848]).

10. *Id.* at 240-41. ALFRED MARSHALL, PRINCIPLES OF ECONOMICS 243-44 (1952 [1890]), regarded the "village artisan who...makes things on his own account for sale to his neighbours" as "rare."

11. F. TAUSSIG, WAGES AND CAPITAL: AN EXAMINATION OF THE WAGES FUND DOCTRINE 111, 112, 71 (1896). Another late-nineteenth-century American economist did impute a "residual share" to wages but not in a sense implicating the assumption of risk relevant here. Francis Walker, *The*

Source of Business Profits, 1 Q.J. ECON. 265, 282 (1887). For a critique, see GEORGE GUNTON, PRINCIPLES OF SOCIAL ECONOMICS 180-81 (1897).

12. Taussig received a law degree in addition to a doctorate in economics from Harvard in the 1880s. 3 JOSEPH DORFMAN, THE ECONOMIC MIND IN AMERICAN CIVILIZATION: 1865-1918, at 264-45 (1949). He was doubtless one of the only such dual-degreed academics at that time and perhaps even the first in the United States.

13. TAUSSIG, WAGES AND CAPITAL at 72-73.

14. An early American political economist made the same point when he stated that "the pedler with his pack, who makes wages only, although employed in the same business which, on a large scale, produces what are usually termed profits," also takes the risk of success. 1 H. CAREY, PRINCIPLES OF POLITICAL ECONOMY 325 (1837).

15. *See* Marc Linder, *Towards Universal Worker Coverage under the National Labor Relations Act: Making Room for Uncontrolled Employees, Dependent Contractors, and Employee-Like Persons*, 66 U. DET. L. REV. 555 (1989).

16. *See* Arthur Hadley, *Profits*, in 3 CYCLOPAEDIA OF POLITICAL SCIENCE, POLITICAL ECONOMY AND OF THE POLITICAL HISTORY OF THE UNITED STATES 375, 376 (John Lalor ed. 1884) ("once engaged in business he cannot go out of it when he fails to make the expected profit, without sacrificing a great part of his invested capital and losing the chance of ever again doing business on the same terms"). This reasoning later supported a disqualification for unemployment compensation benefits to unemployed workers who become self-employed on the ground that the need to valorize the invested capital was inconsistent with unavailability for work: "The fact that a man has set himself up in business implies an intention to continue operations, particularly where, because of investment of capital...it would be difficult or to his economic disadvantage to wind up his business immediately." 2 Fed. Security Agency, Unemployment Compensation Interpretation Service: Benefit Series 326, 329 (944-Minn. A, Decision of App. Tribunal, Sept. 14, 1938). In order to gauge a claimant's subjective intent--that is, whether he was merely trying to eke out an existence while intending to return to the labor market--some states looked to the size of the business, including the capital stock, in preference to a claimant's own allegations. *See id*. at 2234, 2237 (2225-Mich. R, Decision of App. Bd., June 15, 1939); U.S. Employment & Training Adm., Benefit Series Service--Unemployment Insurance, Rep. No. 290-73 (July 1974) (TPU-415.15-69, Idaho A, No. 390-74, Feb. 22, 1974) (worker with no capital investment not disqualified as self-employed). *But see id*. at 1480, 1481 (1772-R.I. A, Decision of Referee, Feb. 22, 1939) ("the making of an investment in the past cannot bar a claimant from receiving compensation if totally unemployed").

17. In this sense it is therefore wrong to assert that "[u]ncertainty of success cannot well affect the wages of common labour, since no man, unless he be to a certain extent a capitalist, unless he have a fund for his intermediate support, can devote himself to an employment in which success is uncertain." NASSAU SENIOR, AN OUTLINE OF THE SCIENCE OF POLITICAL ECONOMY 209 (1939 [1836]).

18. In a questionnaire he formulated in 1880 to be used as the basis of a statistical investigation of the French working class, Marx posed this question: "[A]t what terms are your wages paid? in other words how long a credit must you give to your master before receiving pay for work done?" Karl Marx, *Questionnaire for Workers*, in I:25 KARL MARX [&] FRIEDRICH ENGELS, GESAMTAUSGABE (MEGA) 199, 204 (1985 [1880]).

19. A turn-of-the-century American political economist combined the positions of Cantillon and Taussig by emphasizing that "wages may also be received by small independent producers who perform their own labor." CHARLES BULLOCK, THE ELEMENTS OF ECONOMICS 271 (2d ed. 1913 [1905]).

20. *See* ERIK WRIGHT, CLASS STRUCTURE AND INCOME DETERMINATION 95 (1979).

21. For very brief interpretations of Smith's view, see SAMUEL HOLLANDER, THE ECONOMICS OF ADAM SMITH 103-104, 115 (1976 [1973]); MAXINE BERG, THE AGE OF MANUFACTURES: INDUSTRY, INNOVATION AND WORK IN BRITAIN 1700-1820, at 59-64, 278-86 (1985).

22. FRITZ MARBACH, THEORIE DES MITTELSTANDES 67 (1942).

23. MARX, ZUR KRITIK DER POLITISCHEN ÖKONOMIE (MANUSKRIPT 1861-1863) at 2180-81. In their dogmatic Marxist work, Baudelot et al. have failed even to reproduce the dogma correctly by arguing syllogistically that because (1) the petty bourgeois "vivent d'une rétrocession de plus-value" and (2) artisans and farmers "n'EXPLOITENT personne et ne sont EXPLOITÉS par personne"; therefore, (3) the petty bourgeoisie does not include artisans or paysans. BAUDELOT, ESTABLET, & MALEMORT, LA PETITE BOURGEOISIE EN FRANCE at 41, 14, 221.

24. MARX, ZUR KRITIK DER POLITISCHEN ÖKONOMIE (MANUSKRIPT 1861-1863) at 2155.

25. A very plastic description of the efforts of one group of self-employed to maintain their hybrid status can be found in the position that physicians in the Am. Med. Ass'n took until recently:

> The AMA opposed any one else, such as an investor, making a return from physicians' labor. The AMA was saying...that there must be no capital formation in medical care (other than what doctors accumulated), that the full return on physicians' labor had to go to physicians, and consequently, by implication, that if medicine required any capital that

doctors themselves could not provide, it would have to be contributed gratis by the community, instead of by investors looking for a profit.

PAUL STARR, THE SOCIAL TRANSFORMATION OF AMERICAN MEDICINE 216 (1982).

26. John Wilson, *The Political Economy of Contract Farming*, REV. RADICAL POL. ECON., Winter 1986, at 47, 56. For an early example of a contract farming relationship in which Campbell Soup Co. treated carrot farmers as de facto piece-rate workers, see Campbell Soup Co. v. Wentz, 172 F.2d 80 (3d Cir. 1948).

27. *See* ARONSON, SELF-EMPLOYMENT at 43; Marc Linder, *Self-Employment as a Cyclical Escape from Unemployment: A Case Study of the Construction Industry in the United States During the Postwar Period*, 2 RESEARCH IN SOC. OF WORK: PERIPHERAL WORKERS 261, 262 (1983). *See also* STEWART CLEGG, PAUL BOREHAM, & GEOFF DOW, CLASS, POLITICS, AND THE ECONOMY 81 (1986) ("craftspeople who purvey manual skills which might otherwise be for sale as wage-labour").

28. ARONSON, SELF-EMPLOYMENT at 118-19.

29. *Id.* at xi.

30. *Id.* at ix.

31. *Id.* at xi. This is Schumpeter's narrow, not Frank Knight's broader, sense. *See* DAVID EVANS & LINDA LEIGHTON, SELF-EMPLOYMENT SELECTION AND EARNINGS OVER THE LIFE CYCLE 3 (U.S. Small Bus. Adm., Dec. 1987): "Self-employed workers are certainly Knightean entrepreneurs because they have control over their workplace and they bear risk as residual income claimants." Evans and Leighton's *petitio principii* is obvious: the whole point of analysis is whether in fact these criteria are met.

32. ARONSON, SELF-EMPLOYMENT at xii.

33. *See* Daniel Bertaux & Isabelle Bertaux-Wiame,*Artisanal Bakery in France: How It Lives and Why it Survives*, in THE PETITE BOURGEOISIE: COMPARATIVE STUDIES OF THE UNEASY STRATUM 155-81 (F. Bechhofer & B. Elliott ed. 1981); Carl Cuneo, *Has the Traditional Petite Bourgeoisie Persisted?* 9 CANAD. J. SOC. 269, 293-94 (1984); Harriet Friedmann, *Patriarchal Commodity Production*, SOCIAL ANALYSIS, Dec. 1986, at 47-55.

34. In fact, the BLS/BOC data on the unincorporated self-employed already include partners in such a way that it is not possible to go behind and to correct them. *See* MANUAL at D6-24.

35. Similarly, BEVERLY LOZANO, THE INVISIBLE WORK FORCE: TRANSFORMING AMERICAN BUSINESS WITH OUTSIDE AND HOME-BASED WORKERS 11 (1989), who correctly observes that the BOC cannot ask or answer the subtle questions (concerning independence, autonomy, access to profits, number of clients, who controls the pace of work, sets the price, and

owns the equipment) necessary to identify a third category of those she calls "informal workers," fails to see that the same deficiencies render the prevailing dichotomy between the self-employed and employees equally unsubstantiated.

36. INTERNATIONAL LABOUR OFFICE, THE PROMOTION OF SELF-EMPLOYMENT 1-2 (Int'l Lab. Conf., 77th Sess., Rep. VII, 1990)

37. Catherine Hakim, *Self-Employment in Britain: Recent Trends and Current Issues*, 2 WORK, EMPLOYMENT & SOCIETY 421, 434 (1988).

38. George Steinmetz and Erik Wright, *The Fall and Rise of the Petty Bourgeoisie: Changing Patterns of Self-Employment in the Postwar United States*, 94 AM. J. SOC. 973, 979 (1989). Aronson's claim that Steinmetz and Wright "have explained the rise in nonfarm self-employment as an anticapitalist development" is wholly without foundation. *See* ARONSON, SELF-EMPLOYMENT at 118.

39. 3 MARX, DAS KAPITAL at 882. *See also* THOMAS CARVER, PRINCIPLES OF POLITICAL ECONOMY 385-86 (1919) ("In many small enterprises the independent business man does his own work and is therefore a laborer...and furnishes his own capital and is therefore his own capitalist").

40. 3 MARX, DAS KAPITAL at 882.

41. In fact, since the self-employed presumably work with an inferior capital stock, the level of self-exploitation may even exceed that obtaining in the dominant sector.

42. Steinmetz and Wright, *The Fall and Rise of the Petty Bourgeoisie* at 980.

43. *See* Marc Linder and John Houghton, *Self-Employment and the Petty Bourgeoisie: Comment on Steinmetz and Wright*, 96 AM. J. SOC. 727, 729 (1990). Marx himself merely names--rather than solves--the problem when he says that nonemploying independent artisans or farmers sell commodities rather than their labor. MARX, ZUR KRITIK DER POLITISCHEN ÖKONOMIE (MANUSKRIPT 1861-1863) at 2179.

44. This essence is expressed in French and German, where the self-employed are called *indépendants* and *Selbständige*, respectively. *See* 10/1 JACOB GRIMM & WILHELM GRIMM, DEUTSCHES WÖRTERBUCH 494 (1905) ("selbständig" as adjective: independent in economic or legal sense). Germans have eschewed such linguistically available coinages as *Selbstbeschäftigte, Selbstbeschäftiger, Selbstangestellte, Selbstarbeitgeber*, or *Selbstarbeitnehmer*. The mere fact that a linguistic community constructs some workers as *independent*, however, does not explain that independence. As a French legal scholar noted, defining economic dependence by reference to receiving income for an activity compensated by others is "fuzzy" "in contemporary societies where practically all the citizens are economically dependent on one another." JEAN-JACQUES DUPEYROUX, SÉCURITÉ SOCIALE 244 (1967).

45. Frank Bechhofer & Brian Elliott, *The Voice of Small Business and the Politics of Survival*, SOCIOLOGICAL REV., Feb. 1978, at 57, 61.

46. EMIL GRÜNBERG, DER MITTELSTAND IN DER KAPITALISTISCHEN GESELLSCHAFT: EINE ÖKONOMISCHE UND SOZIOLOGISCHE UNTERSUCHUNG 168 (1932).

47. If, moreover, half of all men shifting from employee status to self-employment also change their industry or occupation, EVANS & LEIGHTON, SELF-EMPLOYMENT SELECTION AND EARNINGS at 3, it is questionable whether the capital they bring is competitively relevant. WILLIAM FORM, DIVIDED WE STAND: WORKING-CLASS STRATIFICATION IN AMERICA 30-31 (1985), adduces work autonomy, property ownership, above-average occupational skills, and favored ascriptive status (i.e., male, white, native-born) as the characteristic resources of the self-employed. Only the first two distinguish the self-employed from employees, whereby autonomy derives largely from ownership of the means of production (and unusual skills, which may be viewed as human capital).

48. MARCIA LEVY, SELF-EMPLOYMENT IN THE COVERED WORK FORCE 22 (Soc. Sec. Adm. Staff Paper No. 19, 1975), exaggerated in stating that the data confirm "[t]he typical picture of self-employed individuals as farmers, shopkeepers, or professional persons engaged in their own practice."

49. George Steinmetz & Erik Wright, *Reply to Linder and Houghton*, 96 AM. J. SOC. 736, 738-39 (1990).

50. It is not even in law--let alone socioeconomically--the case that the "labor-only self-employed" are in reality employees only if they "sell their labor power only to one contractor or capitalist rather than to a variety of contractors and...do not sell their products directly to consumers." Steinmetz & Wright, *Reply to Linder and Houghton* at 739 n.5. *See* Marc Linder, *Employees, Not-So-Independent Contractors, and the Case of Migrant Farmworkers: A Challenge to the "Law and Economics" Agency Doctrine*, 15 N.Y.U. REV. L. & SOC. CHANGE 435, 469-71 (1986-87).

51. *Id*. at 469-70.

52. *See* MARC LINDER, THE EMPLOYMENT RELATIONSHIP IN ANGLO-AMERICAN LAW: A HISTORICAL PERSPECTIVE 11-14 (1989).

53. Marx refers to the "independent artisan, who works for stray customers." MARX, ZUR KRITIK DER POLITISCHEN ÖKONOMIE (MANUSKRIPT 1861-1863) at 2133. For a schematic explanation of various outwork and homework relationships, see LINDER, THE EMPLOYMENT RELATIONSHIP IN ANGLO-AMERICAN LAW at 6-11; GERALD JAYNES, BRANCHES WITHOUT ROOTS: GENESIS OF THE BLACK WORKING CLASS IN THE AMERICAN SOUTH, 1862-1882, at 26-29 (1986).

54. ERIK WRIGHT, CLASSES 53 (1985).

55. *Id.* at 103 n.39. For mathematical proof of how unequal exchange can generate a division of nonemploying independent producers into exploited and exploiters, see JOHN ROEMER, A GENERAL THEORY OF EXPLOITATION AND CLASS 123-32 (1982); *idem, New Directions in the Marxian Theory of Exploitation and Class*, in ANALYTICAL MARXISM 81, 84-90 (J. Roemer ed. 1985 [1982]). For incisive criticism of Roemer's overall revision of Marx, see W. Anderson & Frank Thompson, *Neoclassical Marxism*, 52 SCI. & SOC. 215 (1988).

56. WRIGHT, CLASSES at 62 n.47.

57.   Under circumstances in which the self-employed are economically insecure, it is difficult to claim that they are autonomous in their work, that they are truly free to make their own decisions and be their own bosses while surviving as well. ...
If we think of the "free" artisan and shopkeeper in the same terms, we cannot fail to observe how penury, long hours, panicky fear of losing essential customers, and bankruptcy are commonly associated with the condition of self-employment.... Indeed, it might be argued that such oppressive conditions are typical of self-employment, success being the exception. Beggars and ragpickers, after all, are self-employed.

ELIOT FREIDSON, PROFESSIONAL POWERS: A STUDY OF THE INSTITUTIONALIZATION OF FORMAL KNOWLEDGE 124 (1986).

58. That is, other than the self-exploiter herself. Ontogeny recapitulates phylogeny here: just as it was once said that it was senseless for workers in a socialist state to strike against themselves, a self-employed worker would have to be schizophrenic to take action against herself. But then the hybrid model posits the self-employed as literally schizoid ("cut up into two persons").

59. "The self-employed are isolated workers who do not come together politically.... If the self-employed cannot act in their self-interest, they cannot link up with other employees to increase working-class political power." WILLIAM FORM, DIVIDED WE STAND at 263. *See also* William Form, *Self-Employed Manual Workers: Petty Bourgeois or Working Class?* 60 SOCIAL FORCES 1050, 1062-65 (1982) (self-employed are more conservative than employees). For a historical discussion of the reverse process--the integration of isolated workers into formal proletarian positions--in terms of organization and consciousness, see LINDER, EUROPEAN LABOR ARISTOCRACIES at 202-205.

60. FREIDSON, PROFESSIONAL POWERS at 124-25.

61. *See* WILLIAM REDDY, MONEY AND LIBERTY IN MODERN EUROPE: A CRITIQUE OF HISTORICAL UNDERSTANDING ch. 3 (1987).

62. For a critique, see Marc Linder, *What Is an Employee? Why It Does, But Should Not, Matter*, 7 LAW & INEQUALITY 155, 172 n.75 (1989).

63. THOMAS CARVER, PRINCIPLES OF POLITICAL ECONOMY at 378-79, 402.

64. *See* Marc Linder, *Employees, Not-So-Independent Contractors, and the Case of Migrant Farmworkers* at 470-71.

65. *See* DIETER BÖGENHOLD, DIE SELBSTÄNDIGEN: ZUR SOZIOLOGIE DEZENTRALER PRODUKTION 218 (1985). TOM ELFRING, SERVICE SECTOR EMPLOYMENT IN ADVANCED ECONOMIES: A COMPARATIVE ANALYSIS OF ITS IMPLICATIONS FOR ECONOMIC GROWTH 137 (1988), mentions peddlers, shoe cleaners, small-scale retailers, and repairers as among those pushed into self-employment "because it is their only option." Or as Irving Leveson, *Some Determinants of Non-Farm Self-Employment*, MONTHLY LAB. REV., May 1968, at 11, 16, framed the issue, "a prerequisite for access to self-employment as a vehicle for social mobility may be the attainment of a minimum occupational level."

66. Harold Aurand, *Self-Employment: Last Resort for the Unemployed*, INT'L SOC. SCI. REV., Winter 1983, at 7, 9 (discussing coal miners in the 1930s).

67. JAMES WOOD, EMPLOYMENT EXPERIENCE OF PATERSON BROAD-SILK WORKERS, 1926-36: A STUDY OF INTERMITTENCY OF EMPLOYMENT IN A DECLINING INDUSTRY 32-33 (WPA Nat'l Research Proj. 1939), quoting SILK TEXTILE WORK ASSIGNMENT BOARD, REPORT UPON CONTRACT WEAVING IN THE RAYON AND SILK INDUSTRY 4 (mimeo. 4387, 1935) (latter document, according to RLIN, OCLC, and 546 NATIONAL UNION CATALOG: PRE-1956 IMPRINTS 156 col. 1 (1978), held only by John Crerar Library, which was folded into University of Chicago Library, which in turn sold document to Detroit Public Library, which lost it). *See generally*, ALFRED OXENFELDT, NEW FIRMS AND FREE ENTERPRISE: PRE-WAR AND POST-WAR ASPECTS 120-23 (1943). Truck and taxicab drivers are contemporary examples of workers who buy their vehicles in order to avoid unemployment. *See* Richard Peterson, John Schmidman, & Kirk Elifson, *Entrepreneurship or Autonomy? Truckers and Cabbies*, in VARIETIES OF WORK 181, 184, 190 (P. Stewart & M. Cantor ed. 1982). For another example of the flight of the unemployed into nominal self-employment, see U.S. BUREAU OF LABOR STATISTICS, IMPACT ON WORKERS AND COMMUNITY OF A PLANT SHUTDOWN IN A DEPRESSED AREA 18 (Bull. No. 1264, 1960). In Britain, too, it has been established that for some, "self-employment represents a second-best alternative to an employee job." While such "involuntary entrants...seek only to provide themselves with a job," even among the voluntary, some "seek[] only to 'own their own job.'" Catherine Hakim, *New Recruits to Self-Employment in the 1980s*, 97 EMPLOYMENT GAZETTE 286, 290, 291 (1989). *See also* JAMES TREBLE, URBAN POVERTY IN BRITAIN 1870-1914, at 47-49 (1979) (hawking as response to cyclical unemployment).

68. Even in the professions such as medicine and law, "[t]he relative status of the salaried and independent groups may be reversed during cyclical depressions when large numbers of previously salaried individuals may become unemployed and enter individual practice because they find it impossible to obtain salaried employment." MILTON FRIEDMAN & SIMON

KUZNETS, INCOME FROM INDEPENDENT PROFESSIONAL PRACTICE 297 (1945). More recently, self-employed accountants, doctors, and lawyers, appear to have had higher earnings than their employee counterparts. *See* Eugene Becker, *Self-Employed Workers: An Update to 1983*, MONTHLY LAB. REV., July 1984, at 14, 18.

69. In this regard it is wrong that if the self-employed in hard times drive themselves and families harder, "[i]t is largely a private question as to how badly or how well they treat themselves in terms of hours and conditions of work." INTERNATIONAL LABOUR OFFICE, THE PROMOTION OF SELF-EMPLOYMENT 5 (Int'l Lab. Conf., 77th Sess., Rep. VII, 1990). Through the force of competition, such substandard labor conditions may have an impact on formal employees. Such entities have therefore often been called "'cockroach' shops." *See* WOOD, EMPLOYMENT EXPERIENCE OF PATERSON BROAD-SILK WORKERS, 1926-36 at 33.

70. As has long been recognized, a large or even increasing number of self-employed in a branch may indicate overcrowding rather than prosperity. *See* ANNETTE LEPPERT-FÖGEN, DIE DEKLASSIERTE KLASSE: STUDIEN ZUR GESCHICHTE UND IDEOLOGIE DES KLEINBÜRGERTUMS 19, 19 n.20 (1974).

71. *See* Kurt Bauman, *Characteristics of the Low-Income Self-Employed*, 40 INDUS. REL. RES. ASS'N PROC. 339, 340 (1987) (data include the incorporated self-employed). *See also* David Evans & Linda Leighton, *Some Empirical Aspects of Entrepreneurship*, 79 AM. ECON. REV. 519, 521 (1989) ("Poorer wage workers--that is, unemployed workers, lower-paid wage workers, and men who have changed jobs a lot--are more likely to enter self-employment...all else equal. These results are consistent with the view of some sociologists that 'misfits' are pushed into entrepreneurship").

72. JOSEPH PHILLIPS, THE SELF-EMPLOYED IN THE UNITED STATES 51 (1962).

73. MARTIN WEITZMAN, THE SHARE ECONOMY: CONQUERING STAGFLATION (1984), generalizes this claim to all employment.

74. *Reply to Linder and Houghton* at 737 n.2.

75. For a sketch of an explanation of this phenomenon emphasizing the central role of social norms, see ROBERT SOLOW, THE LABOR MARKET AS A SOCIAL INSTITUTION 28-50 (1990).

76. Lloyd Reynolds, *Cutthroat Competition*, 30 AM. ECON. REV. 736, 747 n.29 (1940).

77. *See* Martha Loufti, *Self-Employment Patterns and Policy Issues in Europe*, 130 INT'L. LAB. REV. 1, 17 (1991).

78. SOLOW, THE LABOR MARKET AS A SOCIAL INSTITUTION at 39.

79. *See infra* ch. 5.

80. *See, e.g.*, MICHAEL PIORE, BIRDS OF PASSAGE: MIGRANT LABOR AND INDUSTRIAL SOCIETIES 95-98 (1979).

81. *See* Otto Nathan, *Favorable Economic Implications of the Fair Labor Standards Act*, 6 LAW & CONTEMP. PROBS. 416, 417 (1939); PAUL SAMUELSON, ECONOMICS 577 n.2 (9th ed. 1973 [1948]).

82. 4 PARL. DEB. H.C. (5th ser.) 382 (1909) (Mr. Balfour); Robert Hale, *Minimum Wages and the Constitution*, 36 COLUM. L. REV. 629, 630 (1936).

83. For criticism of the neoclassical analysis of the labor market, see SOLOW, THE LABOR MARKET AS A SOCIAL INSTITUTION.

84. Steve Balkin, *Self-Employment Assistance Programs in the United States Targeted to Low-Income Disadvantaged People*, in 40 INDUS. REL. RES. ASS'N PROC. 356, 359-60 (1987). *See also* STEVE BALKIN, SELF-EMPLOYMENT FOR LOW-INCOME PEOPLE (1989).

85. *See generally*, BELOUS, THE CONTINGENT ECONOMY.

86. David Rabban, *Distinguishing Excluded Managers from Covered Professionals under the NLRA*, 89 COLUM. L. REV. 1775, 1845, n.327 (1989), sharing Freidson's perspective, argues that "[w]hen demand for their services is high, salaried professionals often have substantially more autonomy than self-employed 'free' professionals who have difficulty attracting clients or who are dependent on only a few clients."

4

Substance

"Independents" [whose] independence consisted in the necessity of independently bearing the misery without the social protection which the employees enjoyed.[1]

Who Are the Self-Employed?

[T]he self-employed are a highly diverse category of workers.... Their diversity and uniqueness have undoubtedly contributed to their being treated as a nuisance in most research on the psychology of work. One suspects that a reason for frequently classifying all the self-employed together in occupational status codes is that it facilitates their elimination from analysis.[2]

From 1975 to 1990, the crucial years of the alleged "renaissance of the self-employed,"[3] the number of (unincorporated) self-employed as a share of all nonagricultural employed rose only marginally--from 6.9 per cent to 7.7 per cent (table 1).[4] Significantly, the growth in the absolute number and the rate of increase of self-employed women--whose claim to economic independence is much more tenuous than men's[5]--exceeded those of men: the number of nonagricultural self-employed women rose by 1,662,000, or 112.3 per cent, while that of men increased by 1,394,000, or 33.0 per cent.[6] Indeed, after the aggregate rate

Farewell to the Self-Employed

of self-employment peaked in 1983, it was only the continued rise in the rate of female self-employment that restrained the decline in the former.

Table 1
Rate of (Unincorporated) Nonagricultural Self-Employment, 1975-1990

	Total	Men	Women
1975	6.9%	8.6%	4.4%
1980	7.3	9.0	5.1
1983	7.8	9.5	5.6
1990	7.7	9.1	6.0

Source: Calculated according to data in U.S. BUREAU OF LABOR STATISTICS, LABOR FORCE STATISTICS DERIVED FROM THE CURRENT POPULATION SURVEY, 1948-87, tab. B-11 at 625-26 (Bull. 2307, 1988); U.S. BUREAU OF LABOR STATISTICS, HANDBOOK OF LABOR STATISTICS (Bull. 2340, 1989), tab. 21 at 112-13; EMPLOYMENT AND EARNINGS, Jan. 1991, tab. 23 at 191.

Scrutiny of the shifts in the industrial and occupational locations of the self-employed as disclosed by a variety of sources may shed light on the solidity of their status. If the focus is narrowed to the years 1976 to 1983, which Steinmetz and Wright single out as the core years of the relative rise of the self-employed,[7] total nonagricultural self-employment grew by thirty-five per cent. Disproportionately high growth rates were recorded in the following six distinctly dependent occupations, which alone accounted for thirty per cent (513,000) of the aggregate increase of (1,736,000) self-employed: hucksters[8] (216 per cent); maids, janitors, and cleaners (170 per cent); truck drivers (70 per cent); child care workers (67 per cent); taxi drivers (63 per cent); and hairdressers and cosmetologists (34 per cent).[9]

For at least a half-century, the service, construction, and retail industries have accounted for about four-fifths of all unincorporated self-employed.[10] From 1979 to 1988, while the total number of nonfarm sole proprietorships filing returns with the Internal Revenue Service (IRS) rose by forty-six per cent, from 9,343,603 to 13,679,302,[11] service businesses increased by seventy-six per cent--from 3,654,001 to 6,456,871. Thus, new service businesses alone accounted for almost two-thirds (65%) of the total net increase. Within services, the largest individual increases were recorded for miscellaneous personal services: 580,998 (244 per cent); other business services: 564,701 (173 per cent); management/public relations: 336,913 (130 per cent); services to buildings: 196,637 (143 per cent); computer/data processing: 120,936 (539 per cent); and beauty shops: 85,999 (36 per cent).[12] In other words, the increases were concentrated in businesses requiring little or no physical or human capital and those requiring significant formalized credentials.[13]

Many of these entities, of course, may be large employers, the existence of which says little or nothing about the course of self-employment. More relevant here are unpublished CPS data on the unincorporated self-employed. They show that between 1983, when the BLS/BOC introduced a new occupational classification, and 1988, services accounted for twenty-eight per cent of the increase in total nonagricultural self-employment and was the only sector in which the rate of self-employment rose. Even more revealingly, the increase of almost a quarter-million self-employed in four occupations--maid, janitor, hairdresser, and child care worker--alone accounted for nine-tenths of the increase within the service sector and more than one-quarter of the entire growth of nonagricultural self-employment.[14] These are precisely the kinds of jobs that prompt the strongest doubts about their classification as self-employment.

A more precise picture of the service businesses in the late 1980s emerges from the 1987 Census of Service Industries. Of the 6,254,512 establishments returned in that year, seventy-nine per cent were individual proprietorships, seventy-four per cent were without payroll, and seventy per cent individual proprietorships without payroll. The average receipts of all establishments without payroll amounted to $21,000, compared to $475,000 for those with payroll.[15] If the receipts were $21,000, it may be assumed that the net income of the average service proprietorship with no

employees was only a fraction of that amount--that is,
considerably less than half of the median earnings of year-
round, full-time workers in 1987 (which were $26,008 for
men and $16,909 for women).[16] Data from earlier censuses
disclose a pronounced trend toward ever more diminutive
one-person service providers. In 1977 only fifty-seven per
cent (1,109,617) of 1,834,713 establishments were individual
proprietorships without payroll;[17] in 1967 and 1963 the
respective shares were fifty-six per cent (666,404 of 1,187,814)
and fifty-two per cent (557,317 of 1,061,673).[18] In 1977, 1967,
and 1963, the average receipts of service establishments
without payroll were ninety-four, 105, and 107 per cent,
respectively, of the median earnings of year-round, full-time
male workers[19]--compared to only eighty-one per cent in
1987.

Table 2 reports, by branch of business, the largest number
of individual proprietorships without payroll[20] in the service
sector in 1987.

Table 2
**Largest Branches in Service Sector by Number of
Individual Proprietorships without Payroll, 1987 and 1977**

Branch	1987 Number	% of All Establishments	1977 Number	% of All Establishments	% Increase 1977-1987
All	4,386,405	70	1,048,501	57	318
Health services[a]	279,640	56	NA[b]	NA	NA
Beauty shops	252,199	75	119,344	61	111
Building services	238,276	82	38,948	58	512

Table 2 (*cont.*)

Branch	1987		1977		% In-
	Number	% of All Estab-lishments	Number	% of All Estab-lishments	crease 1977-1987
Child day care	221,780	89	157[c]	1	141260
Auto repair	178,221	59	67,279	44	165
Accounting/ book-keeping	175,512	70	84,501	67	107
Theatrical producers/ enter-tainers	169,783	91	58,832	87	186
Legal services	129,136	47	70,605	42	83
Engi-neering/ archi-tectural	123,656	63	NA[d]	NA	NA
Computer services	97,988	70	4,557	28	2050
Medical doctors	97,467	33	51,727	27	88

Source: Calculated according to data in U.S. BUREAU OF THE CENSUS, 1987 CENSUS OF SERVICE INDUSTRIES: NONEMPLOYER STATISTICS SERIES: MIDWEST tab. 1 at 2-3-2-9; U.S BUREAU OF THE CENSUS, 1977 CENSUS OF SERVICE INDUSTRIES, 1 SUBJECT STATISTICS at 1-12-1-38, 1-141-1-151, 9-5-9-9, 9-81.

[a]Except medical doctors.
[b]Other than physicians' offices, this branch included 254,919 establishments. Excluding the rubric "not elsewhere classified (n.e.c.)," 27,943 establishments were individual proprietorships without payroll. The n.e.c. category included an additional 111,534 establishments without payroll, but these were not broken out according to ownership form. Calculated according to data in *id.* at 8-3 and 8-37.
[c]These data overstate the number of nonemploying proprietorships since they include all ownership forms of organization. In 1977, 14,172 taxable child care service establishments were returned, only 157 of which reported no employees. There were an additional 10,641 tax-exempt (i.e., nonprofit) establishments. *Id.,* tab. 30 at 9-63.
[d]In 1977, data for sole proprietorships without payroll were not published separately for this branch. Of 75,583 establishments, 50,541 were sole proprietorships and 34,403 establishments without payroll. 1977 CENSUS OF SERVICE INDUSTRIES, 1 SUBJECT STATISTICS at 9-7.

Farewell to the Self-Employed

Table 2 shows both an explosion in the number of isolated workers, such as janitors, hairdressers, and child care attendants engaged in pseudo-self-employment,[21] who perform services at the low end of the spectrum of skill, technology, capital, and income, and an increase in independent professionals[22] at the high end.[23]

The increasingly insubstantial character of isolated workers' activities is replicated in the construction industry (table 3).

Table 3
Construction Industry Establishments
without Payroll, 1972, 1982, and 1987

	Number	% of All Establishments in Category
All		
1972	482,865	52%
1982	912,452	67
1987	1,368,322	72
Specialty Trades		
1972	384,343	59
1982	700,833	70
1987	1,062,226	76

Source: Calculated according to data in U.S. BUREAU OF THE CENSUS, 1972 CENSUS OF CONSTRUCTION INDUSTRIES, 1 INDUSTRY AND SPECIAL STATISTICS tab. A1 at 1-3 (1976); U.S. BUREAU OF THE CENSUS, 1987 CENSUS OF CONSTRUCTION INDUSTRIES, INDUSTRY SERIES, UNITED STATES SUMMARY: ESTABLISHMENTS WITH AND WITHOUT PAYROLL tab. 1 at 7 (1990) (excluding land subdividers and developers).

The number of construction establishments without payroll almost tripled during these fifteen years, while their share of all establishments in the industry rose from little more than half to almost three-quarters. The very modest incomes such solo workers were able to generate can be gauged by the average value of business done (that is, including costs) by specialty trade "contractors" without payroll; in 1987, 1982, and 1972 it amounted to only $32,000, $27,000, and $13,000, respectively, compared to $597,000, $444,000, and $212,000, respectively, for those with payroll. The two largest specialties were considerably smaller: in 1987, 166,591 solo painters/paperhangers on the average did only $22,000 in business, and 337,935 carpenters averaged $24,000.[24] Overall in 1987, sixty-nine per cent of all specialty trade contractors without payroll did work for less than $25,000; in 1972, forty-one per cent had done less than the equivalent inflation-adjusted figure of $10,000.[25]

In retail trade, the third large sector harboring considerable numbers of self-employed, the data also confirm subproletarian incomes of the proprietors. Isolated workers, however, do not predominate as they do in services and construction, nor do they display the same monolithic trend toward proliferation. At the most recent business census in 1987, 916,048 establishments without payroll accounted for thirty-eight per cent of all establishments; their average sales of $51,000 amounted to approximately one-twentieth of that of establishments with payroll.[26] Of these retail establishments without payroll, sixteen per cent reported sales of $10,000-$25,000, eleven per cent $5,000-$10,000, and sixteen per cent less than $5,000. Because twenty per cent did not operate during the entire year and were not included in the sales breakdown, these groups accounted for fifty-four per cent of year-round establishments without payroll.[27] Ten years earlier,[28] only 551,447, or thirty per cent of 1,855,068, retail establishments were without payroll.[29] The numbers and shares of retail establishments without payroll in the 1960s were similar to those in 1977.[30]

The branches that recorded the largest number of retail establishments without payroll (as a percentage of all stores) in 1987 are identified in table 4.[31]

Table 4
Largest Branches in Retail Trade by
Number of Establishments without Payroll, 1987

Branch	Number of Establish-ments	% of All Establish-ments in in Branch	Average Sales ($000)
All	916,048	38	51
Eating/ drinking	99,080	20	47
Used merchan-dise	74,502	83	23
Furniture/ furnishings	70,359	39	47
Grocery	59,632	30	92
Used car dealer	59,573	80	125
Apparel	47,976	24	40
Gift/ souvenir	46,672	59	21
Sporting goods	28,198	57	42
Florist	22,819	46	28
Gas service station	22,432	16	124

Source: Calculated according to data in U.S. BUREAU OF THE CENSUS, 1987 CENSUS OF RETAIL TRADE, SPECIAL REPORT SERIES: SELECTED STATISTICS tab. 2 at 1-4-1-9 (1991); U.S. BUREAU OF THE CENSUS, 1987 CENSUS OF RETAIL TRADE, NONEMPLOYER STATISTICS SERIES, NORTHEAST tab. 1 at 1-3-1-4 (1990).

Once costs are deducted from such average sales, it is clear that many of these solo retailers--in particular the large numbers of establishments with sales much below the average--also receive incomes far below those of an average employee.[32] When long store hours and the widespread use of unpaid family workers are taken into account, the aggregate working and living conditions of such families may be far inferior to those of outright employees.

Income and Class

> [M]ore than one-seventh of the self-employed earned less than the minimum wage.[33]

> In the poorest parts of the country...self-employment is frequently the only manner in which a living income can be put together.[34]

If those classified as self-employed are viewed not as a homogeneous class defined by their uniquely hybrid relationship to labor and the means of production but instead as composed of heterogeneous sectors including proletarianized and lumpen strata, then the loss of the criterion of the capacity to capture part of their own surplus labor[35] will no longer distinguish them from employees. Once this criterion ceases to apply to the nominally self-employed, the distributional pattern of income will overlap with that of the working class.

Overall, the literature agrees, employees' income exceeds that of the self-employed:[36] "On average, wage-and-salary work pays substantially better than self-employment."[37] Moreover, "[t]he central fact about the earnings of the self-employed in the recent period of expansion is their decline from a relatively more favorable level to a relatively less favorable level in comparison with the average earnings of employees."[38] Social security data reveal a steady upward trend in the average annual total earnings of wage and salary workers as a share of those of the self-employed from 1968 forward: 1955, eighty per cent; 1960, eighty-three per cent; 1965, sixty-seven per cent; 1970, seventy-two per cent; 1975, seventy-five per cent; 1980, nintey-six per cent; 1988, 128 per cent.[39] Unpublished CPS data show that the mean income of wage and salary workers as a share of that of nonfarm self-employed men (women) rose from 1974 to 1984 from 110 per cent (176 per cent) to 130 per cent (189 per cent).[40]

Unpublished CPS data also reveal that the median annual earnings of year-round, full-time (unincorporated) self-employed were considerably lower than those of their employee counterparts. In 1987, the male self-employed earned 83.2 per cent[41] and self-employed women only 61.4 per cent as much as wage and salary workers.[42] With regard to specific occupations, the shares that the self-employed attained vis-à-vis employees appear in table 5.

Table 5
Median Annual Earnings of Year-Round, Full-Time Self-Employed as a Share of Those of Wage and Salary Workers, Selected Occupations, 1987

Occupation	%
Managerial	68
Professional	119
Technician	104
Sales	91
Services	78
Mechanic-repairer	51
Construction	79
Precision production	59
Operator	97
Transport	103
Handler	71
Cleaning & building service	80
Personal service	82

Source: Calculated according to data in U.S. BLS, CURRENT POPULATION SURVEY (unpub. tabulations 1987).

It shows that the income of the self-employed is much more skewed than that of employees, again suggesting that they are heterogeneous strata rather than a unitary class. Thus, in 1987, even among those employed fulltime and yearround, the self-employed displayed a much more bipolar distribution of income than did employees. Whereas 9.8 per cent of employees earned less than $10,000, 27.0 per cent of the self-employed did; at the other end of the scale, 2.2 per cent of employees reported earnings of more than $75,000 compared to 5.0 per cent of the self-employed.[43] A calculation including the incorporated self-employed shows similar results (table 6).[44]

Table 6
Distributional Extremes of Income among Year-Round, Full-Time Employees and Self-Employed, 1982

	<$5,000	>$30,000
Wage and salary workers	1.2%	17.3%
Incorporated self-employed	4.6	50.5
Unincorporated self-employed	19.1	23.5

Source: U.S. SMALL BUS. ADM'N, THE STATE OF SMALL BUSINESS [1986] tab. 4.12 at 130 (1986).

In seeking to identify differences between employees and self-employed that might be relevant to explaining their respective earnings, one researcher notes that "[t]he obvious major difference, in principle, is in their ownership, responsibility, and control over physical capital." This difference implies first "that the entire yield of the capital investment will belong to its owner and that there will be a strong incentive to utilize plant, equipment, and tools more efficiently. Second, the self-employed worker, as entrepreneur, should be compensated for the risk of loss of capital and, as worker, for job loss should the business venture fail."[45] The first point follows from or is at least consistent with Marx's conceptualization of independent producers as workers whose ability to interpose capital enables them to prevent their suppliers and customers from capturing all of the surplus value they create. The problem is that empirical studies show little advantage accruing to the self-employed from capital ownership, perhaps because of the small scale of enterprise and the low quality of capital;

moreover, in recessions, underemployed self-employed may accept lower earnings as a means of preserving their capital investment and as an alternative to unemployment when they are not eligible for unemployment insurance benefits.[46]

One available inference from these data--albeit one that the aforementioned researcher does not draw[47]--is that such nominal self-employed are not and should not be categorized as independent economic agents.   This inference is also consistent with the finding that half of all male employees switching to self-employment change industry or occupation,[48] which suggests that impulses other than the contemplated use of accumulated skills and training may motivate a significant segment of those shifting to nominal self-employment.

The political importance of the intersection between class and income lies in the sphere of ideology. According to one influential formulation:

> If we consider only the economic grounds of determining the societal division into classes, the demarcation at the low end is clear insofar as the non-independent owner of labor power only, i.e., he who in principle is always dependent on the labor market, would never be petty bourgeois [*Mittelständler*], but would always have to be a proletarian. Nevertheless even the economic (i.e., not only the ideological) demarcation at the low end has its difficulties. Such difficulties surface as soon as one thinks of the *independent* owner of only his own labor power, of the small master or dealer with only other people's operating funds.... The income-poor hairdresser, small cabinet-maker, retail dealer, tailor is despite the low income conceptually not a proletarian, and he does not feel himself to be such either. He has at his disposal, apart from his labor power, modest means of production and tools--but still means of production and tools. Furthermore, he does not enter the labor market in order to sell his labor power to be placed at someone else's disposal. He employs it himself and remains in freedom a poor man. In spite of the possibly meager income, small dealers, artisans, or small producers are therefore in principle never proletarians.[49]

This approach may become empirically fruitful only to the extent that it does not commit a *petitio principii*, which can be avoided only if criteria are articulated to identify those who do not sell their labor power on the labor market.

The sole criterion that Marbach develops is whether the worker in question sells directly to a noncapitalist consumer or, alternatively, to a firm not in the same product market and hence unable to control him. A solo house painter with minimal tools (brushes and a ladder or scaffolding) earning less than the average worker may serve as a contemporary example. Although his individual customers do not tell him how to paint, it is not clear that a painting contractor-employer would interfere significantly with the routine details of his work either. If he is competing with large numbers of other solo painters (as well as with employing contractors), the force of competition through the price system will impose on him a certain level of technology, techniques, tools, materials, methods, speed, and intensity almost as surely as if he were an employee. To be sure, if he is willing to make do with a subaverage level of income, he may be able to escape some of these competitively enforced restrictions. To the extent that he is prepared to trade off relief from a personal workplace boss for lower income, he may be living in a kind of solipsistic world. Yet this would not conform to the classical image of the self-employed as enjoying financially solid independence--and not merely heightened risk.[50]

In order to illuminate just how compressed the stratum of economically independent self-employed is, a unique set of data are set out from a period in which the self-employed figured much more prominently than they do today. At the time of the introduction of the federal income tax in the United States, the working class was effectively exempt from tax liability because the income threshold was set so high.[51] It is, therefore, possible to use the returns as a class matrix. For one year only, 1916, the Commissioner of Internal Revenue published income data by occupation, on the basis of which the self-employed/petty bourgeoisie and bourgeoisie can be fairly segregated out (table 7).[52]

Table 7
Distribution of Net Income by Occupation, 1916

Occupation	Number of Persons	% of Persons in Occupation Returned at 1910 Census	% of All Returns	% of All Net Income
Total	437,036	—	100	100
Capitalists: investors & speculators	85,465	NA	20	27
Merchants & dealers: storekeepers, jobbers, & commission merchants	54,363	4	12	13
Corporation officials	53,060	NA	12	11
Employees: superintendents, office, & foremen	38,388	NA	9	4
Manufacturers	23,631	10	5	9
Lawyers & judges	21,273	19	5	4
Medical profession[a]	20,348	7	5	2
Agriculturists	14,407	0.2	3	2
Commercial travelers	12,274	5	3	1

Table 7 (*cont.*)

Occupation	Number of Persons	% of Persons in Occupation Returned at 1910 Census	% of All Returns	% of All Net Income
Brokers: all other	7,479	21	2	3
Insurance agents	7,243	8	2	1
Engineers	6,628	11	2	1
Bankers	6,518	NA	1	3
Real estate brokers	6,146	5	1	1
Military	5,459	7	1	0.5
Accounting	4,229	NA	1	0.4
Public service: civil	2,992	1	1	0.3
Teachers	2,919	0.5	1	0.3
Stock/bond brokers	2,839	21	1	2
Hotel proprietors & restaurateurs	2,752	NA	1	0.5
Mine owners/operators	2,554	18	1	2
Authors	2,529	7	1	0.4

Table 7 (*cont.*)

Occupation	Number of Persons	% of Persons in Occupation Returned at 1910 Census	% of All Returns	% of All Net Income
Labor, skilled & unskilled	2,304	NA	0.5	0.3
Clergymen	1,671	1	0.4	0.2
Architects	1,419	9	0.3	0.2
Insurance brokers	1,414	NA	0.3	0.3
Lumbermen	1,319	11	0.3	0.3
Saloon keepers	1,311	2	0.3	0.1
Theatrical profession	914	0.5	0.2	0.2
Theatrical business: owners, managers	811	3	0.2	0.2
Artists	786	NA	0.2	0.1

Source: Calculated according to data in STATISTICS OF INCOME FOR 1916: COMPILED FROM THE RETURNS FOR 1916 UNDER THE DIRECTION OF THE COMMISSIONER OF INTERNAL REVENUE, H. Doc. No. 1169, 65th Cong., 2d Sess. at 7, tab. 6 at 31 (1918).
[a]The fact that the occupation includes nurses may account for the relatively low percentage of high-income persons in occupation.

With a few moderately heroic assumptions, these occupations can be reclassified under the rubrics in table 8.

Table 8
Distribution of Net Income by Class, 1916

Class	% of All Returns	% of All Net Income
Capitalists/employers	43	56
Capitalists		
Merchants		
Manufacturers		
Agriculturists		
Bankers		
Mine owners		
Lumbermen		
Hotel/Saloon keepers		
Theater owners		
Employees	13	5
Supervisors		
Military		
Civil servants		
Teachers		
Laborers		
Professions	15	9
Lawyers		
Medicine		
Engineers		
Accountants		
Authors		
Clergy		
Architects		
Actors/Artists		
Ambiguous	21	19
Corporation officials		
Travelers		
Insurance Agents		
Real estate/Stock brokers		

The major assumption is that without employing others, no person in the class of employers could have been engaged in a solo producing or retail business[53] generating five to six times as much income as the annual wages of the average worker.[54] This assumption thus eliminates the backbone of the pure petty bourgeoisie, that is, the nonemploying, nonprofessional old middle class, from the ranks of the taxably wealthy.[55] The class of taxable professionals, which includes only between one-fifth and one one-hundredth of all professionals, surely embraces some self-employed; yet how many of the lawyers and doctors, for example, worked alone, without employees, is unknown.   The major taxonomic problem arises among the corporate officials, brokers, and agents.   Many of the officials may have been highly paid executive employees of firms they did not own; those who were owners were presumably by and large not solo operators of incorporated businesses. Thus, this numerically predominant segment was only partly self-employed, but only few were probably pure petty bourgeois. Among the agents and brokers, many may have been employees, but some were in business on their own, and some of these may have operated more or less alone.

Women as Self-Employed:
The Quintessential Disguised Proletarians

> [I]t is not surprising to find an above-average incidence of poverty among the self-employed.[56]

Dramatic growth of self-employment among women[57] has fueled the notional rise in self-employment since the mid-1970s.[58] From 1979 to 1983 the number of unincorporated self-employed women increased five times faster than men[59] and from 1975 to 1988, women as a share of the self-employed rose from 23.7 per cent to 32.7 per cent.[60] Two characteristics crucially distinguish female self-employed from their male counterparts. First, even much more so than is the case among men, their incomes are much lower than the wages and salaries received by employees in corresponding occupations.[61]   Second, the hallmark of female self-employment is the virtual absence of the traditional professional self-employed (such as physicians, dentists, accountants, and lawyers) and its concentration in heteronomous and low-paid occupations. In 1980, for example, the census of population showed that the seven occupations of cosmetologist, food service worker, cleaning and building service worker, secretary, cashier, bookkeeper, and retail sales worker--which are almost on their face redolent of economic and personal dependence--alone accounted for one-third of all self-employed women outside agriculture.[62]

The average earnings of self-employed women are well below those of wage and salary workers, and this gap has widened. Those of full-time, full-year self-employed women amount to little more than half of those of their employee counterparts.[63] Even incorporated self-employed women do not fare much better.[64] Consequently, the recorded rise in female self-employment may merely be disguising a tendency for women to subsidize their otherwise uncompensated reproductive labor: "[W]omen who provide market goods and services while working in their homes may be compensated for lower money earnings by the increase in utility derived from being able to devote more time to child rearing and homemaking."[65] That self-employment among women is even less substantial than among men is also reflected in their less frequent use of capital.[66]

A special study done in connection with the 1970 census disclosed the insubstantial character of self-employed women (table 9).

Farewell to the Self-Employed

Table 9
Distribution of High Incomes among
Male and Female Employees and Self-Employed, 1969

	>$15,000	>$50,000
Men		
Employees	3,835,188	133,919
Self-Employed	1,000,308	95,931
Women		
Employees	158,921	5,985
Self-Employed	40,019	2,293

Source: Calculated according to data in U.S. BUREAU OF THE CENSUS, CENSUS OF POPULATION: 1970, SUBJECT REPORTS: FINAL REPORT PC(2)-7F: OCCUPATIONS OF PERSONS WITH HIGH EARNINGS tab. 14 at 95-97 (1973). The data refer to the experienced civilian labor force, which includes the experienced unemployed, who had worked at any time in the past.

The minuscule number of highly paid self-employed women and the relatively small percentage of all self-employed women they represent underscore the disproportionately nominal nature of female self-employment.[67] Although there were about five times as many self-employed men as women, forty-two times as many men as women reported incomes in excess of $50,000. Viewed another way, two per cent of self-employed men, but only 0.2 per cent of self-employed women reached that level of income.[68] Of unincorporated women, 32.5 per cent earned less than $5,000, and seven per cent of incorporated earned more than $30,000.[69]

Unpublished data from the CPS for 1987 show that the situation did not improve for self-employed women during the intervening two decades (table 10).

Table 10
Distributional Extremes of Earnings among
Year-Round, Full-Time Male and Female
Employees and Self-Employed, 1987

	< $10,000	> $75,000
Men		
Employees	6.7%	3.4%
Self-Employed	21.6	5.9
Women		
Employees	14.4	0.3
Self-Employed	47.0	1.9

Source: Calculated according to data furnished by BLS, CURRENT POPULATION SURVEY (unpub. tabulations, 1987). The highest earnings bracket for which data were collected was over $75,000.

Three times as many self-employed men as women reached the highest income level. At the other extreme, whereas almost half of all female self-employed earned less than $10,000, little more than one-fifth of the males fell into this group. The pronounced bipolarity of earnings as between female self-employed and employees was also greater than among males.

NOTES

1. HANS SPEIER, DIE ANGESTELLTEN VOR DEM NATIONALSOZIALISMUS: EIN BEITRAG ZUM VERSTÄNDNIS DER DEUTSCHEN SOZIALSTRUKTUR 1918-1933, at 65 (1989 [1977]).

2. Dov Eden, *Self-Employed Workers: A Comparison Group for Organizational Psychology*, 9 OCCUPATIONAL BEHAVIOR AND HUMAN PERFORMANCE 186, 212 (1973).

3. Thomas Hagelstange, *Niedergang oder Renaissance der Selbständigen? Statistische Daten zur Entwicklung in der EG und in Nordamerika*, ZEITSCHRIFT FÜR SOZIOLOGIE, Apr. 1988, at 142 (denying renaissance).

4. Calculated according to data in U.S. BUREAU OF LABOR STATISTICS, HANDBOOK OF LABOR STATISTICS tab. 21 at 112 (Bull. 2340, 1989); and EMPLOYMENT AND EARNINGS, Jan. 1991, tab. 23 at 191.

5. *See infra* at 78-81.

6. Calculated according to data in U.S. BUREAU OF LABOR STATISTICS, HANDBOOK OF LABOR STATISTICS, tab. 21 at 113 (Bull. 2340, 1989); EMPLOYMENT AND EARNINGS, Jan. 1991, tab. 23 at 191.

7. Steinmetz & Wright, *The Fall and Rise of the Petty Bourgeoisie* tab. A1 at 1010.

8. By 1983 BLS/BOC changed their description to "street and door-to-door sales workers."

9. Calculated according to data from U.S. BUREAU OF LABOR STATISTICS, CURRENT POPULATION SURVEY (unpub. tabulations, 1976 and 1983). These data include only the unincorporated self-employed.

10. Calculated according to data in SPEC. COMM. TO STUDY PROBLEMS OF AMERICAN SMALL BUSINESS, 78TH CONG., 1ST SESS., SMALL BUSINESS PROBLEMS: SMALL BUSINESS WANTS OLD-AGE SECURITY tab. 2 at 33 (Sen. Comm. Print. No. 17, 1943); U.S. BUREAU OF ECONOMIC ANALYSIS, THE NATIONAL INCOME AND PRODUCT ACCOUNTS OF THE UNITED STATES, 1929-82: STATISTICAL TABLES tab. 6.9B at 282 (1986); EMPLOYMENT AND EARNINGS, Jan. 1991, tab. 24 at 192.

11. Although those operating full-time businesses rose from 5.99 million to 6.46 million from 1981 to 1985, the rate declined from 9.3% to 9.1%. U.S. SMALL BUS. ADM'N, STATE OF SMALL BUSINESS 1989, at 37-38 (1989).

12. INTERNAL REVENUE SERVICE, STATISTICS OF INCOME--1979-1980 SOLE PROPRIETORSHIP RETURNS tab. 1 at 10-15 (1982); Louella Ballenger, *Sole Proprietorship Returns, 1988*, SOI BULLETIN, Summer, 1990, at 39, tab. 1 at 43-46.

13. The expansion of the business service industry is itself in part a reflection of efforts by firms to contract out peripheral parts of their work in order to take advantage of the lower wages and "very low incidence of unionization" prevailing in that sector. *See* Wayne Howe, *The Business Services Industry Sets Pace in Employment Growth*, MONTHLY LAB. REV., Apr. 1986, at 29, 34-35.

14. Calculated according to data furnished by U.S. BUREAU OF LABOR STATISTICS, CURRENT POPULATION SURVEY 1983-88 (unpub. tabulations, 1989).

15. U.S. BUREAU OF THE CENSUS, 1987 CENSUS OF SERVICE INDUSTRIES: NONEMPLOYER STATISTICS SERIES: MIDWEST tab. 1 at 2-3 (1990) (with data for United States); *see also* U.S. BUREAU OF THE CENSUS, 1987 CENSUS OF SERVICE INDUSTRIES, SUBJECT SERIES: ESTABLISHMENTS AND FIRM SIZE

(INCLUDING LEGAL FORM OF ORGANIZATION) A-2 (1990) (containing data only on firms and establishments with payroll). No data were broken out on receipts for individual proprietorships, which presumably would have been even lower than $20,000.

16. U.S. BUREAU OF THE CENSUS, MONEY INCOME OF HOUSEHOLDS, FAMILIES, AND PERSONS IN THE UNITED STATES: 1987 tab. A at 2 (Current Pop. Rep., Ser. P-60, No. 162, 1989). It must also be taken into account that if a self-employed worker must buy medical insurance for the family and disability and life insurance, "an employee earning $60,000 may well discover it takes self-employment income of $100,000 to have the same net." Jan Rosen, *Your Money: Caution Is Urged On Retiring Early*, N.Y. Times, June 8, 1991, at 18, col. 1, 3.

17. U.S BUREAU OF THE CENSUS, 1977 CENSUS OF SERVICE INDUSTRIES, 1 SUBJECT STATISTICS tab. 1 at 1-6 (1981) (data on establishments without payroll calculated by subtracting data on establishments "with payroll" from those on "all" establishments). Of 1,834,713 establishments, 973,581 had no employees; *id*. tab. 2 at 1-39 (discrepancy presumably stems from exclusion from data on number of employees of establishments not operating entire year). Of 1,763,992 firms, 1,109,617 had no employees; *id*. tab. 5 at 1-116.

18. U.S. BUREAU OF THE CENSUS, 1967 CENSUS OF BUSINESS, SELECTED SERVICES, AREA STATISTICS: UNITED STATES tab. 1 at 1-6-1-7 (1970) (calculated by subtracting data for establishments with payroll from those for all establishments).

19. Calculated according to data in *id*.; MONEY INCOME OF HOUSEHOLDS, FAMILIES, AND PERSONS IN THE UNITED STATES: 1987 tab. A at 2 and tab. A-1 at 178; U.S BUREAU OF THE CENSUS, 1977 CENSUS OF SERVICE INDUSTRIES, 1 SUBJECT STATISTICS tab. 1 at 1-6.

20. The data for all establishments (including incorporated entities) without payroll are very similar--increasing by 317 per cent from 1977 to 1987, while individual proprietorships rose by 318 per cent. The figures for the individual branches track those for the proprietorships too.

21. The BOC does not obtain data on nonemployers directly from them but rather from the IRS based on the Schedule C that self-employed taxpayers file. *See* U.S. BUREAU OF THE CENSUS, 1987 CENSUS OF SERVICE INDUSTRIES: GEOGRAPHIC AREA SERIES: UNITED STATES A-1 (1989). Thus, for example, a hairdresser who must "rent her chair" from the owner of a beauty shop who treats her as self-employed will file a Schedule C to document expenses to be set off against income. Transformed into a census datum, each such hairdresser will count as a nonemploying, individual proprietorship "beauty shop," although in fact one shop may employ several such hairdressers.

22. That almost one-half of all lawyers' offices and one-third of all physicians' offices are individual proprietorships without payroll seems implausible. To be sure, in some cases a spouse might be an unpaid secretary, assistant, nurse, or receptionist but not on this order of magnitude. That large numbers of lawyers and doctors actually work alone--for example, answer their own telephone and door--also fails to accord with experience. When questioned about this issue, the chief of the services branch of the BOC conjectured that many nonemployers might be working part-time or at a second job or that they might really be employees or consultants at other full-time jobs. Telephone interview with Jack Moody (May 21, 1991). This explanation may be plausible in other occupations, but it does not ring true for doctors and lawyers.

23. Unfortunately, the BOC did not break out the numbers for child day care before 1987. Other groups encompassing large numbers of businesses could have been included depending on how broadly the category was defined.

24. Calculated according to data in U.S. BUREAU OF THE CENSUS, 1972 CENSUS OF CONSTRUCTION INDUSTRIES, 1 INDUSTRY AND SPECIAL STATISTICS tab. A2 at 1-4 (1976); U.S. BUREAU OF THE CENSUS, 1987 CENSUS OF CONSTRUCTION INDUSTRIES, INDUSTRY SERIES, UNITED STATES SUMMARY: ESTABLISHMENTS WITH AND WITHOUT PAYROLL tab. 1 at 7 (1990). In 1972, "receipts" rather than "value of business done" were recorded.

25. Calculated according to data in U.S. BUREAU OF THE CENSUS, 1972 CENSUS OF CONSTRUCTION INDUSTRIES, INDUSTRY SERIES: U.S. SUMMARY tab. A2 at 1-5; U.S. BUREAU OF THE CENSUS, 1987 CENSUS OF CONSTRUCTION INDUSTRIES, INDUSTRY SERIES, UNITED STATES SUMMARY: ESTABLISHMENTS WITH AND WITHOUT PAYROLL tab. 2 at 9. The size of specialty trade contractor individual proprietorships without payroll was even smaller. *See* U.S. BUREAU OF THE CENSUS, 1987 CENSUS OF CONSTRUCTION INDUSTRIES, SUBJECT SERIES: LEGAL FORM OF ORGANIZATION AND TYPE OF OPERATION tab. 1 at 6 (1990) (average value of business done $30,000). If in 1972 seventy per cent of individual proprietors had no payroll, by 1987 the figure had risen to eighty-nine per cent. *Id.* tab. 1 at 5; U.S. BUREAU OF THE CENSUS, 1972 CENSUS OF CONSTRUCTION INDUSTRIES, SPECIAL REPORT SERIES: TYPE OF OPERATION AND LEGAL FORM OF ORGANIZATION tab. 1 at 4 (1975).

26. Calculated according to data in U.S. BUREAU OF THE CENSUS, 1987 CENSUS OF RETAIL TRADE, NONEMPLOYER STATISTICS SERIES, NORTHEAST tab. 1 at 1-3 (1990) (817,318 individual proprietorships without payroll accounted for eighty-nine per cent of all establishments without payroll).

27. Calculated according to data in U.S. BUREAU OF THE CENSUS, 1987 CENSUS OF RETAIL TRADE, SPECIAL REPORT SERIES: SELECTED STATISTICS tab. 2 at 1-4 (1991).

28. In 1982, 491,114 (31.2%) of 1,923,228 establishments reported no paid employees and averaged $42,000 in sales. U.S. BUREAU OF THE CENSUS, 1982 CENSUS OF RETAIL TRADE, INDUSTRY SERIES, ESTABLISHMENT AND FIRM SIZE (INCLUDING LEGAL FORM OF ORGANIZATION) tab. 5 at 1-107 (1985).

29. 1 U.S. BUREAU OF THE CENSUS, 1977 CENSUS OF RETAIL TRADE, SUBJECT STATISTICS tab. 1 at 1-8 (1981) (calculated by subtracting "with payroll" from "all" data). Of 1,855,068 establishments, 463,785 reported having no paid employees; *id.*, tab. 2 at 1-35. Of 1,567,071 firms, 551,447 (thirty-five per cent) reported no paid employees; *id.*, tab. 5 at 1-100. Of 1,855,068 establishments, 1,003,667 were individual proprietorships (497,584 of which were without payroll); *id.* tab. 7 at 1-127.

30. U.S. BUREAU OF THE CENSUS, 1967 CENSUS OF BUSINESS, 1 RETAIL TRADE--SUBJECT REPORTS, U.S. SUMMARY tab. 1 at 1-4-1-5 (1971) (571,778/501,844 [32%/29%] of 1,763,324/1,707,931 establishments without payroll in 1967/1963 [calculated by subtracting "with payroll" from "all" data]).

31. The branches selected are to some extent arbitrary; using more or less comprehensive classifications would have led to a different selection and rank order. The comparable data for establishments without payroll in 1977 were as follows: eating and drinking, 59,452 (16%); grocery, 52,200 (29%); furniture/furnishings, 46,837 (57%); gas service station, 29,942 (17%); apparel, 25,313 (18%); used merchandise, 35,352 (71%); used car dealers, 23,729 (64%); gift/novelty/souvenir, 16,940 (50%); florist, 9,283 (32%). 1 U.S. BUREAU OF THE CENSUS, 1977 CENSUS OF RETAIL TRADE, SUBJECT STATISTICS tab. 1 at 1-11-1-32 (1981). In 1967 and 1963, respectively, were recorded 89,445 and 112,709 grocery stores (41% and 46%), and 50,869 and 45,610 gas stations (24% and 22%). Calculated according to data in U.S. BUREAU OF THE CENSUS, 1967 CENSUS OF BUSINESS, 1 RETAIL TRADE--SUBJECT REPORTS, U.S. SUMMARY tab. 1 at 1-4-1-5.

32. Of the three branches with above-average sales, gas service station franchisees most clearly approximate employees. *Cf.* Shell Oil Co. v. Marinello, 63 N.J. 402, 307 A.2d 598 (1973), *cert. denied*, 415 U.S. 920 (1974). Selling commodities with high unit prices such as used cars is apparently one way in which a single person with little human capital can generate relatively high annual sales.

33. U.S. SMALL BUSINESS ADMINISTRATION, THE STATE OF SMALL BUSINESS: A REPORT OF THE PRESIDENT 131 (1986).

34. The Times (London), Aug. 13, 1976, at 13, col. 7 (letter).

35. *See* WRIGHT, CLASS STRUCTURE AND INCOME DETERMINATION at 95-96, 104 (exploitation by monopoly capital of petty bourgeoisie through market reduces latter's income).

36. *See, e.g.*, ILO, THE PROMOTION OF SELF-EMPLOYMENT tab. 8 at 72 (with the exception of West Germany). Even Wright confirms this gap for controlled groups. WRIGHT, CLASS STRUCTURE AND INCOME DETERMINATION at 96, 150-54. This differential is subject to the reservation that a 1983 IRS study showed that self-employeds (as well as those with largely cash incomes) reported only forty-seven per cent of their income compared with ninety-four per cent among taxpayers in general. *See* Daniel Goleman, *Tax Tip: If It's Lump Sum, Cheating Is More Likely*, N.Y. Times, Apr. 13, 1991, at 6, col. 3. *See also* CARL SIMON & ANN WITTE, BEATING THE SYSTEM: THE UNDERGROUND ECONOMY 10-15 (1982) (on underreporting and nonreporting of income by self-employeds); DAVID PYLE, TAX EVASION AND THE BLACK ECONOMY 62-67 (1989) (data for Britain). On the other hand, taking into account the nonwage compensation of wage and salary earners would widen the gap. *See* ARONSON, SELF-EMPLOYMENT at 47.

37. U.S. SMALL BUSINESS ADMINISTRATION, THE STATE OF SMALL BUSINESS: A REPORT OF THE PRESIDENT 128 (1986).

38. ARONSON, SELF-EMPLOYMENT at 42. Although the earnings of the incorporated self-employed are greater than those of the unincorporated, most studies ignore the difference "because the overall effect on earnings comparisons would probably be quite small." *Id*. at 43.

39. Calculated according to data in SOC. SEC. BULL., ANNUAL STATISTICAL SUPPLEMENT, 1989 tab. 4.B.2 at 137. The somewhat different development of median annual earnings of wage and salary workers as a percentage of those of the self-employed was for all workers/men/women: 1955: 99/131/86; 1960: 98/123/99; 1965: 86/109/104; 1970: 85/109/117; 1975: 86/106/122; 1980: 99/115/148; 1982: 124/135/171 (peak); 1986: 118/124/153. Calculated according to data in *id*., tab. 4.B3 at 138. Full-time, full-year unincorporated self-employed wholly dependent on their business earned sixty-seven to seventy-three per cent of the median full-time wage and salary worker in 1983. ARONSON, SELF-EMPLOYMENT at 45. The erosion of the self-employed's earnings advantage may have begun in the early 1960s, but it was not until 1980-84 that the curves crossed. *Id*. at 46-7.

40. Calculated according to U.S. SMALL BUS. ADM'N, THE STATE OF SMALL BUSINESS [1986] tab. 4.11 at 129.

41. The mean was 89.5%.

42. Calculated according to data in U.S. BLS, CURRENT POPULATION SURVEY (unpub. tabulations 1987).

43. Calculated according to data in *id*.

44. A sample study of wage earners and self-employed filing for bankruptcy in 1981 confirms this distribution: although the mean income of the latter was higher, at the twenty-fifth percentile, the income of wage earners was $9,500 compared to $7,000 for self-employeds. TERESA SULLIVAN,

ELIZABETH WARREN, & JAY WESTBROOK, AS WE FORGIVE OUR DEBTORS: BANKRUPTCY AND CONSUMER CREDIT IN AMERICA tab. 6.6 at 124 (1991 [1989]).

45. ARONSON, SELF-EMPLOYMENT at 55.

46. *Id*. at 55-56.

47. Aronson finds that the recent growth in self-employment is, in light of the widening gap in income, "perverse" and a "counterintuitive paradox," but ultimately finds all explanations unsatisfactory. *Id*. at xi, 20, 41, 117-25. In particular, he downplays the significance of self-employment as underemployment or adjustment to displacement. Here he purports to rely on an article that allegedly analyzed the relationship between self-employment and unemployment in individual industries: "Among all nonfarm industries, only the construction industry exhibited an increase in self-employment with a general decline in industrial activity." *Id*. at 30. Yet that article expressly analyzed no industry other than construction. *See* Marc Linder, *Self-Employment as a Cyclical Escape from Unemployment: A Case Study of the Construction Industry in the United States During the Postwar Period,* 2 RESEARCH IN SOCIOLOGY OF WORK: PERIPHERAL WORKERS 261, 262 (1983).

48. *See* EVANS & LEIGHTON, SELF-EMPLOYMENT SELECTION AND EARNINGS OVER THE LIFE CYCLE at 3.

49. FRITZ MARBACH, THEORIE DES MITTELSTANDES 111, 227-28 (1942).

50. Then again he might not be exposed to any more risk than a casually employed painter, who works and is paid only when his contractor calls him for a job. What distinguishes him from the solo painter is the latter's effort to seek jobs directly from customers.

51. $3,000 for single persons and $4,000 for married couples (sums in excess of $30,000 and $40,000, respectively, at the present time). *See* SIDNEY RATNER, TAXATION AND DEMOCRACY IN AMERICA tab. C-1 at 577 (unpaginated) (1967 [1942]).

52. STATISTICS OF INCOME FOR 1916: COMPILED FROM THE RETURNS FOR 1916 UNDER THE DIRECTION OF THE COMMISSIONER OF INTERNAL REVENUE, H. Doc. No. 1169, 65th Cong., 2d Sess. (1918).

53. For a tripartite analysis of late-nineteenth-century retail traders (merchant elite, general merchants, and petty merchants) from the perspective of self-employment, see Melanie Archer, *Self-Employment and Occupational Structure in an Industrializing City: Detroit, 1880,* 69 SOC. FORCES 785 (1991); *idem, The Entrepreneurial Family Economy: Family Strategies and Self-Employment in Detroit, 1880,* 15 J. FAM. HIST. 261 (1990).

54. *Cf.* ARONSON, SELF-EMPLOYMENT at 121-23 (if it becomes profitable to hire additional workers, self-employment takes on different meaning; scale effects are arguably crucial, but "the capacity to utilize capital is limited by biological and technological factors"). The estimates of the average annual earnings of employees in 1916 range between $647 and $765. U.S. BUREAU OF THE CENSUS, HISTORICAL STATISTICS OF THE UNITED STATES, COLONIAL TIMES TO 1970, ser. D 723 at 164, ser. D 753 at 167, ser. D 780 at 168 (bicentennial ed. 1975). Of the 437,036 persons filing returns in 1916, 74,066, reporting between $3,000 and $4,000 of net income, were not subject to taxation because their specific exemption exceeded their net income. The class of employees included an above-average percentage of such persons, as did commercial travelers, insurance agents, engineers, and accountants. As a result, the other classes accounted for somewhat higher shares of all returns and net income. *See* STATISTICS OF INCOME FOR 1916 tab. 2 at 20-21, tab. 6c at 126-37.

55. Since fewer than one in twenty-five merchants was rich enough to be taxed, the assumption appears plausible.

56. ARONSON, SELF-EMPLOYMENT at 90.

57. *See* U.S. SMALL BUSINESS ADMINISTRATION, STATE OF SMALL BUSINESS: A REPORT OF THE PRESIDENT 237, chart D.5 at 239 (1990) (since 1963 the number of female nonfarm self-employed has been increasing annually by an average of 63,000 or 4.6%).

58. *See* ARONSON, SELF-EMPLOYMENT at 4.

59. U.S. SMALL BUS. ADM'N, STATE OF SMALL BUSINESS [1986] at 122. Women accounted for one-quarter of the unincorporated but only one-eighth of the incorporated self-employed in 1983. *Id.*, tab. 4.4 at 116.

60. *See* Theresa Devine, The Recent Rise in Female Self-Employment, tab. 1 and fig. 1 (no pagination) (June 30, 1991) (unpublished manuscript). From 1940 to 1980, however, the decennial censuses indicated that the self-employed as a percentage of the male nonagricultural employed declined somewhat less sharply than among women: 1940: 14.8/7.4; 1950: 12.9/5.6; 1960: 11.1/4.6; 1970: 7.7/3.4; 1980: 7.4/3.4 (self-employed as share of men/women). U.S. BUREAU OF THE CENSUS, 1980 CENSUS OF POPULATION, 1 CHARACTERISTICS OF THE POPULATION, Chapter C: GENERAL SOCIAL AND ECONOMIC CHARACTERISTICS, part 1: UNITED STATES SUMMARY, tab. 91 at 1-48 (1983).

61. *See* Devine, The Recent Rise in Female Self-Employment at 14 (weekly earnings of female self-employed eighty-four per cent of female employees'); Louis Uchitelle, *The New Surge in Self-Employed*, N.Y. Times, Jan. 15, 1991, at C2, col. 1 (summarizing Devine's results); Sheldon Haber, Enrique Lamas, & Jules Lichtenstein, *On Their Own: The Self-Employed and Others in Private Business*, MONTHLY LAB. REV., May 1987, at 17, 20. This relationship obtains in Western Europe as well. *See Self-Employment in OECD Countries*, OECD EMPLOYMENT OUTLOOK, Sept. 1986, at 43, 60, tab. 26 at 62 (female

self-employed earn 40 to 70 per cent of their employee counterparts, with the trend downward).

62. *See* U.S. BUREAU OF THE CENSUS, 1970 CENSUS OF POPULATION, 1 CHARACTERISTICS OF THE POPULATION, part 1: UNITED STATES SUMMARY, tab. 225 at 1-753-1-754 (1973); *idem*, 1980 CENSUS OF POPULATION, 1 CHARACTERISTICS OF THE POPULATION, chap. D: DETAILED POPULATION CHARACTERISTICS, pt. 1: UNITED STATES SUMMARY, tab. 279 at 1-219-1-221 (1984).

63. ARONSON, SELF-EMPLOYMENT at 60, 65-67, tab. 4 at 66.

64. *Id.* at 68-69.

65. *Id.* at 71.

66. *Id.* at 74.

67. The BOC defined self-employed workers as follows: "Own business not incorporated.--Persons who worked for profit or fees in their own unincorporated business, profession, or trade, or who operated a farm. Included here are owner-operators of large stores and manufacturing establishments as well as small merchants, independent craftsmen and professional men, farmers, peddlers, and other persons who conducted enterprises on their own." U.S. BUREAU OF THE CENSUS, CENSUS OF POPULATION: 1970, SUBJECT REPORTS: FINAL REPORT PC(2)-7F: OCCUPATIONS OF PERSONS WITH HIGH EARNINGS vii (1973). The largest highly paid occupations (over $15,000/over $50,000) among self-employed men were physicians: 119,469/33,973 (wage and salary earners: 55,197/9,549); and lawyers: 98,699/15,214 (wage and salary: 54,517/3,109). The largest highly paid occupation among wage and salary workers was engineers (few of whom were self-employed); 111,206 wage and salary construction craftsmen earned more than $15,000 compared to 38,030 self-employed. *Id.* tab. 14 at 95-97.

68. The figure of approximately five million self-employed men and one million self-employed women in the civilian experienced labor force was calculated by subtracting the published figures for wage and salary earners in the experienced civilian labor force from the total experienced civilian labor force since the census did not publish the data separately for the self-employed. The sources are: U.S. BUREAU OF THE CENSUS, CENSUS OF POPULATION: 1970, DETAILED CHARACTERISTICS, FINAL REPORT PC(1)-D1: UNITED STATES SUMMARY, tab. 227 at 1-766, tab. 228 at 1-772 (1973); U.S. BUREAU OF THE CENSUS, CENSUS OF POPULATION: 1970, SUBJECT REPORTS, FINAL REPORT PC(2)-7A: OCCUPATIONAL CHARACTERISTICS, tab. 24 at 476, 490 (1973).

69. U.S. SMALL BUS. ADM'N, STATE OF SMALL BUSINESS [1986] tab. 4.13 at 132.

5

Legislative and Judicial Attitudes
toward the Unemployed Self-Employed

Unions obviously are concerned not to have union standards
undermined by non-union shops. This interest penetrates into self-
employer shops. On the other hand, some of our profoundest
thinkers from Jefferson to Brandeis have stressed the importance
to a democratic society of encouraging self-employer economic
units as a counter-movement to what are deemed to be the dangers
inherent in excessive concentration of economic power.[1]

Organized Labor's Struggle against
Self-Employed Wage Cutters

The tacit positive reevaluation that self-employment has
undergone recently stands out most clearly when contrasted
with the open hostility which it met with at the hands of
unions in the 1930s and 1940s. Prompted by the vast
unemployment of the Depression (and the fear of its
resurgence after demobilization), the labor movement
articulated that antagonism in the course of combating the
spread of self-employment as a tool for cutting wages and
undermining the conditions of employment. Unions acted on
the belief that the self-employed were not a *tertium quid*
poised between workers and capitalists. Instead, the unions'
strategy was predicated on the assumptions that the self-
employed were one or the other and that they had to be
induced by trade union pressure to opt for their appropriate

class position.   Where the self-employed wanted to be employers, the unions not only barred them from membership but in effect demanded that their operations be large enough to warrant a clear separation of capital from labor so that the employer would not compete with his employees by working with his own hands.[2]   Where the self-employed had acquiesced in real employers' insistence that they work alone, unions requested that they become members and cease depressing union standards.[3]

More remarkable than the unions' position was its widespread judicial acceptance and vindication. In landmark litigation reaching several state supreme courts and the U.S. Supreme Court, the unions figured as defendants whose picketing--to protest the usurpation of union jobs under sub-union standards--the self-employed sought to enjoin.   The disparate jurisprudences of labor injunctions, federalism, and free speech that shaped the judicial outcomes are of less interest here than the judges' attitudes toward the character of the conflict between the self-employed and the unions, which often was central to a determination as to whether the parties were engaged in a "labor dispute"--a finding that would have statutorily immunized the picketing.

A typical set of facts--and one reminiscent of the structure of much of today's proliferating self-employment --characterized the successful attempt by baking companies in New York City to compel their unionized employee-drivers to become so-called independent peddlers.   The recent introduction of social security and unemployment insurance payroll taxes had prompted efforts by employers to eliminate these additional costs. As the U.S. Supreme Court found, "[t]he peddler system has serious disadvantages to the peddler himself" because his exclusion from the workers' compensation, unemployment insurance, and social security systems could lead to his (and his family's) becoming "a public charge."[4]   The Court upheld the lawfulness of the union's picketing, which had been sparked by the latter's "alarm[] at the aggressive inroads of this kind of competition upon the employment and living standards of its members."[5]

Recent adjudications, in contrast, project a strikingly different perspective. Where, for example, taxicab companies have perpetrated essentially the same self-employment conversion scheme for precisely the same cost-cutting and anti-union reasons, prominent judges have cynically glorified the imaginary entrepreneurial characteristics of the involuntary self-employed.[6]

A half-century ago, even judges who sympathized with the self-employed[7] by upholding the injunction recognized that they were merely workers:[8] "The businessman-worker operating in an industry...in which he competes with organized workmen may likewise be subjected to the same means of persuasion as any other workman to join the union and conform to the conditions regulating union labor."[9] The enormous sea change in attitudes that has taken place in the last half-century becomes even more salient in the dissent in the same case, which involved a union that sought to enforce a closed shop for milk wagon drivers vis-à-vis two self-employed drivers who refused to hire employees. Reacting to the union's success in persuading the milk brokers to cease doing business with the plaintiffs, the dissenters were more than ready to acquiesce in the union's plan to compel the self-employed to choose between becoming capitalist employers and proletarianized:

> [P]laintiffs...are simply being subjected to the vicissitous competition of free enterprise. Obviously, plaintiffs are not deprived of the right to work or to earn their living merely because in conducting their particular business they are faced with the practical alternative of employing union labor, of choosing another business in which to engage, or of continuing in the same line of work but in the employee status of union workers.[10]

In 1936, too, the Wisconsin Supreme Court displayed a remarkable lack of sympathy for a tile layer whom a union effectively deprived of a livelihood. By working "as a journeyman or a helper at a price and during hours that suit him individually and which are below the standard desired by the unions," his "method of conducting his business brings into the situation a direct attack by him upon the means relied upon by the unions to protect their scale of wages, hours, and working conditions against the cutting of prices and lengthening of hours of work."[11]

This cavalier attitude toward the self-employed stands in sharp contrast to the solicitude embodied in contemporary state rhetoric for the welfare of the self-employed. Surprisingly, the Reagan-era enthusiasm for self-employment has been not so much a celebration of entrepreneurialism as the making a virtue of a necessity: self-employment as a refuge from unemployment. What has been lost is the insight that the unions and the judiciary developed in the 1930s and 1940s into self-employment as provoking an intra-working-class race to the bottom.

For many years, the only aspect of unemployment that caught the attention of analysts of self-employment was their interrelationship over the business cycle.[12] Specifically, researchers asked whether self-employment acted as a safety valve enabling unemployed employees to make an alternative living during periods of high unemployment.[13] As unemployment in the 1980s reached levels theretofore unprecedented during the postwar period,[14] national states in Europe and the United States intervened in ways that gave new contours to the relationship between unemployment and self-employment. In addition, even earlier, administrative agencies and courts, in adjudicating claims for unemployment insurance compensation, had displayed modes of understanding the structure of self-employment and its interaction with unemployment that transcended the conventional socioeconomic framework.

Self-Employment for the Poor: State-Sponsored Interpenetration of Unemployment and Self-Employment

[W]e're convinced that there are thousands of people in the unemployment lines today...who are capable of becoming self-employed. ... If we cannot offer a decent job at a decent wage for everyone who wants one, the least we can do is offer them the opportunity to create their own.[15]

[A] person who previously engaged in crime might find entrepreneurial activities more suitable than wage employment. This might be especially true if one's wage work opportunities were in the secondary labor market. There is no authoritarian boss; one can set work rules, and there is risk. If one desires to work less than a 40-hour week, come to work drunk, or use inappropriate language, self-employed persons can do these things and not get fired. They may lose customers and hence income, but they can still retain their self-created job. Furthermore, it can be expected that the experience of greater control and independence associated with direct participation in the market will have a humanizing influence. ... It is incorrect to think that a self-employed person does not have a boss. The market is the boss. It is very exacting, but it is diffuse. Supervision, via the market, is diffuse.[16]

During the 1980s, arguably prompted by the Reagan administration's celebration of free enterprise and its simultaneous helplessness in the face of persistently high levels of unemployment, the state for the first time began to implement policies that treat self-employment both as a destination of the poor and unemployed and as a source of unemployment. This shift in program content reflected an arresting phenomenon during the 1970s: not only was the percentage of unemployed becoming self-employed greater than that among the employed, but the gap widened.[17] This unprecedented practical devaluation of self-employment now coexists--albeit irreconcilably and unconsciously--with the traditional rhetoric: "Let us empower a few more people to pursue the American dream."[18]

Congress has touted "legislation to remove impediments to economic independence faced by self-employed AFDC recipients" by permitting them to "work [their] way off public assistance by starting [their own] business."[19] The Displaced Homemakers Self-Sufficiency Assistance Act provides training in self-employment for those who had performed uncompensated work at home and lost their source of income support.[20] Such efforts are taking place within the context of a more grandiose plan for fostering "micro-enterprises" qua "self-employment for the poor."[21] With the spotlight on such "micro-enterprises" as "hawkers and street vendors," the campaign has gone global: a proposed Self-Sufficiency for the

Poor Act of 1987 would have extended the program to the Third World.[22]

At about the same time, Congress amended the Joint Training Partnership Act to include among the eligible dislocated workers those who "were self-employed (including farmers) and are unemployed as a result of general economic conditions in the community...or because of natural disasters."[23] The statutory and regulatory wording indicate that the self-employed were being treated like employees in the sense that only those who did not bring about their unemployment through their own fault would be covered.[24] This recognition that the self-employed do not live in a solipsistic world[25] but are instead subject to the same economic insecurities as other workers marks a further watershed in the gradual demolition of the misconceptualization. The eligibility of the self-employed, like other working poor, for the earned income credit[26] and food stamps[27] is further testimony to this approaching parity.

The 1980s also witnessed the first experiments in the United States with ushering the unemployed into self-employment. Although the British and French programs, which make unemployment insurance payments to unemployed persons starting their own business--thus exempting them from the rule that they be looking for employment--have been found wanting,[28] Congress in 1987 authorized pilot programs involving lump-sum payments.[29] Pertinent here are not the details of the design or implementation[30] but rather the fact itself of state acknowledgment of the essential equivalence and fungibility of employment and self-employment among dependent workers.

Judicial Treatment of the Unemployed, Paper Incorporated, Solo Self-Employed

> [A]mong all of the self-employed, those who form private corporations (in which they may be the only employee) are likely to be the most fully petty bourgeois in their class situation.[31]

The true lumpen-bourgeoisie...*employ* no workers at all: the proprietors and their family members do the work, frequently sweating themselves day and night. ... Here, at the bottom of the twentieth-century business world, lies the owner-operator who, in the classic image, is the independent man in the city.[32]

Whether the sole employee/stockholder of an incorporated business is deemed eligible for unemployment compensation may be a significant clue as to the societal evaluation of his or her status as a financially autonomous bourgeois or as a dependent worker. Arguably the most penetrating social analysis of this issue involved a case that arose in California in the 1970s.[33] The California Unemployment Insurance Appeals Board ("Board") determined that a cameraman-director who had received ($1,428 in) unemployment insurance benefits during a six-month period was not entitled to these payments because he was the president and sole shareholder of his corporation. Before incorporating in 1969 on the advice of his lawyer in order to limit his personal liability, Jack Cooperman had been both a "sole proprietor" and a member of a film craft union.[34] Incorporation did not affect his operations in any way.[35]

The lower court judge, who ruled in Cooperman's favor, remarked at trial that "this is just a Mickey Mouse little corporation, it's an alter ego of this man, and he is just out there scratching around to get a little employment for himself. [H]is activities were directed solely toward his own self-employment."[36] In affirming the trial court ruling, the intermediate court of appeal emphasized that because the corporation (which had no assets) and Cooperman were identical, it would be unjust to deprive an unemployed person working in an erratic labor market of benefits "for the mere reason that he does business as a corporation rather than as a sole proprietor."[37] Its programmatic reasoning ran as follows:

> In this modern age when an ever increasing number of people including professional people engaged in the rendition of personal services, incorporate themselves in order to continue to render personal services but in corporate form, such a distinction

between the sole proprietor and the incorporated proprietor would be palpably injust and a denial of even-handed treatment.[38]

Because, the court continued, the public policy of the state of California is to stabilize purchasing power by means of a compulsory unemployment fund, "the figurehead title of president" should not thwart Cooperman's eligibility.[39]

The court appeared unfazed by and/or oblivious of the converse: that it was conferring unemployment benefits on an ineligible self-employed person "for the mere reason that he does business as a corporation rather than as a sole proprietor." Nowhere does the court suggest that the Board should countenance a tender of unemployment insurance taxes from sole proprietors[40] who would like a modicum of protection from the rigors of the market.[41]

Although little force may inhere in the logic of *Cooperman*,[42] the importance of the case lies in the judiciary's perception that such self-employed are de facto employees characterized by identically the same vulnerabilities and needs as covered workers.[43] To the extent that this judgment is accurate, it militates in favor of classifying the incorporated self-employed as employees and yet also against the cavalier presumption that BLS and BOC erred in reclassifying the incorporated self-employed as employees in 1967.[44]

Are the Self-Employed Subject to the Same Vicissitudes as Employees? Judicial Treatment of Unemployed Secondary Self-Employed Workers[45]

> As a general rule, self-employed workers are able to make arrangements for obtaining a mid-day meal. I regret that I cannot allow them the special cheese ration.[46]

As an instructive comparison, note may also be taken of the other chief pattern involving the claims of alleged self-employed to unemployment insurance benefits. This situation arises where the claims of employees who have become unemployed are denied or challenged on the ground that in the interim they had been engaged in a secondary job as self-employed, which disqualifies them. In the future this constellation[47] may give rise to repeated litigation since these secondary self-employed are the fastest growing segment of the self-employed.[48] Their tenuous hold on independence was underscored by the Small Business Administration, which observed that their numbers quadrupled between 1979 and 1983 as employees sought to compensate for shorter hours and as employers sought to reduce costs by using "independent contractors" to avoid payroll taxes and union-related costs.[49] By 1989, 1,965,000 (or twenty-nine per cent) of the 6,767,000 wage and salary workers with second jobs reported themselves as self-employed in those jobs.[50]

At issue in these cases is the possibility that

> where a person divides his *time and labor* between work for another and potentially profitable work for himself, as where, e.g., a factory worker also operates, say, a store, a farm or a work-shop, a suspension of work at the factory may not and probably does not expose him to the rigors of unemployment which the Law is designed to alleviate.[51]

The regimes adopted by the states vary widely.[52] The most restrictive approach embodies an automatic blanket disqualification for benefits for any period during which a worker is self-employed.[53] An intermediate rule has evolved in order to correct "a gross inequity against some partially self-employed individuals as against individuals who performed the same services for wages while in the employ of another."[54] It takes the form of an exception for workers who are self-employed "by reason of continued participation without substantial change during a period of unemployment in any activity including farming operations undertaken while customarily employed by an employer in full-time work...and continued subsequent to separation from such work when such activity is not engaged in as a primary source of livelihood."[55] The most expansive judicial interpretations of statutes that are silent on the status of unemployed workers who take up self-employment have rejected the position that "'self-employment and unemployment are contradictory terms.'"[56]   Motivated by the desire to avoid the irrational result of "plac[ing] an unemployed individual who is unable to secure employment from a third-party in the position of having to remain completely idle or else entirely forego his claim,"[57] such courts have created parity between unemployed self-employeds and part-time employees.

Several socially and jurisprudentially arresting cases may illustrate social attitudes toward equalizing the legal protection of the two groups. In the first, a fifty-seven-year-old sheet metal worker who had been employed at a shipyard during World War II, suspecting that at the close of the war he would be laid off and have difficulty securing other employment, quit in August 1945 in order to devote himself fulltime to a roofing business that he had begun as a sideline while still an employee.[58] He earned about thirty-five dollars weekly--considerably less than the average gross weekly earnings of manufacturing workers[59] at the time--from August until November 1945, when he was forced to abandon his business as a result of a lack of materials.   Three administrative adjudicators and a trial court sustained his entitlement to benefits on the ground that his separation from his roofing business, in which he was employed, was due to a lack of work and therefore involuntary. The trial court judge, noting that "[t]he most attractive feature of what we have been lately calling the American system of free enterprise is the liberty of choice open to all men," rejected the employer's position, inter alia, because it would mean "that an employe is without good cause who, faced by an imminent lay-off, seeks economic security without recourse to the compensation law."[60]   The shipbuilding company, which was his base-year employer, contested the claim on the ground that once he left its employ, he was no longer an eligible employee but a disqualified independent contractor.[61]

The Supreme Court of Pennsylvania reversed on the ground that the statute was intended to protect those who become unemployed while working for wages--from which "class" those who "voluntarily removed themselves" "become independently engaged in a business of their own."[62]   In denying benefits to "an unemployed businessman,"[63] the court stressed that

> [t]he law does not make Pennsylvania employers the insurers...of the private ventures of their employees. [I]f he "gambles" with his job as an employee in the hope of becoming a businessman and an employer himself he cannot expect to find that the "game" is one in which all the possible gains are to be his while the losses...are to be borne chiefly by his last employer. [S]ince he had renounced his status as a "wage earner" in order to become a "businessman" his failure in the latter role did not automatically restore him to the status of an "unemployed employee."[64]

The point here is not to analyze whether the court interpreted the state unemployment statute correctly[65] but simply to document the rigid class line that the court preferred to draw between employees and the self-employed, who were put on notice that they would have to take the bitter (insecurity) with the sweet (independence).[66]

A more recent case involved several employees of a motor corporation who, upon being laid off, pooled their resources to open a watch repair shop. For the two months of their unemployment each averaged less than a dollar per day in income.[67] Rejecting as a "cliche" that self-employment and unemployment were mutually exclusive, the Supreme Court of Michigan applied the test of "genuine attachment to the labor market," which served "to differentiate the business or professional man, who temporarily attaches himself to the industrial market, from the workman who seeks a temporary augmentation of funds in a period of lay-off."[68] This court, in other words, recognized a broad area of overlap within which workers remained protected employees despite transient shifts into proletaroid activities unassociated with a capitalist employer.[69] Only at the other extreme, where small business owners or professionals sought to smuggle themselves into the state protective system, was the court prepared to draw the line excluding them from the working class.[70]

By far the most thought-provoking case in this series is *Slocum Straw Works v. Industrial Commission*,[71] a 1939 case in which the Supreme Court of Wisconsin interpreted a provision in that state's unemployment compensation statute declaring ineligible for benefits workers who (1) were "customarily self-employed," (2) did not work at least fifteen hours per week for at least twenty weeks, (3) worked at their self-employment thirty or more weeks in the year preceding the termination, and (4) could return to that (or similar) self-employment after the termination.[72] The claimant, Marie Rybacki, was a married woman (living with her husband, child, and father in the father's house) who each year for ten years had had a highly paid job as a "'highly skilled' straw hat sewing operator" from December to April at a seasonally operating factory and was then laid off.[73] The employer, having denied benefits on the ground that Rybacki "was self-employed as a housewife,"[74] appealed the initial contrary determination.   The Appeal Tribunal of the Wisconsin Industrial Commission affirmed that determination on these grounds:

> Since the reason for suspending benefits to one who is customarily self-employed is the probability of substantial income from such self-employment, it follows that such enterprise must be undertaken for profit. ...
> These...principles would eliminate from consideration as self-employment certain services which practically everyone performs for himself with the idea of saving money, such as, gardening, laundering, repairing, cooking, housework, and other similar economy measures.
> The performance of household duties by a housewife does not constitute self-employment within the meaning of section 108.04(5)(g). A household is not a business enterprise; rather, services in and about the household are primarily economy measures performed pursuant to a status as contrasted with services performed for gain in a business or contractual relationship.[75]

When the employer appealed the matter to the Circuit Court for Dane County, the socioeconomic stakes became manifest:

> The situation of this employee obviously is of much importance to married women in Wisconsin industry. It is also of substantial concern to the industries themselves. As plaintiff says in its brief: "The trifling amount involved...would not warrant the

effort involved, but the application of the principle has become an important financial problem in this industry, which has made the case assume importance as a test case to judicially determine what is meant in the law by 'self-employment.'"[76]

The trial court was acutely aware of the fact that the employer's assertions--in particular, that Rybacki employed a maid to take care of the child and house while she worked for wages and that she failed to seek gainful employment from April to December[77]--

> lend color to a belief that this particular woman, by virtue of her financial position, may not represent the most deserving case for unemployment compensation benefits. However, we must not lose sight of the general principle which will affect thousands of married women not so fortunately situated. There is a limit to which the law may individualize. Rules of general application must govern.[78]

In pursuit of justice in general and "deal[ing] with the average,"[79] the trial judge analyzed the employer's claim as arguing for a per se ban on benefits for married women, which might prompt employers to discriminate in hiring against men and unmarried women in order to avoid payment of benefits.[80]   By the same token, the judge wondered aloud whether the logic of the employer's argument might not be applicable to "the reverse situation where the husband may be temporarily unemployed and is doing the chores around the home."[81] In order to avoid the palpably absurd result that virtually everyone with a home might be deemed self-employed and therefore ineligible for benefits, the judge stated that only where an unemployed person was "earn[ing] an economic subsistence, not in the employ of another" would he or she be "outside of the presumably needy class."[82] But where a wage-earning wife loses her paid employment, although "she unquestionably is doing things of value to her family...[h]er concentration upon household duties does not restore that earning power, does not add one cent to income."[83]

The Supreme Court of Wisconsin reversed all the administrative tribunals and the lower court and held that Rybacki was ineligible for benefits (in effect) because the commodification of reproductive labor as embodied in the monetization of the wife/mother/daughter's labor when transferred to a hired domestic servant[84] disclosed the theretofore hidden value of her self-employment to the court:[85] "So far as the family unit is concerned, there is a monetary return from the services of the wife which results in a saving of the family income."[86] The court thus provided Marxists and feminists[87] with an object lesson in the statutory perversity that can result from recognizing reproductive labor as commensurable with employment[88]--an ironic outcome in light of the court's socioeconomically hollowed-out notion of self-employment[89] and superficial analysis of the proletarian character of the worker's attachment to the labor market.[90]

The logic of *Slocum Straw Works* found its counterpart in contemporaneous agency decisions involving men with farm ties. Upon becoming unemployed, one worker who owned a farm "[b]y his own energy and with his own labor...raised sufficient crops and earned enough from his farm to furnish his family with food."[91] Like Rybacki, this claimant hired a laborer to work on the farm while he had been employed. Because it was customary to pay farm laborers in the produce of the farm, the Pennsylvania Unemployment Compensation Board of Review ruled in 1938 that "[i]f the claimant were working for another farmer and received in kind enough foodstuffs to feed his family of six and a surplus to sell for over $100 per year...he would be receiving substantial wages."[92]

That the principle underlying these cases is the hypothetical monetization of uncompensated labor (and/or the products thereof) becomes plain in a claim by a single man without relatives or even a home of his own. He was initially disqualified for benefits because he "received board and lodging in exchange for making himself useful" on a farm. But the Michigan Unemployment Compensation Commission reversed this determination in 1939 on the ground that because the farm was large enough to warrant the services of a hired laborer and no one was ever so employed there, "the claimant could not be said to have replaced another employee."[93]

Disqualification of the unemployed worker-farmer seems to make more intuitive sense than that of the housewife because only as to the former is it literally not the case that "the law of property...coerces him into wage-work under penalty of starvation."[94] Whereas ownership of the land (and the relevant equipment) makes the unemployed worker-farmer the mythical self-employed who, by controlling his inputs, "can produce food" and thus avoid "working for factory owners,"[95] the housewife merely has access to a businessman-husband who can afford to subsidize the opportunity cost of her paid employment (that is, the maid's wage).[96] Is the only relevant difference between the two the fact that the farmer secures subsistence directly--without exchange--while the housewife, by replacing the maid, releases money that can be spent on subsistence? That such a difference may not be significant is suggested by supposing that instead of taking care of a household, Rybacki had operated a beauty parlor (or provided day care) in her house (which she closed down entirely or hired another to operate from December to April in order to take advantage of the higher wages in the factory). Should she have been denied benefits had she refused to resume hairdressing? If she had no significant capital investment, would it make any less sense to require every unemployed person to try home hairdressing or similar personal-service self-employment?

Light may be shed on this question by two lines of cases. The first involved a barber who, after having been an employee, leased the barber shop and hired another barber to work there in his stead in exchange for three-quarters of the gross receipts; after paying an additional fifteen per cent in rent, the claimant allegedly earned fifty dollars per month, although he testified that he received no income. While looking for work as a hospital orderly, at which he had had more experience than as a barber, he did not want to fire his employee and to do the barbering himself "because he feels if the individual engaged as a barber needs the work, the claimant is also reluctant to sit around the shop and wait for business."[97] Benefits were denied on the ground that he was not unemployed because "he could work full time, if he desired to do so" and thus "controll[ed] his own employment or lack of it."[98] Is it socioeconomically justifiable to penalize the self-selected loser at musical employment chairs? Since one of these two workers had to become unemployed,[99] what macroeconomic sense does it make to deprive the one who formally leased the shop of benefits?

Since the entitlement to unemployment insurance benefits is not means tested but only employment tested, an unemployed millionaire who can subsist on her interest or dividends would not be ineligible for benefits. Even if she were the passive owner of all the stock of a corporation but did not work there in any capacity, she would not be self-employed and hence would not be required to go through the motions of asking the corporation to give her a paying job in lieu of going on the dole. But apparently if she customarily cut others' hair in her house, her eligibility for benefits would be contingent on her prior unsuccessful effort to return to hairdressing.

The other line of cases is generated by a provision in the unemployment insurance statute of Iowa (and of several other states) disqualifying for benefits an unemployed person who "has failed, without good cause...to return to his customary self-employment (if any) when so directed by the commission."[100] Where it was not reasonable to return to customary self-employment because there was no market for such services and/or it promised no "reasonable return," the unemployed were dispensed from the requirement.[101] But perhaps the most tantalizing decisions have been made under the Iowa statute, which was amended in 1939 to include this unique definition:

> An employee shall be deemed to be engaged in "his customary self-employment"...during the periods in which he customarily devotes the major portion of his working time and efforts: (1) to his individual enterprises and interests; or (2) to her duties as housewife; or (3) to attending classes and preparing his studies for any school or college.[102]

A literal reading of these two provisions suggests the following scenario: Upon applying for unemployment benefits, a married woman is directed by the state agency to return to her duties as housewife. She states that although she is ready, willing, and able to accept new wage employment, she refuses to darn her husband's socks and prefers to spend her days at the public library reading George Eliot's novels. The agency then disqualifies her. In two cases decided in 1939, the Appeals Tribunal of the Iowa Unemployment Compensation Commission underwrote this logic. One claimant was let off the hook because relatives living in her house made it unnecessary for her to "remain at home to take care of the duties of a housewife."[103] The other had performed enough full-time work in the recent past to overcome the presumption that she had "customarily devoted the major portion of her time and efforts to attending to her duties as a housewife."[104] In other words, persistent dereliction of housewifely duty served as an exemption. The dramatic rise in labor force participation rates among married women during the past several decades may prove useful to them in Iowa--where these provisions are still in force.[105]

If the impoverished and exceedingly attenuated notion of self-employment in the unemployed housewife cases is placed in the context of the housewife as exploited[106] by one who does not employ her (namely, her husband and/or his employer),[107] the resulting structure strikingly confirms the illusory solipsistic character of self-employment.

NOTES

1. International Bhd. of Teamsters, Local 309 v. Hanke, 339 U.S. 470, 475 (1950) (per Frankfurter, J.).

2. *See, e.g.*, Senn v. Tile Layers Protective Union, Local No. 5, 301 U.S. 468 (1937), *aff'g* Senn v. Tile Layers Protective Union, Local No. 5, 222 Wis. 383, 268 N.W. 270 (1936); Boro Park Sanitary Live Poultry Market, Inc. v. Heller, 280 N.Y. 481, 21 N.E.2d 687 (1939); Bautista v. Jones, 25 Cal.2d 746, 155 P.2d 343 (1945).

3. *See, e.g.*, International Bhd. of Teamsters, Local 309 v. Hanke, 339 U.S. 470 (1950), *aff'g* Hanke v. International Bhd. of Teamsters, Local 309, 33 Wash.2d 646, 207 P.2d 206 (1949).

4. Bakery & Pastry Drivers & Helpers Local 802 of Teamsters v. Wohl, 315 U.S. 769, 770-71 (1942).

5. *Id.* at 771.

6. *See, e.g.*, Local 777, Democratic Union Org. Comm. v. NLRB, 603 F.2d 862 (D.C. Cir. 1978). This case involved a complaint that the employer had committed an unfair labor practice by refusing to bargain with the union. For an extended critique, see Marc Linder, *Towards Universal Worker Coverage under the National Labor Relations Act: Making Room for Uncontrolled Employees, Dependent Contractors, and Employee-Like Persons*, 66 U. DET. L. REV. 555 (1989). *But see* Fugazy Continental Corp., 231 N.L.R.B. 1344 (1977), *enforced*, 603 F.2d 214 (2d Cir. 1979) (drivers who had paid thousands of dollars for limousine franchises were employees).

7. Interestingly, the courts in these cases did not use the term *self-employed* until Justice Frankfurter did so at mid-century. International Bhd. of Teamsters v. Hanke, 339 U.S. at 476.

8. This is not to say that they did not also view them as entrepreneurs in the making. The dissent in *Senn* is a splendid example:

> Business in contracting for such work as tile laying ordinarily begins with small beginnings, and if successful gradually extends to more considerable proportions. The plaintiff's road to success in such business is blocked, and the entry into such business is blocked to every worker by the requirement...[--]that no contractor shall work with his own hands...[--which] would foreclose every worker...from entering the contracting business unless he has or is able to procure capital otherwise not necessary for entry into and prosecution of the business to success. ... The practice upheld by the court is Un-American.

Senn, 268 N.W. at 275-76.

9. Bautista v. Jones, 155 P.2d at 345.

10. *Id.* at 357.

11. *Senn*, 268 N.W. at 272.

12. *See, e.g.*, John Bregger, *Self-Employment in the United States*, MONTHLY LAB. REV., Jan. 1963, at 37; Robert Ray, *A Report on Self-Employed Americans in 1973, id.*, Jan. 1975, at 49; Linder, *Self-Employment as a Cyclical Escape from Unemployment*; Eugene Becker, *Self-Employed Workers: An Update to 1983*, MONTHLY LAB. REV., Mar. 1984, at 14; *Self-Employment in OECD Countries*, in OECD EMPLOYMENT OUTLOOK, Sept. 1986, at 43, 59-60.

13. By way of contrast, Adam Smith observed that "[i]n dear years...poor independent workmen frequently consume the little stocks with which they used to supply themselves with the materials of their work, and are obliged to become journeymen for their subsistence." SMITH, WEALTH OF NATIONS at 83.

14. *See* GÖRAN THERBORN, WHY SOME PEOPLES ARE MORE UNEMPLOYED THAN OTHERS: THE STRANGE PARADOX OF GROWTH AND UNEMPLOYMENT (1986).

15. 131 CONG. REC. E 1044 (Mar. 21, 1985) (Rep. Wyden, introducing the Self-Employment Opportunity Act of 1985).

16. STEVEN BALKIN, SELF-EMPLOYMENT FOR LOW-INCOME PEOPLE 3-4 (1989).

17. In 1971 5.43% of unemployed and 3.72% of wage workers shifted to self-employment; by 1980, the corresponding figures were 9.02% and 2.84%. EVANS & LEIGHTON, SELF-EMPLOYMENT SELECTION AND EARNINGS OVER THE LIFE CYCLE tab. 5.6 at 68.

18. 131 CONG. REC. E 1349 (Apr. 4, 1985) (Rep. Gebhardt, co-sponsor of the Self-Opportunity Act of 1985).

19. 136 CONG. REC. E 3131 (Oct. 4, 1990) (Rep. Kennelly).

20. Pub. L. No. 101-554, 104 Stat. 2751 (1990). *See also* U.S. DEP'T OF LABOR, FROM HOMEMAKING TO ENTREPRENEURSHIP: A READINESS TRAINING PROGRAM (1985).

21. *Self-Employment for the Poor: The Potential of Micro-Enterprise Credit Programs: Hearing Before the House Select Comm. on Hunger*, 100th Cong., 2d Sess. (1988).

22. *Micro-Enterprise Development Legislation: Hearing Before the Subcomm. on International Economic Trade and Policy of the House Comm. on Foreign Affairs*, 100th Cong., 1st Sess. 6, 4 (1988).

23. Joint Training Partnership Act Amendments of 1986, Pub. L. No. 99-496, § 11, 100 Stat. 1261, 1264 (1986) (codified at 29 U.S.C. § 1651(a)(1)(D) (Supp. 1991)).

24. The focus for employees was on layoffs and plant closures. 29 U.S.C. § 1651(a)(1)(A) and (B) (Supp. 1991). Among the self-employed, the prominent criterion was failure of their major suppliers or customers. 20 C.F.R. § 631.3(c) (1990). The original impetus for inclusion of the self-employed appears to have been concern for farmers. *See* S. REP. NO. 99-317, 99th Cong., 2d Sess. 5 (1986); H. REP. NO. 99-754, 99th Cong., 2d Sess. 9-11 (1986); 132 CONG. REC. H 5289-90 (Aug. 11, 1986) (Rep. Lightfoot).

25. *But see* ERIK WRIGHT, CLASS STRUCTURE AND INCOME DETERMINATION 104 (1979) ("Petty bourgeois income is self-earned income").

26. 26 U.S.C. § 32(c)(2)(A)(ii) (Supp. 1991) (earned income includes net earnings from self-employment); 26 C.F.R. § 1.43-2(c)(2)(iii [*sic*; should read ii]) (1991) (minus net loss).

27. Food Stamp Act of 1977, 7 U.S.C. § 2014(f)(1)(A) (Supp. 1991).

28. *See, e.g.*, Marc Bendick, Jr. & Mary Egan, *Transfer Payment Diversion for Small Business Development: British and French Experience*, 40 INDUS. & LAB. REL. REV. 528 (1987); Report of the Subcomm. on the Foreign Experience of the Task Force on Economic Adjustment and Worker Dislocation, *Evaluation of Programs to Assist Displaced Workers in Foreign Industrialized Countries,* in ECONOMIC ADJUSTMENT AND WORKER DISLOCATION IN A COMPETITIVE SOCIETY: REPORT OF THE SECRETARY OF LABOR'S TASK FORCE ON ECONOMIC ADJUSTMENT AND WORKER DISLOCATION 24 (1986); Beatrice Reubens, *Unemployment Insurance in Western Europe: Responses to High Unemployment, 1973-1983,* in UNEMPLOYMENT INSURANCE: THE SECOND HALF-CENTURY 173, 196-97 (W. Hansen & J. Byers ed. 1990); ARONSON, SELF-EMPLOYMENT at 103.

29. *See* Omnibus Budget Reconciliation Act of 1987, Pub. L. No. 100-203, § 9152, 101 Stat. 1330, 1330-322 (1987).

30. *See, e.g.*, BNA, DAILY LAB. REP., Oct. 19, 1987, at A-12 (LEXIS); Peter Kilborn, *Novel Program for the Jobless Aims to Create Entrepreneurs*, N.Y. Times, May 16, 1990, at 1, col. 7 (nat. ed.); Glenn Rifkin, *From Unemployment, Into Self-Employment, id.*, Sept. 19, 1991, at C1, col. 4 (nat. ed.). Congress did not adopt an initiative to "address[] business community concerns over the use of unemployment insurance funds, to which they contribute, toward the start-up of potential competition," by prohibiting the use of the self-employment allowances for starting the business. *See* 133 CONG. REC. S 18,405 (Dec. 18, 1987) (Sen. Heinz). On the possibility that such subsidies are merely zero-sum games in which others are displaced, see ARONSON, SELF-EMPLOYMENT at 102.

31. Steinmetz & Wright, *Reply to Linder and Houghton* at 738. Mass incorporation by doctors and lawyers may account for the observation that those with graduate school educations are most likely to form incorporated businesses. *See* EVANS & LEIGHTON, SELF-EMPLOYMENT at 39. Aronson's (undocumented) claim--that "[t]he incorporated self-employed are more likely to include entrepreneurs in the classical sense. The majority are managers of small businesses," ARONSON, SELF-EMPLOYMENT at 43 n.2--would arguably be untenable if the employer-owners of substantial firms were ignored and the self-employed were restricted to solo workers.

32. C. WRIGHT MILLS, WHITE COLLAR: THE AMERICAN MIDDLE CLASSES 28-29 (1956 [1951]). The decline of these urban self-employed and their shift to employee status involves no massive shift in status system "but rather the replacement of low-income entrepreneurs (really 'disguised unemployed') by employees." LEBERGOTT, MANPOWER IN ECONOMIC GROWTH at 108-109.

33. Cooperman v. California Unemployment Ins. App. Bd., 49 Cal. App. 3d 1, 122 Cal. Rptr. 127 (1975).

34. The opinion does not explain why Cooperman was not the employee of the entities for which he worked.

35. 49 Cal. App. 3d at 4-5, 122 Cal. Rptr. at 129.

36. 49 Cal. App. 3d at 5, n.2, 122 Cal. Rptr. at 130 n.2.

37. 49 Cal. App. 3d at 8, 122 Cal. Rptr. at 132.

38. 49 Cal. App. 3d at 6, 122 Cal. Rptr. at 132.

39. 49 Cal. App. 3d at 10, 122 Cal. Rptr. at 133.

40. Since 1963, however, California has permitted the self-employed to elect coverage under the disability benefit system of the state unemployment compensation statute. CAL. UNEMPL. INS. CODE § 708.5 (West 1986); Simon v. Unemployment Insurance Appeals Bd., 193 Cal. App. 3d 1076, 238 Cal. Rptr. 589 (1987). To be sure, by 1986 only three per cent of the more than one million eligible self-employed in California so elected. *See Rising Use of Part-Time and Temporary Workers* at 133 (statement of R. Dillon) (an absolute decline since 1975). Yet the entrenchment of this partial and voluntary incorporation of the self-employed may have made it easier for the *Cooperman* court to treat the entitlement of the self-employed to benefits in such a cavalier manner. That statutory incorporation is, in any event, further evidence of the felt need for the assimilation of the self-employed to the status of dependent employees. Since 1953, moreover, California has been the only state to permit employers to elect coverage personally for themselves in the event of unemployment. CAL. UNEMP. INS. CODE § 708 (West Supp. 1991). Positing that "the true basis of the *Cooperman* decision consisted of the fact that the plaintiff's state of unemployment was a matter over which he had no control and one which was not the result of any deliberate decision to tailor the terms of his employment, and particularly his compensation, in such a way as to avail himself of unemployment compensation benefits to which he should not have been entitled," another court of appeal awarded benefits to the president of a small corporation who was a carpenter and employer. Carlsen v. California Unemployment Ins. App. Bd., 64 Cal. App. 3d 577, 588, 134 Cal. Rptr. 581, 588 (1976).

41. On the contrary, the court denied the applicability of its ruling to a hypothetical case in which "an incorporator forms a corporation in order to obtain unemployment insurance benefits which he would not otherwise be entitled to." Cooperman, 49 Cal. App. 3d at 10, 122 Cal. Rptr. at 133. The Board had apparently conceded that Cooperman's self-incorporation was not motivated by the desire for benefits. Although Cooperman's payment of payroll taxes and claim for benefits show that he was certainly not unaware of this advantage of incorporation, possibly the Board wanted to avoid triggering a judicial ruling that would have forced it to engage in the doubtless very difficult task of proving such subjective intent in the future.

42. Although greater plausibility might attach to the view that it would be unjust to impose liability for payroll taxes on the sole employee-stockholder of a corporation who was in principle ineligible to receive benefits, a challenge to the constitutionality of such a regime has been rejected. State v. Sherlock Auction & Realty, Inc., 235 Kan. 232, 678 P.2d 630 (1984).

43. The Supreme Court of Rhode Island adopted a similar position in a contemporaneous case involving a more technical issue.   Agency administrators had denied benefits to a carpenter who was the principal stockholder and president of a corporation on the ground that his very effort to secure work for his company/himself, although unsuccessful and uncompensated (because neither corporation nor the claimant could pay for it), constituted the performance of services inconsistent with being totally unemployed.   Without engaging in the expansive social theorizing of the *Cooperman* court, the Rhode Island judiciary refused to countenance an economically inefficient catch-22 that treated unemployed self-incorporated workers differently than traditional employees. Dumont v. Hackett, 390 A.2d 375 (R.I. 1978).

44. *See infra* ch. 6.

45. Inexplicably, Aronson asserts that "[s]ocial protection is the one area in which governments have recognized that the self-employed are subject to the same hazards as wage and salary workers. Failure of one's own business may mean a spell of unemployment as well as the loss of physical and financial capital." ARONSON, SELF-EMPLOYMENT at 109. Although he observes that public insurance for the self-employed against illness, disease, injury, and unemployment is "virtually nonexistent" in the United States, *id.* at 110, Aronson fails to document such government recognition.

46. 445 Parl. Deb., H.C. (5th ser.) 1441 (1947) (John Strachey, Minister of Food).

47. It is important to keep in mind the socioeconomic ambiguity inherent in self-employment as a secondary job. Although the classification may refer to an employee who takes up a second job 'on his own,' it also includes the self-employed who began waged work to supplement their income but whose own-account income has in the meantime become subsidiary. *See, e.g.,* Harriet Friedman, *World Market, State, and Family Farm: Social Bases of Household Production in the Era of Wage Labor,* 20 COMP. STUD. IN SOC'Y & HIST. 545, 563 (1978).

48. The secondary self-employed are not counted among the officially reported self-employed.

49. U.S. SMALL BUSINESS ADMINISTRATION, THE STATE OF SMALL BUSINESS: A REPORT OF THE PRESIDENT 111-12 (1986).

50. Calculated according to data in John Stinson, Jr., *Multiple Jobholding Up Sharply in the 1980's,* MONTHLY LAB. REV., July 1990, at 3, tab. 4 at 7. Significantly, of these secondary self-employed, 30.0 per cent did all, and 61.8 per cent did some, of that work at home--by far the highest percentages in the nonagricultural sector. *Id.,* tab. 5 at 7. Apart from the large absolute increase, the most striking difference from the situation thirty years earlier is that fifty-seven per cent of the nonagricultural wage and salary workers with a secondary job as self-employed held that position in agriculture in 1958, whereas that figure had declined to twenty-three per cent by 1989.

Calculated according to data in *id.*, tab. 4 at 7; U.S. BUREAU OF THE CENSUS, CURRENT POPULATION REPORTS: LABOR FORCE tab. 1 at 2 (Ser. P-50, No. 88, Apr. 1959). Earlier data were similar; see *idem*, CURRENT POPULATION REPORTS: LABOR FORCE tab. 2 at 4 (Ser. P-50, No. 30, Mar. 13, 1951). Looked at from a different perspective, between 1956 and 1980, nonagricultural self-employment as a share of all nonagricultural secondary jobs almost doubled--from thirteen per cent in 1956 to twenty-five per cent in 1980, dropping again by 1989 to twenty-three per cent. Calculated according to data in 1 U.S. BUREAU OF LABOR STATISTICS, LABOR FORCE STATISTICS DERIVED FROM THE CURRENT POPULATION SURVEY: A DATABOOK tab. C-18 at 725 (Bull. 2096, 1982); Stinson, *Multiple Jobholding*, tab. 4 at 7.

51. Martin v. Unemployment Compensation Bd. of Rev., 174 Pa. Super. 412, 101 A.2d 421, 423 (1953).

52. For an overview of the case law, see Unempl. Ins. Rep. (CCH) ¶ 1901 at 4385 and ¶¶ 1901.20-.398.

53. *See e.g.*, ALA. CODE § 25-4-78 (1990); Miller v. Director, Ala. Dep't of Indus. Rel., 460 So.2d 1326 (Ala. 1984).

54. Department of Lab. & Indus. v. Unemployment Compensation Bd. of Review, 203 Pa. Super. 183, 199 A.2d 475, 477 (1964).

55. PA. STAT. ANN. tit. 43, § 802(h) (Purdon 1991). Much of the reported litigation under this provision has involved the issue of whether work not taken up until after the claimant became unemployed was (absolutely disqualifying) self-employment or wage employment, the income from which would merely be set off against benefits. For examples of the very restrictive adjudications, see Unemployment Compensation Bd. of Review v. Kessler, 365 A.2d 459 (Pa. Commw. 1976); Pavlonis v. Commonwealth Unemployment Compensation Bd. of Review, 426 A.2d 215 (Pa. Commw. 1981).

56. Cumming v. District Unemployment Compensation Bd., 382 A.2d 1010, 1013 (D.C. 1978) (quoting board's position).

57. *Id.* at 1015.

58. Sun Shipbuilding & Dry Dock Co. v. Unemployment Compensation Bd. of Review, 160 Pa. Super. 501, 52 A.2d 362, 263 (1947).

59. *See* THE MIDYEAR ECONOMIC REPORT OF THE PRESIDENT: TO THE CONGRESS, JULY 30, 1948, tab. 9 at 85 (1948) ($44.39 in 1945).

60. Sun Shipbuilding, 52 A.2d at 365. The judge found that the employer had conceded that the employee would have been laid off in December anyway. *Id.* at 364 n.1.

61. 52 A.2d at 364. One puzzling point is that the worker filed his claim on August 30, 1945; *id.* Unless this is a misprint (his claim was allowed as of

Nov. 14), it is unclear how he could have been eligible for benefits while earning thirty-five dollars per week.

62. Sun Shipbuilding & Dry Dock Co. v. Unemployment Compensation Bd. of Review, 358 Pa. 224, 56 A.2d 254, 259 (1948).

63. *Id*. at 261.

64. *Id*. at 260.

65. For an excellent critique of the opinion, see *Note, Unemployment Insurance--A Discussion of the Eligibility Requirements and the Voluntary Leaving Disqualification*, 17 GEO. WASH. L. REV. 447 (1949).

66. *See* Mississippi Employment Security Comm'n v. Medlin, 171 So.2d 496 (Miss. 1965).

67. Bolles v. Appeal Bd. of the Mich. Employment Security Comm'n, 361 Mich. 378, 105 N.W.2d 192 (1960).

68. *Id*. at 195. The opinion, written by Talbot Smith, a former law professor at Berkeley, who also wrote what is arguably the most mordant judicial critique of the so-called control test of employment in interpreting social legislation, is a rare judicial masterpiece of factual directness and lucid reasoning. *See* Powell v. Appeal Bd. of Mich. Employment Sec. Comm'n, 345 Mich. 455, 75 N.W.2d 874, 878-86 (1956) (Smith, J., dissenting).

69. An analogous jurisprudence has developed under the National Labor Relations Act. The National Labor Relations Board may order employers who have discriminatorily discharged employees to reinstate them with back pay. Such employees are then entitled to the difference between what they would have earned had they not been discharged and their actual interim earnings. Both the Board and the reviewing courts of appeal have ruled that for purposes of mitigating the loss of wages, "[s]elf-employment should be treated like any other interim employment." Heinrich Motors, Inc., v. NLRB, 403 F.2d 145, 148 (2d Cir. 1968). Even where the worker's profit from self-employment is not significant, he will not be deemed to have wilfully lost earnings. F.E. Hazard, Ltd. v. Moffitt, 303 N.L.R.B. No. 130, 1991-92 NLRB Dec. (CCH) ¶ 16,768. Since back pay may be awarded only where the interim earnings are less than what the employee's wages would have been, such self-employment must definitionally be sub-bourgeois.

70. *See, e.g.,* Phillips v. Unemployment Compensation Comm'n, 323 Mich. 188, 35 N.W.2d 237 (1948) (lawyer in practice for forty-five years).

71. Slocum Straw Works v. Industrial Comm'n, 232 Wis. 71, 286 N.W. 593 (1939).

72. Wis. Stat. § 108.04(5)(g) (1937).

73. 2 Soc. Sec. Bd., Unemployment Compensation Interpretation Service: Benefit Series 348, 349 (965-Wis. Ct. D., Dane County Cir. Ct., Oct. 28, 1938). In 1937 Rybacki earned $1.073 an hour--considerably in excess of the national average for manufacturing of $0.624. THE MIDYEAR ECONOMIC REPORT OF THE PRESIDENT: TO THE CONGRESS, JULY 30, 1948, tab. 10 at 86 (1948).

74. 2 Soc. Sec. Bd., Unemployment Compensation Interpretation Service: Benefit Series 346 (964-Wis. A, Decision of App. Tribunal, July 1938).

75. *Id.* at 347.

76. Slocum Straw Works v. Industrial Comm'n of Wisconsin, *id.* at 348-49 (965-Wis. Ct. D., Oct. 28, 1938).

77. *Id.* at 349. The Supreme Court made the case confusing by tendentiously neglecting to mention that the Commission contested these contentions.

78. *Id.*

79. *Id.* at 351.

80. *Id.* at 350.

81. *Id.*

82. *Id.* at 350, 351.

83. *Id.* at 351.

84. The Supreme Court neglected to disclose that the maid was Rybacki's sister-in-law. *Id.* at 351.

85. Why the court by the same logic did not regard her as the employee of her husband, who "pa[id] the bills for the support of the family," *id.* at 596, is unclear.

86. Slocum Straw Works v. Industrial Comm'n, 232 Wis. 71, 286 N.W. 593, 598 (1939).

87. *See, e.g.,* Nancy Folbre, *The Unproductive Housewife: Her Evolution in Nineteenth-Century Economic Thought*, 16 SIGNS 463 (1991).

88. "Housewifery as a Business" was a not uncommon trope of early twentieth-century home economics. *See, e.g.,* LYDIA BALDERSTON, HOUSEWIFERY: A MANUAL AND TEXT BOOK ON PRACTICAL HOUSEKEEPING 1-20 (1919).

89. The employer had argued in its brief that self-employment meant "'Attending to one's own affairs.'" Comment, *Unemployment Compensation--"Self-Employment*," 1940 WIS. L. REV. 147, 148 (citing Brief for appellant at 17).

90. Although the court did not articulate this character as a ground of its decision, it appeared impressed that:

> Mrs. Rybacki testified "she used her earnings for extra expenses, clothing, movies, the baby, company and things like that." ... There is no suggestion...that Mrs. Rybacki was obliged to seek employment either for her support or as a contribution to the household expense. The testimony is...that this was amply provided for by her husband.

Slocum Straw Works, 286 N.W. at 595, 596. The court may therefore have tacitly assumed that in 'mixed marriages'--the husband was a capitalist employing several workers, *id.* at 595--in which the proletarian wife unnecessarily continued to work, she ceased being an "unemployed worker" on whom "[t]he burden of irregular employment...falls...with crushing force." 1931 Wis. Laws ch. 20, § 108.01(1) (Spec. Sess.).

91. 1 Soc. Sec. Bd., Unemployment Compensation Interpretation Service: Benefit Series 816, 816 (712-Pa. R, Pennsylvania Unemployment Compensation Bd. of Review, July 26, 1938).

92. *Id.* at 817.

93. 2 Unemployment Compensation Interpretation Service: Benefit Series 1466 (1763-Mich. A, Feb. 17, 1939).

94. Robert Hale, *Coercion and Distribution in a Supposedly Non-Coercive State*, 38 POL. SCI. Q. 470, 472-73 (1923).

95. *Id.* at 473. Two Iowa cases involving laid-off miner-farmers decided the same day illustrate this point: the one who was able to feed his family was disqualified, whereas the one who was not was eligible. 3 Fed. Security Agency, Unemployment Compensation Interpretation Service: Benefits Series 320 (2543-Iowa A, Iowa Unemp. Comp. Comm'n, Decision of App. Tribunal, Aug. 21, 1939); id. at 323 (2544-Iowa R, Iowa Unemp. Comp. Comm'n, Decision of Comm'n, Aug. 21, 1939).

96. In fact, since Rybacki received such an above-average hourly wage, it is plausible that her earnings far exceeded the amount that she paid her sister-in-law.

97. U.S. Employment and Training Adm., Benefit Series Service--Unemployment Insurance TPU-415.15-71 (Hawaii B, No. 437-74, Decision of Referee, May 3, 1974) (Rep. 291-75, Aug. 1974).

98. *Id.*

99. Alternatively, they might have shared the work and both been eligible for partial unemployment benefits.

100. 1937 Iowa Acts ch. 4, § 5(c) at 516. The Social Security Board had recommended that the states not adopt such a requirement because it was not "feasible for the employment security agency to determine that a claimant should again take up some former self-employment." Instead, it suggested

as a more appropriate criterion whether she was unemployed or available for work. Soc. Sec. Bd., Unemployment Comp. Div., Manual of State Employment Security Legislation 503-504 n. (Employment Security Memorandum No. 13, rev. Nov. 1942). For an overview of state statutes with such provisions in the 1940s, see Soc. Sec. Bd., Comparison of State Unemployment Compensation Laws as of December 31, 1945, at 164-65 (Employment Security Memorandum No. 8, rev. Dec. 1945).

101. *See, e.g.*, 2 Fed. Security Agency, Unemployment Compensation Interpretation Service: Benefit Series 607 (1150-R.I. A, R.I. Unemp. Comp. Bd., Decision of Referee, Oct. 14, 1938); *id.* at 1480 (1772-R.I. A, R.I. Unemp. Comp. Bd., Decision of Referee, Feb. 22, 1939).

102. 1939 Iowa Acts ch. 64, § 2 at 93.

103. 3 Fed. Security Agency, Unemployment Compensation Interpretation Service: Benefit Series 53 (2862-Iowa A, Oct. 31, 1939).

104. *Id.* at 206 (2974-Iowa A, Oct. 14, 1939).

105. Iowa Code § 96.5.3 and § 96.19.18 (1991). The phrase "to her duties as housewife" was changed to "to the employee's household duties." Iowa Code § 96.19.18 (1985). The new wording was not the work of the legislature but rather that of the code editor, who "shall edit [the Code] in order that words which designate one gender will be changed to reflect both genders when the provisions of law apply to persons of both genders. The Code editor shall not make any substantive changes." Iowa Code § 14.13.2(1991). If the legislature meant to treat housewives differently in 1939 and has never voted to eliminate that historical discriminatory intent, then, ironically, the code editor exceeded her authority. *See* Des Moines Register, July 31, 1991, at 9A, col. 1 (letter to editor).

106. *See, e.g.*, Herbert Gintis & Samuel Bowles, *Structure and Practice in the Labor Theory of Value*, Rev. Radical Pol. Econ., Winter 1981, at 1, 8-14; Nancy Folbre, *Exploitation Comes Home: A Critique of the Marxian Theory of Family Labour*, 6 Cambridge J. Econ. 317 (1982).

107. A few years after *Slocum*, a trial court in an apparently similar case ruled that "[t]he 'little woman' does not work for her husband. The male spouse is not her employer. She is not his employee." Doughboy Mills, Inc. v. Industrial Comm'n (Cir. Ct., Dane Cty., Aug. 7, 1944) (cited in 12 Unempl. Insur. Rep ¶ 1901.04 Wis. at 52,164 (CCH)).

6

The Question of the Incorporated
Self-Employed

> Congress realized that the income of self-employed
> persons is in most instances a combination of income from both
> labor and invested capital, and deliberately chose not to attempt
> the difficult, if not impossible, task of separating one from the
> other.[1]

The complaint voiced by several researchers that the
exclusion of the incorporated self-employed from the count
has vitiated quantitative and qualitative analysis of self-
employment calls for discussion of a number of interrelated
characteristics of this subgroup.

Was Henry Ford Self-Employed?

> The modern American is not self-employed.... Whether the
> president of General Motors or a floor-sweeper in a Chevrolet
> plant, the "worker" today is what Marx defined as a proletarian: a
> man who sells his labor to those who control the "tools of
> production," in exchange for which he receives a "wage" payment.
> No individual is wealthy enough to own personally the vast capital
> resources required for modern industrial production; hence, we all
> become employees, that is, economic dependents of organizations.
> ... Even those who are self-employed are not necessarily
> economically independent. The local franchised dealer for a
> national corporation may have his economic affairs as effectively

administered by the manufacturer as though he were a direct employee.[2]

The chief vehicle of collecting information on the self-employed, the CPS questionnaire, does not delve into socioeconomically sensitive detail that would enable the BLS/BOC to verify self-reported data on self-employment.[3] In particular, it fails to explore such issues as the share of stock ownership above which it would be appropriate to characterize a corporate president as self-employed. Although the categorization of the president of General Motors as not self-employed appears uncontroversial, what about that of Henry Ford II at the time he or his family owned or controlled a controlling interest in the Ford Motor Company? And with regard to an empirically more relevant phenomenon, what about working shareholders in much smaller incorporated businesses?

Steinmetz and Wright distinguish between "[r]entier capitalists," who do not work for income, and "[e]ntrepreneurial capitalists," who do.[4] The former they describe as "coupon-clipp[ers]...receiving an income strictly from investments."[5] What about owners who do not receive a fixed income but fluctuating (so-called residual) profits and rely largely on their managers? Although they cannot seriously be deemed to "work for profit...in their own business," it is unlikely that the state will compel census respondents to incriminate themselves; it has, after all, been some time since it was socially acceptable to call people "capitalists"[6]--by distinguishing between working and nonworking owners.

So long as a business has a payroll (that is, employees), whether it is incorporated or unincorporated does not affect the class status of the owner. She may be a small capitalist or a large one, but she is neither a dependent worker[7] nor *self*-employed. The question is not so much whether the owners of incorporated businesses should be classified as employees or self-employers but whether it makes sense to lump together manager-owners of large firms with one-person entities regardless of whether the latter are incorporated. In favor of an inclusive grouping, it can be said that it is no less meaningful to classify (the original) Henry Ford and the owner-operator of a one-person hot dog stand as self-employed than to call both the current president of Ford Motor Company and his production-line workers employees. Although there is force to this argument,[8] visiting the improprieties of the latter classification on the former is not a valid justification. If self-employment is viewed as a dual or hybrid category combining labor and (petty) capital, capturing its essence requires a lower and an upper cutoff point. In other words, exclusion must extend to both crypto-employees and crypto-capitalists.

The socioeconomic sense underlying this categorization is rooted in the ontogenetically transitional character of autonomous producers,[9] "who employ no workers, and therefore do not produce as capitalists."[10]

> It is then also the law that economic development distributes the functions to different persons and the artisan or farmer...will either gradually transform himself into a small capitalist, who also exploits other workers, or he will lose his means of production (this may happen at first although he remains their *nominal* proprietor...) and be transformed into a wage laborer.[11]

That this process is not merely cyclical but also secular is shown by the monotonic decline in the rate of self-employment from the poorest to the richest countries today.[12] If the study of the self-employed is not to be a sterile exercise in taxonomy, investigation of their concrete relations remains a research desideratum.

The BOC/BLS's reclassification in 1967 of the incorporated self-employed as employees was part of a larger project to revamp the procedures for collecting data on employment and unemployment in order to implement national economic policies.[13] That expedience rather than theoretical rigor underlay the changes recommended by the so-called Gordon Committee emerges from the guideline that different uses and purposes of data on employment "may require different concepts and definitions." Therefore "no single definition of the labor force...is obviously *the* correct one."[14] Instead, "[e]ach concept should correspond to objectively measurable phenomena and should depend as little as possible on personal opinion or subjective attitudes." Moreover, "the concepts should be operationally feasible. It should be possible to get reliable data at reasonable cost."[15]

The committee's specific interest in the self-employed, to whom "[r]elatively little attention is paid," related to their occupational distribution, analysis of which might contribute to understanding changes in the volume of employment and unemployment.[16] Although the committee maintained that "[b]y the nature of the case, unemployment is almost nonexistent among the self-employed," it also acknowledged that "[c]ertain types of self-employment may rise as workers lose jobs in a business contraction. The apple sellers of the Great Depression are a classic example."[17] The possibility of self-misclassification in household surveys arose because

> [s]ome persons may regard themselves, or are considered by their wives, as self-employed even though they operate an incorporated business and are listed on its payroll as salaried officers or are otherwise on the payroll of an establishment. This would most likely occur among owners of small retail or service establishments or among salesmen who operate on a relatively loose relationship with their organization.[18]

In the construction industry, too, "many workers think of themselves as self-employed or alternate between self-employed and wage or salary work. There is no independent evidence on the number who might be reported as self-employed although they are actually, or at least legally, employees."[19]

When the BLS adopted the recommendations of the Gordon Committee in 1967, it concurred in the view that estimates of self-employment had been too high "because they included some persons who were the operators of small incorporated family enterprises and regarded themselves as proprietors rather than as wage or salary workers. The misclassification of these wage and salary workers as self employed" largely underlay the discrepancies between household and establishment data.[20] In order to segregate the two groups, the CPS inserted a question asking "all persons reported as self employed in a nonfarm business as to whether the business was incorporated."[21] The result "was to reduce the average level of nonfarm self-employment by about 750,000."[22]

To be sure, the BLS/BOC erred in reclassifying *all* incorporated self-employed as employees in 1967 (just as it had erred earlier in classifying them all as self-employed). But such a binary approach is inescapable where, in the absence of a socioeconomically sensitive inquiry, self-identification prevails. The point is not to return to the status quo ante but to determine who among the incorporated and unincorporated self-employed in fact live up to that class status. And neither the owner of a large corporation with many employees nor the dependent carpenter who incorporates in the hope of taking advantage of some tax code provision belongs to the self-employed.

How the Reagan Tax Reforms Inhibited Incorporation by the Self-Employed

> The term "employee" includes...an individual who is a self-employed individual. ... An individual who owns the entire interest in an unincorporated trade or business shall be treated as his own employer.[23]

A number of sociologists and economists have stressed that the CPS undercounts the self-employed because it definitionally excludes the incorporated self-employed, who have been increasing more rapidly than the unincorporated. Steinmetz and Wright, for example, created data on the incorporated self-employed by interpolating and extrapolating from the figures on incorporated self-employment that the BLS did publish on three occasions since BLS/BOC began classifying the incorporated self-employed as employees in 1967. The bench marks they used are: 1967, 850,000; 1976, 1,500,000; 1978, 2,100,000; 1982, 2,800,000.[24] These intervals indicate that Steinmetz and Wright were interpolating and extrapolating on the assumption that the rates of increase among incorporated self-employed were: seventy-six per cent (eight per cent per annum) between 1967 and 1976; forty per cent (twenty per cent per annum) between 1976 and 1978; eighty-seven per cent (fourteen per cent per annum) between 1976 and 1982; and 229 per cent (fifteen per cent per annum) between 1967 and 1982.

In August 1989, the BLS began tabulating (but not publishing) these data--the nonsampling error in which may be so great as to make them worthless[25]--separately once again.   The annual averages outside agriculture were 3,311,000 in 1989 and 3,356,000 for 1990.[26]   The increase from 1982 to 1990 thus amounted to only twenty per cent, or 2.5 per cent annually. Thus Steinmetz and Wright, who do not specify the rate of extrapolation they used for the period after 1982, may have been overestimating the growth during that period by a factor of four- to sixfold.[27]

It was no coincidence that 1982 marked a turning point for incorporation by the self-employed. Until then, such incorporations had been vitally induced by the significant tax-sheltered pension benefits advantage that the incorporated had enjoyed. But the enactment in 1982 of the Tax Equity and Fiscal Responsibility Act (TEFRA),[28] which created virtual pension parity between the unincorporated and incorporated self-employed,[29] reduced the incentive to incorporate. Lowering the highest individual income tax rates below the highest corporate rate in 1986[30] virtually eliminated any tax advantages accruing from incorporation.[31] Tax lawyers predicted at the time that incorporations would fall off,[32] and by 1991 new incorporations did in fact decline to the level they had reached in 1983.[33]

The story, however, is not yet told.   In order to understand why it is misleading, without more, to impute socioeconomic solidity to the incorporated self-employed, it is necessary to trace the legal and economic background of one-person incorporations since World War II.[34] In 1942, Congress amended the Internal Revenue Code (IRC) to authorize employers to establish pension plans for their employees (and themselves insofar as they were employees of the corporation) by providing a tax shelter for part of their wages or salaries (and the accruing interest) until they retired.[35]   This favorable tax treatment of corporate employers and employees in tandem with the advent of steeply progressive individual income tax rates in 1942 created a powerful incentive to incorporate.[36] This corporate privilege prompted a forty-year campaign by the excluded sole proprietors and partners to secure similar tax-sheltered retirement plans.

Led by the American Bar Association and American Medical Association, those in the professions began orchestrating a public relations crusade on behalf of their financially embattled group:

> Excluded from the benefits of social security coverage and precluded (by reason of the unavailability of the corporate form of carrying on his practice) from participation in employees' pension and profit-sharing plans which enjoy special income tax benefits, a lawyer or other professional man who is self-employed, even one with a large income, simply cannot accumulate a competence for himself and his family.[37]

This facially implausible claim of penury was tirelessly embellished during the 1940s and 1950s in professional journals[38] and, especially, at congressional hearings.[39] Repeated lobbying efforts kept the issue before Congress and gained a number of staunch advocates, chief of whom was Representative Keogh.[40]

The argument pressed by the professional associations ran as follows. Because "a member of a partnership is not an employee of the partnership [and a] sole proprietor is not his own employee...he is left out in the cold."[41]   And because lawyers also considered the denial to partners of employee status to be "arbitrary,"[42] the ideological notion of being one's own employer and employee made a noteworthy rhetorical contribution to the campaign for extension of tax-sheltered pension rights.[43]   The professions deemed social security inadequate because "lawyers and doctors and architects and most self-employed people do not want to retire and stop earning money. We like to die with our boots on."[44] As a result, "[m]ost physicians, dentists, and lawyers...would make substantial payments all their lives, only to find at age 65 that they are disqualified to receive benefits because they earn more than $1,000 per year."[45]

Although opposition by the Treasury Department to various bills[46] blocked enactment of tax-sheltered pensions for the self-employed through the 1950s, the long-time lobbying came to a first fruition with the enactment of the Keogh bill amendment to the IRC in 1962,[47] which cut the Gordian knot by treating the self-employed "for retirement purposes as the employers of themselves."[48] The relatively weak opposition to the bill[49] by liberals, populists, and labor unions[50] focused on the bipolar distribution of income among the self-employed:[51]

> The bill singles out for assistance a class of people, the self-employed, who as a group are, generally speaking, least in need or deserving of assistance. ... The most active proponents of the legislation include organized groups of doctors, lawyers, and accountants. It is said that there are more than 6 million self-employed individuals in this country who might benefit by the legislation. However, in fact, according to the estimates of the Treasury Department, about 80 percent of the tax reductions...would be received by self-employed people with an annual income in excess of $10,000, and about 50 percent...by self-employed people with an annual income in excess of $20,000. Now there are about 379,000 self-employed people in the United States with an annual income in excess of $20,000. These people constitute only about 6 percent of the self-employed people subject to this tax.[52]

At the other end of the spectrum,

> there are several million self-employed individuals who are unable to set aside substantial sums of money out of current earnings. These people must spend all of their current earnings to maintain themselves and their families. These are the self-employed who are most in need of assistance in providing for their nonproductive years but this bill is of no assistance whatsoever to this large group.[53]

The Keogh Bill did not create closure. As an Assistant Secretary of the Treasury astutely remarked at the time, the fact that corporate owner-managers still retained certain advantages in terms of the amount of income they were permitted to shelter from taxes created "an artificial tax incentive" for the self-employed to incorporate.[54] And incorporate they did in large numbers during the next two decades. Between 1962 and 1975 the number of new business incorporations rose by seventy-nine per cent; during the following six years alone, the figure increased a further seventy-eight per cent. There then followed the afore-mentioned slackening in the rate of growth, so that new incorporations rose by only twelve per cent from 1981 to 1990.[55]

The proliferation of so-called personal service corporations (PSCs) is particularly relevant to evaluating claims about the disproportionate increase in the incorporated self-employed and their comparative economic solidity. Before the passage of TEFRA in 1982 and the reduction of tax rates in 1986, a number of basic advantages inured to incorporated service providers. First, they could shift the taxation of income from higher individual tax rates to lower corporate tax rates.[56] Second, they could avail themselves of the fringe benefits available to employees--but not to self-employees--such as term life insurance, medical reimbursement plans, and death benefits, the expense of which could be deducted. And third, they benefited from timing differences governing the recognition of income by postponing tax payment through the choice of a corporate fiscal year.[57]

In order to suppress frivolous incorporations, the IRS finally prevailed upon Congress to authorize it to adopt countermeasures designed to eliminate the incentive attaching to the formation of PSCs. Thus TEFRA, in defining a PSC as an entity "the principal activity of which is the performance of personal services [which] are substantially performed by employee-owners," who in turn must own more than ten per cent of the outstanding stock,[58] provides that if

> (1) substantially all of the services of a personal service corporation are performed for (or on behalf of) 1 other...entity, and
> (2) the principal purpose of forming...such personal service corporation is the

> avoidance or evasion of Federal income tax by
> reducing the income of...any employee-owner
> which would not otherwise be available,
> then the Secretary may allocate all income...between such personal
> service corporation and its employee-owners, if such allocation is
> necessary to prevent avoidance or evasion of Federal income tax or
> clearly to reflect the income of the personal service corporation or
> any of its employee-owners.[59]

It was Congress's express purpose in enacting this provision to overturn the results triggered by permissive judicial decisions in cases in which "the corporation served no meaningful business purpose other than to secure tax benefits which would not otherwise be available."[60] In the wake of this congressional action, the IRS has taken the principled interpretive position that if an employee (as opposed to already self-employed person) incorporates a PSC, the IRS will ignore that intermediate layer and tax the common-law employer.[61]

A case that antedates TEFRA will illustrate the point. Two professional hockey players, who had previously been employees of their team, each formed a PSC in which he was the sole shareholder, officer, director, and employee, in order to shelter income in a pension plan. The PSC then entered into an employment contract with the team. At issue was the disallowance by the IRS of pension deductions. Based on the "smallest details" to which the team's control over the players extended, the tax court found that the players were the team's employees; it therefore held against the taxpayers.[62] The dissent stated that the majority had afforded a logical basis for the IRS position "that only 'traditional' independent contractors (i.e., those over whom service-recipients do not exercise 'control') can avail themselves of PSC's while 'traditional' employees cannot."[63] By condoning self-incorporation by those who even under the strict standard of the control test[64] are acknowledged employees, the dissent clearly demonstrated its willingness to dismantle a categorical distinction between employees and self-employees. In reversing the tax court, the court of appeals not only supported this act of conceptual dissolution, but noted in dictum that it would have decided the case the same way had it arisen under § 269A.[65]

Although the practical point may nevertheless have become moot by virtue of the fact that few athletes have incorporated in the past few years because the tax advantages have been reduced,[66] the theoretical point subsists: there can be no presumption that incorporators of one-person PSCs "are likely to be the most fully petty bourgeois."[67] The refutation of this claim in this context is particularly ironic in light of the high incomes received by these conceded employees.[68]

NOTES

1. Delno v. Celebrezze, 347 F.2d 159, 163 n.10 (9th Cir. 1965).

2. MICHAEL REAGAN, THE MANAGED ECONOMY 30 (1970 [1963]).

3. *See supra* ch. 2.

4. Steinmetz & Wright, *The Fall and Rise of the Petty Bourgeoisie* tab. 2 at 979.

5. *Id*. at 979.

6. In 1916, when the Commissioner of Internal Revenue published occupational data for federal personal income tax returns, the rubric "Capitalists: Investors and speculators" accounted for approximately one-fifth of all returns, one-quarter of all net income, and one-third of all income tax. *See* STATISTICS OF INCOME FOR 1916: COMPILED FROM THE RETURNS FOR 1916 UNDER THE DIRECTION OF THE COMMISSIONER OF INTERNAL REVENUE, H. Doc. No. 1169, 65th Cong., 2d Sess. tab. 6 at 31 (1918).

7. Assuming that she is not economically and personally subordinated to some larger entity.

8. *See* Packard Motor Co. v. NLRB, 330 U.S. 485, 493-94 (1947) (Douglas, J., dissenting).

9. Although Marx was referring to artisans and farmers, the unstable state of solo practice also appears to apply to doctors and lawyers. *See* MAGALI LARSON, THE RISE OF PROFESSIONALISM: A SOCIOLOGICAL ANALYSIS 232-33 (1979 [1977]). The decline of self-employed professionals has been associated with increasing capital costs. *See* ARONSON, SELF-EMPLOYMENT at 87.

10. MARX, ZUR KRITIK DER POLITISCHEN ÖKONOMIE (MANUSKRIPT 1861-1863) at 2179.

11. *Id.* at 2181. Earlier Marx had one-sidedly emphasized the falling of the "small Mittelstände...down into the proletariat." KARL MARX AND FRIEDRICH ENGELS, MANIFEST DER KOMMUNISTISCHEN PARTEI, in 4 *idem*, MARX-ENGELS WERKE 469 (1959 [1848]). For a discussion of the applicability of the model to nineteenth-century Germany, see SHULAMIT VOLKOV, THE RISE OF POPULAR ANTIMODERNISM IN GERMANY: THE URBAN MASTER ARTISANS, 1873-1896, at 32-94 (1978). The other extreme of Marx's model is reflected in the characterization of the one-man shop as an "embryo employer." WILLIAM WEYFORTH, THE ORGANIZABILITY OF LABOR 183 (1917).

12. ILO, THE PROMOTION OF SELF-EMPLOYMENT tab. 1 at 8.

13. In this context, one author has charged that "[c]oncepts and statistical measures regarding employment...are conceptual artifacts which...have no reality in and of themselves." Stanley Moses, *Labor Supply Concept: Political Economy of Conceptual Change*, in 3 COUNTING THE LABOR FORCE: READINGS IN LABOR FORCE STATISTICS, App. 96, 103 (Diane Werneke ed., Nat'l Comm'n on Employment & Unemployment Statistics, 1979) (reprinted from ANNALS of the Am. Ass'n of Pol. Soc. Sci., March 1975, at 36).

14. PRESIDENT'S COMMITTEE TO APPRAISE EMPLOYMENT AND UNEMPLOYMENT STATISTICS, MEASURING EMPLOYMENT AND UNEMPLOYMENT 42 (1962).

15. *Id.* at 43.

16. *Id.* at 57-58.

17. *Id.* at 57. In other words, the committee one-sidedly focused on underemployment.

18. *Id.* at 368.

19. *Id.* at 370.

20. Robert Stein, *New Definitions for Employment and Unemployment*, EMPLOYMENT AND EARNINGS AND MONTHLY REP. ON THE LAB. FORCE, Feb. 1967, at 3, 7.

21. *Id.* at 7-8.

22. *Id.* at 10.

23. 26 U.S.C. §§ 401 (c)(1)(A) and (4) (Supp. 1991). *But see* Peckham v. Board of Trustees of the Int'l Bhd. of Painters, 653 F.2d 424 (10th Cir. 1981) (self-employed sole proprietor cannot qualify as an employee under ERISA).

24. Steinmetz & Wright, *The Fall and Rise of the Petty Bourgeoisie* at 988-90. It is unclear why they use 850,000 for 1967 since BLS estimated at the time that the reclassification reduced the number of self-employed by about 750,000. *See* Stein, *New Definitions for Employment and Unemployment* at 10.

25. *See supra* ch. 2. The Small Business Administration, using unpublished data from the CPS, has published data offering greater detail about the incorporated self-employed. Apart from the unreliability resulting from nonsampling errors, the small numbers of respondents who would both be incorporated self-employed and fall under other (e.g., occupational) rubrics cast doubt on the accuracy of cross-tabulations. According to these data, the incorporated self-employed rose 33.3 per cent from 1979 to 1983 compared to 6.9 per cent for the unincorporated, accounting for twenty per cent of all self-employed (including employees with self-employment) in May 1983. U.S. SMALL BUSINESS ADMINISTRATION, THE STATE OF SMALL BUSINESS: A REPORT TO THE PRESIDENT tab. 4.2 at 112, tab. 4.3 at 114 (1986). Those with four or more years of college represented 28.3 per cent of full-time unincorporated self-employed but 44.0 per cent of the incorporated. *Id.*, tab. 4.6 at 118. The incorporated were more concentrated in manufacturing and wholesale trade and less so in services than the unincorporated, more in executive, administrative, and managerial, but equally in professional specialty occupations. *Id.*, tab. A4.17 at 146-47.

26. For both years, 133,000 incorporated self-employed were reported in agriculture. The seasonally unadjusted figures for March 1991 are 3,257,000 and 117,000, respectively. Unpublished CPS data, BLS, furnished by John Stinson, Apr. 18, 1991.

27. On their assumption that incorporation continued on its path steep even after 1983, see Steinmetz & Wright, *Reply to Linder and Houghton* at 737.

28. TEFRA, Pub. L. No. 97-248, Title II, § 250(a), 96 Stat. 528 (1982).

29. H. CONF. REP. NO. 760, 97th Cong., 2d Sess., 1982 U.S. Code Cong. & Adm. News 1190, 1394-95 (TEFRA creates parity under qualified plan rules for corporations, S corporations, and self-employed).

30. During the Reagan administration, the highest corporate tax rate was reduced from forty-six per cent to thirty-four per cent, while the highest personal income tax rate fell from seventy per cent to twenty-eight per cent. *See* 26 U.S.C. §§ 1, 11 (1976, 1982, and 1988).

31. On the other hand:

> [T]he watchwords of savvy owners of privately held concerns, especially after the 1986 tax revision cut personal rates below those on business income, have been "zero out the corporation." Rent to your company, lend to your company, be an employee or contractor for your company--do what you can to put the expenses on the company's books and the pay-outs on yours.

Tim Ferguson, *Elite's Earnings Are Exposed and Taxed...and It's a Scandal?* *Wall St. J.*, May 14, 1991, at A17, col. 3, 4.

32. *See, e.g.*, J. Philipps, J. McNider, & D. Riley, *Origins of Tax Law: The History of the Personal Service Corporation*, 40 WASH. & LEE L. REV. 433, 455 (1983) (particularly with regard to personal service corporations). *But see Looking for Tax Breaks? Incorporate Yourself*, BUS. WK., Aug. 27, 1984, at 87-88 (Personal Business page) (still touting one-person corporations on the ground that such entities could put more into pensions--without mentioning the impact of TEFRA--and emphasizing lower corporate tax rates).

33. SURVEY OF CURRENT BUS., Feb. 1991, chart at C-2; BUS. CONDITIONS DIG., July 1989, Tab. C at 98. These data, collected by Dun & Bradstreet from filings with the state secretaries of state, are independent of the CPS data, although they corroborate the trend. These data are consistent with other findings, based on unpublished CPS data, that the rate of incorporated self-employment for white men peaked in 1982. See EVANS & LEIGHTON, SELF-EMPLOYMENT SELECTION AND EARNINGS OVER THE LIFE CYCLE tab. 3.3 at 29.

34. For a comprehensive overview of the relevant provisions in the Internal Revenue Code from the 1920s to 1969, see Isidore Goodman, *Legislative Development of the Federal Tax Treatment of Pension and Profit-Sharing Plans*, 49 TAXES 226 (1971); a brief summary is contained in WILLIAM GREENOUGH & FRANCIS KING, PENSION PLANS AND PUBLIC POLICY 59-63 (1976).

35. Revenue Act of 1942, ch. 619, § 165, 56 Stat. 798, 862 (1942).

36. *See* Philipps, McNider, & Riley, *Origins of Tax Law* at 441.

37. Harry Rudick, *More about Professions for Partners: A Better Solution Than Pension Plans?*, 33 A.B.A.J. 1001, 1001 (1947) (author was law professor at N.Y.U. and practiced at large corporate law firm).

38. *See, e.g.*, Victor Wolder, *The Forgotten Man of Taxes*, 24 TAXES 970 (1946).

39. *See, e.g., Revenue Revisions, 1947-48: Hearings Before the House Comm. on Ways and Means*, 80th Cong., 1st Sess. 1699, 1717 (1947) (testimony of Harry Silverson and Victor Wolder); *Individual Income Tax Reduction: Hearings Before the Sen. Comm. on Finance*, 81st Cong., 1st Sess. 408 (1947) (testimony of Harry Silverson).

40. *See* 97 CONG. REC. 8808 (1951) (remarks of Sen. Ives); *id.* at A4292 (remarks of Rep. Keogh); 98 CONG. REC. A4083 (1952) (remarks of Rep. Keogh); Eugene Keogh, *Pensions for the Self-Employed*, 100 EST. & TR. 175 (1961).

41. *Postponement of Income Tax Set Aside for Retirement: Hearings Before the House Comm. on Ways and Means*, 82d Cong., 2d Sess. 63 (1952) (statement of L. Rapp, N.Y.S. Bar Ass'n).

42. *See* John Nicholson, *Pensions for Partners: Tax Laws Are Unfair to Lawyers and Firms*, 33 A.B.A.J. 302, 303 (1947).

43. Significantly, part of the bar opposed simple integration of partnerships into § 165 on the ground that the statutory prohibition of discrimination in favor of owner-employees would seriously curtail the benefits to any but the largest law partnerships. *See* Rudick, *More about Pensions for Partners* at 1002.

44. *Postponement of Income Tax Set Aside for Retirement* at 26 (testimony of George Roberts).

45. 100 CONG. REC. A5086 (1954) (remarks of Rep. Cretella).

46. The Treasury opposed these schemes inter alia because, by distributing "relief more in proportion to the saving abilities of taxpayers than in proportion to their earned income," they undermined the principle of ability to pay. *Postponement of Income Tax on Income Set Aside for Retirement* at 46, 49 (statement of Treasury Dep't).

47. Self-Employed Individuals Tax Retirement Act of 1962, Pub. L. No. 87-792, 76 Stat. 809 (1962).

48. H. REP. NO. 378: SELF-EMPLOYED INDIVIDUALS TAX RETIREMENT ACT OF 1961, 87th Cong., 1st Sess. 1 (1961).

49. Only four senators voted against the bill. 108 CONG. REC. 18847 (1962).

50. The AFL-CIO opposed the Keogh Bill because very few employees actually benefited from existing corporate pensions plans. *See Pension Plans for Owner-Managers of Corporations: Hearings Before the Sen. Comm. on Finance*, 86th Cong., 2d Sess. 106-109 (1960) (testimony of Peter Henle, AFL-CIO).

51. This general bipolarity was not inconsistent with further heterogeneity within highly paid professional groups. For data on self-employed doctors and lawyers, see 108 CONG. REC. 18840 (1962) (Sen. Douglas).

52. S. REP. NO. 992: SELF-EMPLOYED INDIVIDUALS TAX RETIREMENT ACT OF 1961, 87th Cong., 1st Sess. 56, 58 (1961) (minority views of Sen. Gore and Douglas).

53. 108 CONG. REC. at 18801 (Sen. Gore).

54. *Self-Employed Individuals' Retirement Act: Hearings Before the Sen. Comm. on Finance*, 87th Cong., 1st Sess. 22 (1961) (statement of Stanley Surrey).

55. Calculated according to data in U.S. BUREAU OF ECONOMIC ANALYSIS, BUSINESS STATISTICS, 1961-88, at 21 (26th ed. 1989); SURVEY OF CURRENT BUSINESS, Feb. 1991, at tab. C-2. By the same token, it was not the case that the increase in incorporations in the 1960s and 1970s was merely a reflection of growing business formation. Thus, according to IRS tax return data, from 1960 to 1970, proprietorship (including farm) returns rose only three per cent

compared to forty-six per cent for corporation returns. Calculated according to data in U.S. BUREAU OF THE CENSUS, HISTORICAL STATISTICS OF THE UNITED STATES, COLONIAL TIMES TO 1970, part 2, series V-4 and V-10 at 911 (bicentennial ed. 1975). During the same period, the number of new incorporations rose by forty-five per cent. Calculated according to *id.*, series V-21 at 912. From 1970 to 1980, nonfarm proprietorships (i.e., businesses, not tax returns) rose fifty per cent compared to sixty-three per cent for corporations. Calculated according to data in U.S. BUREAU OF THE CENSUS, STATISTICAL ABSTRACT OF THE UNITED STATES: 1990, tab. 858 at 521 (110th ed. 1990). But according to other IRS data, the number of proprietorship returns rose 107 per cent from 1970 to 1980. Calculated according to SOI BULL., Fall 1990, tab. 10 at 113. From 1980 to 1987, the number of proprietorships rose by ten per cent compared to thirty-three per cent for corporations. Calculated according to data in SOI BULL., Fall 1990, tab. 10 at 113, tab. 13 at 115. *See also* IRS, STATISTICS OF INCOME: SOURCE BOOK: SOLE PROPRIETORSHIP RETURNS 1957-1984, at iii (chart) (1986). Moreover, the number of S corporation returns increased by 112 per cent from 1970 to 1980 and by 107 per cent from 1980 to 1987. Calculated according to *id.*, tab. 13 at 115.

56. In 1982 the rates were forty-one per cent and 26.5 per cent on the first $100,000. This shift, however, benefited only those who caused the PSC to retain and to accumulate some of its earnings instead of distributing all of its income as deductible expenses.

57. *See* Philipps, McNider, & Riley, *Origins of Tax Law* at 434-35.

58. 26 U.S.C. § 269A (b)(1) and (2) (1988).

59. 26 U.S.C. § 269A (a) (1988). For the proposed regulation to this section, see § 1.269A-1, 48 FED. REG. 13,438 (1983).

60. H. CONF. REP. NO. 760, 97th Cong., 2d Sess., 1982 U.S. CODE CONG. & ADM. NEWS 1190, 1406 (specifically mentioning Keller v. Commissioner, 77 T.C. 1014 (1981)).

61. *See* Gen. Couns. Mem. 39,553 (Feb. 2, 1986); Tech. Adv. Mem. 86-25-003 (Feb. 28, 1986). *See generally*, DANIEL MORGAN & YALE GOLDBERG, EMPLOYEES AND INDEPENDENT CONTRACTORS ¶611 (1990).

62. Sargent v. Commissioner, 93 T.C. 572, 579-80 (1989).

63. 93 T.C. at 588.

64. For a comparison of the control test and the economic reality of dependence test, see Marc Linder, *The Joint Employment Doctrine: Clarifying Joint Legislative-Judicial Confusion*, 10 HAMLINE J. PUB. L. & POL. 321, 323-28 (1989).

65. Sargent v. Commissioner, 929 F.2d 1252 (8th Cir. 1991).

66. Wall St. J., Apr. 11, 1991, at B4, col. 2. Two relatively minor respects in which parity between the incorporated and unincorporated self-employed has not been achieved involve loans to pension plan participants and the deductibility of the cost of health insurance. *See* 131 CONG. REC. E 2636 (June 6, 1985) (Rep. Jeffords); 137 CONG. REC. E 1121 (Mar. 22, 1991) (Rep. McDade).

67. Steinmetz & Wright, *Reply to Linder and Houghton* at 738.

68. One tax-evasive action that has not been affected by changes in the tax code during the 1980s has been incorporation calculated to relieve taxpayers of social security tax liability by having the corporation pay out their compensation in the form of "dividends," which as unearned income are not subject to the Federal Insurance Contributions Act, 26 U.S.C. §§ 3101-3128 (1989), Self-Employment Contributions Act, 26 U.S.C. §§ 1401-1403 (1988), or the Federal Unemployment Tax Act, 26 U.S.C. §§ 3301-3311 (1989). This maneuver is also designed to avoid the reduction or elimination of benefits that is triggered when social security old-age insurance recipients report earned income in excess of certain threshold amounts before the age of seventy. 42 U.S.C. § 403(b) (Supp. 1991); MERTON BERNSTEIN & JOAN BERNSTEIN, SOCIAL SECURITY: THE SYSTEM THAT WORKS 24-26, 292 (1989 [1988]). Although the courts have by and large dealt rudely with such incorporations, reported litigation suggests that lawyers continue to advise clients to engage in them. *See, e.g.*, Ludeking v. Finch, 421 F.2d 499 (8th Cir. 1970) (HEW empowered to reclassify S corporation dividends as wages); Joseph Radtke, S.C. v. United States, 712 F. Supp. 143 (E.D. Wis. 1989), *aff'd*, 895 F.2d 1196 (7th Cir. 1990) (where lawyer is sole incorporator, director, shareholder, and full-time employee of S corporation and takes all his compensation as "dividends," they are FICA-taxable wages); *accord*, Spicer Accounting, Inc. v. United States, 66 A.F.T.R.2d 90-5806 (9th Cir. 1990). The position of the IRS is enunciated at Rev. Rul. 74-44, 1974-1 C.B. 287 (two shareholders in an electing small business corporation paying themselves "dividends" in lieu of reasonable compensation for their services actually received wages to which FICA tax liability attached). Even in one case where the court ruled for the taxpayer by finding that his income was not earned income, that ruling may have boomeranged on the taxpayer when the court remanded for a determination as to whether his preretirement and preincorporation income were earned income; if they were then found not to be, his retirement benefits would be subject to reduction because his credited earnings in covered employed would be lower. Bunch v. Schweiker, 681 F.2d 249, 250-52 (4th Cir. 1982). Although it is unclear how evading the social security tax pays off when the price is double taxation of the "dividends"--of the corporation as profits and of the individual as personal income--perhaps the mind-set is the same animating ('irrational') people who self-convert to self-employment because they believe that the effective FICA tax is higher than the Self Employment Contributions Act tax. *See* Robert Moore, *Self-Employment and the Incidence of the Payroll Tax*, 36 NAT'L TAX J. 491, 499 (1983). *See also* EVANS & LEIGHTON, SELF-EMPLOYMENT SELECTION AND EARNINGS OVER THE LIFE CYCLE at 41 (according to

econometric model, FICA tax increases lower the rate of unincorporated self-employment while raising that of the incorporated).

In fact, relatively few incorporated entities appear to be trying to represent all their profits as dividends since the vast majority have at least some payroll. Corporations without payroll as a percentage of all establishments without payroll developed as follows: 1987: retail--5.5; services--3.5; construction--3.1; 1977: retail--2.5; services--2.2; 1972: retail--2.3; services--1.8; construction industry--1.5. Calculated according to data in U.S. BUREAU OF THE CENSUS, 1972 CENSUS OF CONSTRUCTION INDUSTRIES, 1 INDUSTRY AND SPECIAL STATISTICS, tab. 1 at 4 (1976); *idem*, 1972 CENSUS OF SELECTED SERVICE INDUSTRIES, 1 SUMMARY AND SUBJECT STATISTICS, tab. 3 at 1-129 (1976); *idem*, 1977 CENSUS OF SERVICE INDUSTRIES, 1 SUBJECT STATISTICS, tab. 7 at 1-141 (1981); *idem*, 1 1972 CENSUS OF RETAIL TRADE: SUMMARY AND SUBJECT STATISTICS, tab. 3 at 1-118 (*Establishment and Firm Size (Including Legal Form of Organization)*) (1976); *idem*, 1977 CENSUS OF RETAIL TRADE, 1 SUBJECT STATISTICS, tab. 7 at 1-127 (1981); *idem*, 1987 CENSUS OF CONSTRUCTION INDUSTRIES, SUBJECT SERIES: LEGAL FORM OF ORGANIZATION AND TYPE OF OPERATION tab. 1 at 5 (1990); *idem*, 1987 CENSUS OF RETAIL TRADE, NONEMPLOYER STATISTICS SERIES: NORTHEAST tab. 1 at 1-3 (1990); *idem*, 1987 CENSUS OF SERVICE INDUSTRIES, NONEMPLOYER STATISTICS SERIES: NORTHWEST tab. 1 at 2-3 (1990). Data for 1982 are omitted because "[d]ata for most establishments without payroll were extracted from information reported by businesses on...(IRS) Form 1040, Schedule C. These data could not be published as planned because many businesses were miscoded by IRS into miscellaneous categories rather than being classified in the specific kind of business." U.S. BUREAU OF THE CENSUS, 1982 CENSUS OF SERVICE INDUSTRIES, GEOGRAPHIC AREA SERIES: UNITED STATES VI (1984). *See also* U.S. BUREAU OF THE CENSUS, 1987 CENSUS OF SERVICE INDUSTRIES, GEOGRAPHIC AREA SERIES: UNITED STATES A-2 (1989) ("In 1982, data for nonemployer firms...were published at the United States level only").

7

Conclusion:
Dissolution and Reconstitution

[S]ome of these so-called independent contractors are about as independent as Charley McCarthy without Edgar Bergen.[1]

Even if complainant, in the eyes of the law, is an independent contractor, he is in the same practical position as any poor man hunting or holding part time service as an employe.[2]

When the majority of the constitutional committee convening in Frankfurt on Main in 1848 recommended to the plenum that the franchise be limited to the self-employed (*Selbständige*), thus excluding all artisan apprentices, workers, messengers, and day laborers, Bruno Hildebrand, a professor of economics, argued that such a step would discriminate against half of the male population as not being emancipated. He criticized the "conceptualization [*Begriffsbestimmung*]" of the term *selbständig* itself because "[p]recisely the persons whom it [the constitutional committee] excludes are largely economically more independent [*selbständiger*] than those whom it admits to suffrage. It is...the many small masters who are down and out, are in want, and currently must qualify as proletarians."[3] The greater half of the masters, whose incomes were lower than that of the lowest daily wage in German factories, were "unfortunately nothing more than proletarians, who just like the day laborers, live from hand to mouth."[4] Hildebrand then posed a series of rhetorical questions designed to underscore the spurious and threadbare character of the alleged bright line between proletarians and self-employed workers:

> [W]ho is more independent [*selbständig*], who is economically in a more independent position? the individual small master shoemaker, who with all his belongings belongs to the leather dealer and depends on the benevolence of his creditor, or the journeyman artisan, who at any moment can abrogate his contract? Who is more independent, the thousands of master weavers, who fetch their yarn for work from their patron every week and with their whole existence are tied to his favor, or the factory workers, who in rivalry with the machines have practiced their strength and can enter new contracts everywhere?[5]

Tailoring his analysis to a specific context, Hildebrand clearly articulated the issue of whether any principled political justification underlay or flowed from a formal but hollow and misleading economic distinction between employees and the self-employed. The transition to universal adult suffrage in many societies has witnessed the same or similar debates[6] that triggered the conclusion that degrees of formal economic dependence were irrelevant to the entitlement to participation in political processes. But the controversy over the converse issue--whether the economically allegedly more independent group should be protected by the same socioeconomic measures that employees have secured--has proved to be a more protracted one. Yet as transposed and adapted to this other arena, the old arguments for exclusion and segregation continue to make little sense.

This claim can best be probed by examining the post-World War II debate over the inclusion of the self-employed in the social security old-age and survivors insurance system. That brisk ideological opposition to the assimilation of the self-employed has yielded to acknowledgment of the broad interpenetration of employees and self-employees offers strong support for the argument that the socioeconomic basis of self-employment has itself undergone a transformation. In the congressional discussion of coverage of the nonfarm, nonprofessional self-employed in 1949-50, the ranking

Republican on the Senate Finance Committee, Senator Millikin, spoke for those who insisted on the existence of a chasm between employees and self-employers:

> They have a choice of whether they want to become workers or whether they want to be proprietors. If they choose to be proprietors, they choose to take the opportunity for larger gains than the worker gets and suffer the chance of larger losses. Is there not an inconsistency?
>
> ...
>
> On the theory that it is somewhat fallacious to say that an individual employee can bargain at arm's length with large employers. And there was a social need for giving the employee this kind of protection. When you get into the field of the self-employed and independent contractors, you are bringing the benefits of the system to a category of people who...come in under an entirely different philosophy.
>
> ...
>
> A man...has to make a fundamental decision. He is either going to take what security he can get out of being an employee, with whatever certainty there is of getting a wage envelope at the end of the week, or he is going to take his chances as an employer or as an independent contractor, with the benefits that accompany that, when there are any, and take the losses when they occur.[7]

To Millikin's controlling, albeit abstract, principle of risk his interlocutors counterposed the practical problem of "whether the self-employed who have reached the age of retirement without resources, and there will be a considerable proportion of them--it is in the very nature of the competitive economy that there are failures as well as successes--...are going to have something better than charity."[8] The confrontation dissolved, however, when Millikin conceded that "a fellow who has misjudged those risks can be just as needy as an industrial worker,"[9] and his opponents were constrained to agree with him that conferring coverage on the self-employed represented a break with the original principles of social security.[10]

This mutual accommodation, which facilitated the admission of the urban nonprofessional self-employed in 1950,[11] was a watershed because it marked a definitive recognition of the socioeconomic reality of a blurred frontier between employees and self-employed in terms of income and security and an abandonment of fundamentalism concerning the tie between risk and self-responsibility. Indeed, one of the practical points advanced in favor of inclusion of the self-employed in the old-age pension program was precisely the fact that the frequent movement between employee and self-employee status deprived such workers of part of their pension credits.[12] To be sure, the debate flared up again briefly over the admission of farmers,[13] lawyers,[14] and physicians[15] in the 1950s and 1960s. But these rearguard actions were doomed; the principle of assimilation had been established. Promotion by the state of accelerated circulation among the unemployed, self-employed, and employees beginning in the 1980s strikingly demonstrates just how far the ideology of self-contained self-employment has been eroded during the postwar period.

Ironically, in spite of this sea change, even some Marxists woodenly champion shibboleths of a class taxonomy that operate to fracture and disable a more united front of workers precisely when the current phase of economic restructuring is sapping whatever vitality the distinction may once have had. Many are the ways in which employers can cause their dependent workers to appear to be working on their own. Imposing entrepreneurial-like risk on workers is one particularly obfuscating way, and since the risk of not being offered any work and hence of not receiving any income has been crystallized out by economists over the past 250 years as the most prominent negative hallmark of self-employment,[16] it is worth dwelling on the manipulability of its form and the frailty of its substance.

Private duty nurses, for example, may work directly for those (or the families of those) to whom they tend, or they may work through a registry. The BOC automatically classifies all such workers as self-employed rather than as employees of the registry (let alone of the families).[17] But what in fact is the difference between such nurses and those who are on the payroll of a nursing agency that does not pay the nurses for their waiting time[18] (whether spent at the agency or at home)? Indeed, as "the temporary help industry" has come to "provide[] an alternative to traditional sources of personnel for temporary duty--nursing registries which find assignments for self-employed nurses for a fee and on-call pools operated by hospitals,"[19] this equivalence is no longer speculative. Although even the risk of loss of income (rather than of capital) is not a rigorous criterion of independence,[20] unilateral imposition of such risk by employers is so arbitrary as to deprive it of any significance at all as a distinguishing characteristic of independence.[21]

Risk, however, no longer seems to be necessary to identify the self-employed when a federal trial judge can hold--and three federal appellate judges can take seriously--the claim that undocumented Mexican laborers whom a gold and silver mining firm housed in its camp and paid a daily flat-rate wage invariant to productivity might not be the company's employees,[22] or a congressman can introduce a bill to amend the IRC so as to classify as "self-employed" non-English speaking, unskilled Vietnamese seafood processing workers merely because they are paid on a piece rate and "frequently will move around a state or even the country as they perceive more desirable employment opportunities."[23] Far too little appreciated is how arbitrarily or culturally constructed the designation may be.[24]

It is time to recognize that the self-employed as a "class of worker"--in contradistinction to the petty bourgeoisie as a social class[25]--do not constitute a theoretically coherent category. The identification of the two has been too facile.[26] Those who have been labeled self-employed are not identical with the petty bourgeoisie, who include small capitalists; in addition, many of these self-employed are not part of the petty bourgeoisie at all but are merely isolated workers. If analysis of the petty bourgeoisie as a political-economic actor is to retain its vitality,[27] it must be grounded in a more intelligible conceptual framework.

Parsimony of logic, overall coherence of analysis, and the ability to make sense of the political economy of work and class suggest that if the notion of *self*-employment is to live up to its solipsistic aspirations, it must exclude all those who, because they employ and exploit others,[28] are not economically self-sustaining.[29] But even this criterion is inadequate because few of those who nominally meet this solipsistic standard display the requisite substantive characteristics.[30]   In particular, they must own enough physical or human capital to enable them to avoid the exploitation and control or domination characteristic of the antagonistic wage labor-capital relationship. They must, in other words, be independent enough to avoid having to sell and place at the disposal of others their labor power. This independence of the labor market extends to the process of production itself, where owning and possessing the skill to operate their own means of production places them beyond capital's grasp.

To spell out these criteria is virtually to explain why a historically dwindling number of workers can meet them. The semi-solipsistic world of simple commodity production as situated within the capitalist mode of production, to the extent that it ever made socioeconomic sense,[31] was more meaningful when the size and productivity of the competing capitalist entities had not yet made a mockery of the self-employeds' independence.   As the capital threshold for successful competition--that is, the minimum optimal scale for taking advantage of minimum unit costs[32]--rose, it became increasingly implausible that any solo worker could both accumulate that amount of capital and set in motion and valorize it alone.[33]   Although market niches always crop up for small entities in the interstices between large-scale capitalist firms, eventually they too become subject to the economies of scale that drive them into ever more diminutive kinds of economic activity.[34]   To be sure, the self-employed are not would-be steel producers stymied by the cost of competitive technology. Yet to elude the snares of direct or indirect exploitation and dependence, self-employed workers would literally be required to locate an enclave in which they could shelter themselves from oligopolistic landlords, suppliers of materials or equipment, buyers, and creditors, who, through market (or quasi-production) relations, mimic the exploitation of a traditional capitalist employer.[35]

> The very names used in reference to the self-employed suggest a degree of economic well-being which does not correspond with the facts. The term "independent" is a good example of this: "Independent proprietor," "independent contractor," "independent businessman"--the only thing these men are independent of is an employer. In every other respect their competitors, customers, the wholesaler, banker, landlord, etc.--dictate to the small businessman much as would an employer. They do so somewhat less directly perhaps. But by limiting the amount of business he does, by influencing the prices he charges, by determining the margin of profit he shall retain for himself, or by granting or withholding credit, they make him quite as dependent economically as is the person who works for others.[36]

Doubtless workers do exist who are "remote from the classic social predicament to which Marx, outstandingly, had drawn attention."[37] Someone who makes jewelry by hand and sells it on the street might fit the description, particularly if he faced no large-scale capitalist competitors. Whether this jewelry producer-merchant's income exceeds or falls below the range of working-class incomes is not an essential determinant of his class position. But the fact that even relatively solvent economic agents may require their employers, contractees, or customers to finance the purchase of their means of subsistence through installment payments[38] suggests that income as a derivative, market-oriented criterion of class may be a sensitive indicator of the progressively diminished class scope of economic independence. Income is, moreover, a means of distinguishing the successful self-exploiters from the failures. The former manage to generate supra-working-class income by virtue of replicating (or perhaps even surpassing) the kind of exploitation to which they would be subject as outright employees and appropriating at least part of their labor that would have been appropriated by their capitalist employers; the latter do not even benefit from their self-exploitation.

Ironically, however, from the perspective of the propagandistic drawing power of the ideology of self-employment as an escape from oppressive employment into self-directed entrepreneurialism, it is precisely this linchpin of self-employment as ideal type that would daunt and dissuade potential entrants: that success presupposes the reproduction of the most disheartening aspects of employment. In particular, mimetic self-exploitation preserves the epochal distinction between the employer's time and the employee's own time that presumably underlies the romantic yearning to escape the boss's time clock.[39]

The thrust of this discussion suggests that the category of self-employed is grossly overinclusive and should be disbanded and then replaced by several distinct constituents, who should be redistributed among other classes.[40] The reform proposal outlined here is meant to serve only as a modification of the prevailing socioeconomic taxonomy; that is, it is designed to guide data collecting for the purpose of class analysis.[41] The proposal is not designed to promote a yet more subtle set of legal classifications or dichotomies.[42] Instead of a more refined test to identify and segregate dependent workers for purposes of protective statutes,[43] the chief desideratum in this area of the law is decommissioning the dysfunctional distinction between employees and self-employees altogether.[44]

The first comprises small capitalist-employers, who should not be viewed as *self*-employed because their employees contribute to the reproduction of their capital and income.[45] This group is part of the capitalist class, and its activities should not be studied as labor market phenomena.

The second group encompasses the 'independents,' whose human and cultural capital confers upon them their special status. Yet even these professionals' independence has been contested:

> First, self-employment may not even offer a living. ... Under circumstances in which the self-employed are economically insecure, it is difficult to claim that they are autonomous in their work, that they are truly free to make their own decisions and be their own bosses while surviving as well. In the case of medicine, history is littered with circumstances in which physicians had to fit their diagnoses and their remedies to the prejudices of their patrons.... And in the case of law it is not difficult to find circumstances in which the self-employed were dominated and controlled by their clients...as are even elite law firm lawyers serving powerful clients today.[46]

Even abstracting from the issue, for example, of how many doctors and lawyers in "solo" practice really work without exploiting nurses,[47] secretaries, and other assistants and associates, the sociotechnologically determined constantly rising minimum level of physical investment in tandem with the accumulation and centralization of corporate capital in the hospital industry[48] may be in the process, if not of proletarianizing them, at least of inflicting on them "a profound loss of autonomy."[49]

The third group consists of the those who in the nineteenth century qualified as the members par excellence of the petty bourgeoisie: shopkeepers[50] and independent artisans.[51] For Marx, the interesting class issue involved the latter: could they by their labor alone set into motion enough capital to enable them to prevent their suppliers, customers, creditors, and landlords from appropriating a sufficiently significant share of their surplus labor to distinguish the artisans from proletarians?[52] Even more so today than then, it appears increasingly difficult for one person to accumulate and to valorize such threshold amounts of capital as would generate incomes outside the range of their employee counterparts. In this sense, they replicate the problem just adumbrated for the professions although the appropriation of a significant level of human capital may alleviate this dilemma. Dynamically, over time, this group shades off into the fourth and last group.

Franchisees, too, belong to the third group.[53] To the extent that they are left "with virtually no autonomy and independence *despite* a major investment of funds in their business,"[54] they may be more analogous to managers (who have assumed a risk of loss of capital) than to the traditional self-employed.[55] The fact that the number of the more loosely controlled trade-name franchises (e.g., automobile dealerships and gas stations) declined continuously from 1972 to 1988 from 262,100 to 140,820, while the number of business-format franchises (such as fast-food restaurants), the day-to-day operation of which franchisors can regulate by means of prescribing standards and quality controls, almost doubled (from 189,640 to 368,458),[56] supports this thesis.[57]

Special attention should be paid to the last group: the "loners,"[58] the "isolated" (or "proletaroid"),[59] who merely sell their labor power because they do not own the means of production, have no autonomy with regard to the labor process,[60] and receive very low incomes, which make a mockery of any sense of independence.[61] Socioeconomic class analysis would be furthered if the BOC collected data on whether the alleged self-employed employ others.[62] If the West German definitional guideline--"decisive is the economic independence"[63]--is taken as a cue, the self-employed would not, for example, include the underground self-employed; these are the so-called "Mole People," who live in a railroad tunnel in Manhattan but of whom "[p]robably most are self-employed."[64] These are the "independents," the only content of whose "independence consist[s] in the necessity or bearing the[ir] misery independently."[65]

The isolated would also embrace "informal" workers, who are "'disguised wage labor'" or "'self-employed proletarians'" subject to "the worst features of both worlds: They face the risks of self-employment and simultaneously confront the wage worker's dependence on capital."[66] For example, home computer workers would probably be classified by the BOC as self-employed, yet even as to these relatively highly skilled workers who may own or lease more equipment than most other home workers, this "label is...misleading" because "informal workers can be so thoroughly dependent on the enterprises to which they are connected that they call to mind the wage worker's dependence on an employer."[67] Relatively few such workers have health insurance, and some earn less than the minimum wage[68]--in part because they are not compensated for work-related tasks "which would fall within regular on-site work hours."[69] Moreover, even when employers relinquish direct supervision over the pace and quality of work, it reappears in payment by result, which in turn generates increased competition, longer hours, and greater insecurity:[70] "[T]he deadline ensures that regardless of the hour at which outside workers choose to *begin* their working day, they will either extend it or increase its pace to the point at which the deadline can be met."[71] Consequently, the work of isolated workers "is in fact characterized by mechanisms of external control that, however subtle they might be, result in external pressures that determine the pace of work and the design of the product as effectively as does the direct supervision to which wage workers are subject."[72]

Such workers, who are characterized by unstable earnings and lack of job security, autonomy, or independence,[73] should not be confused with small capitalists or independents. That they have accepted or had imposed on them some measure of income risk does not transform them into entrepreneurs,[74] especially where the total structural relationship in which they are embedded systemically disables them from becoming capital accumulators. If they share with employees the categorical class characteristic of being deprived of the ability to accumulate sufficient capital to leave the working class, then employers' tactics of manipulating them into assuming risk should not be allowed to obscure their situation.[75] The solidity of their membership in the dependent working class is underscored in those cases in which they must "slip back into" undisputed employee status when their "business dips"[76]--to prop up not their accumulation but their subsistence.

The perceived increase in self-employment must be understood as one segment of the impressive continuing growth of temporally, spatially, and/or organizationally atomized workers.[77] These contingent workers are estimated to make up as much as a quarter of the work force in the United States.[78] Part-time workers alone now account for almost one-fifth of national employment.[79] Although far smaller in number, temporary workers have experienced extraordinary growth since the early 1980s. Temporary-help supply firms--on whose payroll temporary workers remain while they are supervised by the customer firms--alone may employ upwards of one million workers.[80] These figures do not include temporary workers hired directly by firms or so-called leased employees.[81]

Common to all of these variants of "just-in-time-employment" is that "[t]he employer is paying only for the time needed." But the unspoken converse of the fact that "[t]he largest cost-saving advantage in contingent employment systems is reduction in paid non-productive time"[82] is that employers have succeeded in shifting to workers the consequences of the firms' own entrepreneurial failure to reorganize the flow of work so as to reduce "non-productive time."[83] Just-in-time-employment practices are merely a more subtle way of ordering employees to clock out. In both cases, employers manage to impose the risk of gaps in employment, and hence income, on their workers.[84] Because this risk has been deemed the most telling distinction between employees and self-employers, once this sizable sector of acknowledged employees has been compelled to accept responsibility for piecing together enough part-time and temporary jobs to secure a living wage, the categorical distinction collapses. If the labor force is sufficiently vulnerable, it no longer matters whether the employer treats these workers as employees or self-employed.[85] The rise in nominal self-employment then emerges as an epiphenomenon of the contingent work force.[86] Consistent with this overall pattern, even the increase in the self-employed was fueled by part timers.[87]

Whether the contingent workers' isolation results from the part-time or temporary nature of the relationship or from performing the work in the workers' homes[88] or in the interstices between a labor supplier and labor employer,[89] it is this separation and segregation--rather than the rhetorical (petty) independence of being a propertied laborer--that distinguish the lower echelons of the self-employed from the historical petty bourgeoisie.[90] And it is also this quasi-quarantine that may ultimately exert a much greater impact on the structure of class relationships than any other aspect of pseudo-self-employment.[91] As Adam Smith recognized more than two centuries ago: "A poor independent workman...in his separate independent state, is less liable to the temptations of bad company, which in large manufactories so frequently ruin the morals of the other."[92]

If the study of the self-employed is motivated by class analysis, it is revealing that Marx as a revolutionary politician was much less obsessed than sociologists today with the niceties of taxonomy.[93] In preparing a "Questionnaire for Workers" in 1880 to serve as the basis of a statistical inquiry for French socialists, he included the following question:

> If you work at home, state the conditions of your working room; whether you use only tools or also little machines; whether you employ your wife and children or other helpmates, adults or children, male or female; whether you work for private customers or for an "entrepreneur;" whether you engage directly with him or through middlemen.[94]

For Marx, then, those engaged in workerlike activities under workerlike conditions were categorically and politically members of the working class[95] regardless of the phenomenological confusion capitalists were able to disseminate through manipulation of forms of payment, assumption of risk, and visibility to the customer.[96]

However this controversy is ultimately resolved by future societal development, the salient point remains the political-ideological import of the isolation of low-income loners from both the employing-exploiting class and the spatially-organizationally aggregated wage-earning class.[97] Whatever the taxonomic position and active role of the self-employed within the class structure may have been in the past, the pronounced decline of the unionized working class[98] and the concomitant proliferation of a largely "'on-demand,'"[99] "at-risk,"[100] and contingent work force only marginally integrated into the social wage[101] may contribute to the assimilation of all these working-class strata.[102] If, in addition, the latter mobilize to consolidate and to intensify the trend toward parity of state protective programs for the self-employed,[103] the distinction between employees and self-employees may eventually become moot.[104] Finally, adoption of a guaranteed social income decoupled from the employment relationship would virtually eliminate the distinctive socioeconomic character of self-employment altogether.[105]

Self-employment as a mass phenomenon long ago lost the struggle against colonization by the capitalist labor market; it can no longer function as a refuge of independence from class domination.   To the extent that even the largest individual capital is "wholly dependent for its survival...on a vast network of laws, protection, services, inducements, constraints, and coercions provided by innumerable governments" without which "the firm would instantly disappear,"[106] political-economic conflict that once focused on the place of production shifts its locus in part to the state.[107] Here even those whose employer is obscured may be in a better position to perceive life chances and to articulate interests in common with the rest of the dependent laboring population.[108] Such a prospect becomes plausible, however, only where it is palpably true that "only...the *form*" distinguishes the exploitation of the two groups: "The exploiter is the same: *capital*."[109]

NOTES

1. *Exploiting Workers by Misclassifying Them as Independent Contractors: Hearing Before the Employment and Housing Subcomm. of the House Comm. on Government Operations*, 102d Cong., 1st Sess. 2 (1991) (Rep. Tom Lantos).

2. Suchodolski v. American Fed'n of Labor, 127 N.J.Eq. 511, 512 (1940).

3. 7 STENOGRAPHISCHER BERICHT ÜBER DIE VERHANDLUNGEN DER DEUTSCHEN CONSTITUIERENDEN NATIONALVERSAMMLUNG ZU FRANKFURT AM MAIN 5285 (F. Wigard ed. 1848-49).

4. *Id*. at 5285-86.

5. *Id*. at 5286.

6. On the debate in England in 1867, see LINDER, EUROPEAN LABOR ARISTOCRACIES at 100-103.

7. *Social Security Revision* at 95, 491-92.

8. *Id*. at 2095 (testimony of Sumner Slichter).

9. *Id*. at 2094.

10. *See, e.g., id*. at 491 (testimony of Marion Folsom, treasurer of Eastman Kodak, member of Committee on Economic Security Advisory Council, and future Secretary of HEW). Arthur Altmeyer, the Commissioner of Social Security, sidestepped the question; *id*. at 95.

11. Ch. 809, § 104(a), 64 Stat. 492 (1950).

12. *Social Security Revision* at 95 (testimony of A. Altmeyer); SMALL BUSINESS PROBLEMS at 20-22.

13. For Senator George, who had supported coverage of the urban self-employed in 1950, inclusion of farmers smacked of "creeping socialism." 100 CONG. REC. 15,409 (1954).

14. For a sample of the debate within the profession, see Harold Love, *Social Security and Retirement Plans for Lawyers: It Need Not Mean Socialism*, 38 A.B.A.J. 463 (1952); Arthur Larson, *Social Security and Self-Employed Lawyers: A Plea for Re-evaluation*, 39 A.B.A.J. 971 (1953); Allen Oliver, *Lawyers and Social Security: No Need for Change*, 40 A.B.A.J. 586 (1954).

15. *See* 111 CONG. REC. 16,104-109 (1965).

16. *See supra* ch. 3.

17. *See supra* ch. 2.

18. On the compensability of waiting time under the Fair Labor Standards Act, see Marc Linder, *Class Struggle at the Door: The Origins of the Portal-to-Portal Act of 1947*, 39 BUFFALO L. REV. 53 (1991). Although "the avilability on the premises of manpower which can be made available to a customer on short notice is something of value to an employer," 117 CONG. REC. 21192 (1971) (Rep. Mikva), temporary employee firms do not compensate the waiting time of their "people," whom they cynically regard as their "inventory." *Day Laborer Protection Act of 1971: Hearings Before the Special Subcomm. of the House Comm. on Education and Labor*, 92d Cong., 1st Sess. 75 (1972) (testimony of Elmer Winter, President of Manpower, Inc.).

19. Max Carey & Kim Hazelbaker, *Employment Growth in the Temporary Help Industry*, MONTHLY LAB. REV., Apr. 1986, at 37, 41.

20. *See* Linder, *The Joint Employment Doctrine* at 323 n.14.

21. *See* Linder, *Towards Universal Worker Coverage under the National Labor Relations Act* at 585-92; *idem, From Street Urchins to Little Merchants* at 860; SPEIER, DIE ANGESTELLTEN VOR DEM NATIONALSOZIALISMUS at 65.

22. *See* General Investment Corp. v. United States, 823 F.2d 337 (9th Cir. 1987). *See generally, Employee-Independent Contractor Issues: Hearing Before the Subcomm. on Commerce, Consumer, and Monetary Affairs of the House Government Operations Comm.*, 101st Cong., 1st Sess. (1989). Aronson is quadruply incorrect in asserting that "[t]hus far, the federal courts have upheld the very strict standards developed under wage-hour legislation to determine the legitimacy of claims of independent contractors. Those standards...have been applied in...workers' compensation and unemployment insurance." ARONSON, SELF-EMPLOYMENT at 114. The standards are not strict nor have they have been uniformly upheld; the standards used under workers' compensation and unemployment insurance are different and more relaxed than wage-hour standards; and finally it is not the claims of

independent contractors that constitute the abuse but rather the claims of employers that their employees are independent contractors. *See generally*, MARC LINDER, THE EMPLOYMENT RELATIONSHIP IN ANGLO-AMERICAN LAW: A HISTORICAL PERSPECTIVE (1989). On schemes devised by building firms in Britain to enable their workers to become self-employed while continuing to work for them, see De N. Clark, *Industrial Law and the Labour-Only Sub-Contract*, 30 MOD. L. REV. 6, 11 (1967).

23. 133 Cong. Rec. E 4877 (Dec. 18, 1987) (LEXIS) (Rep. Tauzin). A federal district court's ruling that these workers were also not employees under the Fair Labor Standards Act was overturned in McLaughlin v. Seafood, Inc., 867 F.2d 875 (5th Cir. 1989).

24. For example, in France, models are salaried employees of modeling agencies; in the United States, most are deemed independent contractors. *See* Gordon Mott, *Male Models Chase A Dream in Paris*, N.Y. Times, Sept. 30, 1987, at 19, col. 1, 21 (nat. ed.). Inexplicably, even a Marxist sociologist can speculate that "people who do various kinds of contract work may say that they work for someone else, even though they are in fact self-employed." WRIGHT, CLASS STRUCTURE AND INCOME DISTRIBUTION at 154.

25. For dogmatic overviews of Marx's writings on the petty bourgeoisie, see 2 HAL DRAPER, KARL MARX'S THEORY OF REVOLUTION: THE POLITICS OF SOCIAL CLASSES 288-316 (1978); MICHAEL MAUKE, DIE KLASSENTHEORIE VON MARX UND ENGELS 61-68 (1973 [1970]).

26. *See* Linder & Houghton, *Self-Employment and the Petty Bourgeoisie*.

27. Belgium, for example, has developed a range of corporativist representation for "the middle classes" since the beginning of the twentieth century. *See* Arrêté royal instituant au ministère de l'industrie et du travail un Office des classes moyennes, Jan. 15, 1906, No. 10, at 65; Arrêté royal portant réglement organique du Ministère des Affaires économiques et des Classes moyennes, Dec. 11, 1939, No. 865, at 6252, 6258 (creation of direction générale des classes moyennes "en vue de l'encouragement ou de la defense des intérêsts des classes moyennes"); Recueil des lois et arrêtés royaux, June 15, 1954, No. 494, at 2818-21 (creation of Ministère des Classes moyennes/Ministerie van Middenstand). The statutory term designating this class within Belgian social legislation is "independent workers" ("travailleurs indépendants"; the Flemish counterpart, "zelfstandigen," is cognate to the German term). *See, e.g.*, Arrêté royal organisant le statut social des travailleurs indépendants, July 27, 1967, No. 1053, at 3236. For detailed narratives of the origins and evolution of this representation and legislation, which includes an account of initial resistance to inclusion by the independents, see VINGT ANS AU SERVICE DES CLASSES MOYENNES (Institut Belge d'information et de Documentation ed. 1974); INSTITUT NATIONAL D'ASSURANCES SOCIALES POUR TRAVAILLEURS INDÈPENDANTS, 50 ANS D' ALLOCATIONS FAMILIALES, 30 ANS DE PENSIONS, 20 ANS DE STATUT SOCIAL (1988). The ministry's political charge transcends that of its nearest ideological counterpart in the United States, the Small Business

Administration, which has its roots in antimonopoly, procompetitive movements, and was, at least originally, heavily oriented toward securing for small business a larger share of federal government contracts. *See* ADDISON PARRIS, THE SMALL BUSINESS ADMINISTRATION (1968). The National Association of the Self-Employed, which was founded in 1981, appears to be a relatively nonpolitical service organization offering group medical insurance and other benefits to its 300,000 members. *See* SELF-EMPLOYED AMERICA, March/April 1991.

28. *But see* Howard Aldrich & Jane Weiss, *Differentiation within the United States Capitalist Class: Workforce Size and Income Differences*, 46 AM. SOC. REV. 279 (1981) (arguing that distinction between small employers and nonemploying petty bourgeoisie is unnecessary for analyzing income differences). On the connection between self-exploitation of the self-employed and their exploitation of their employees, see JOHN GALBRAITH, ECONOMICS AND THE PUBLIC PURPOSE 73-75 (1973).

29. Where the alleged self-employed worker patriarchally presides over (and perhaps even exploits) co-working unpaid family members, he forfeits his status just as if he hired nonfamily employees. If, on the other hand, the family operates as a democratically organized cooperative undertaking, it may as a unit be self-employing--subject to the proviso set forth in the text. As a sociohistorical matter, it is important to recall that "[t]he idea of an individual male wage-earner supporting his family was unfamiliar in the first half of the nineteenth century. It was assumed that all members of the household contributed to the family enterprise in agriculture, trade, manufacture or handicraft." Catherine Hakim, *Census Reports as Documentary Evidence: The Census Commentaries 1801-1951,* 28 SOCIOLOGICAL REV. 551, 554 (1980).

30. Indeed, even some of those who appear to be employers are themselves employees of larger entities. *See* Walling v. Twyeffort, Inc., 158 F.2d 944 (2d Cir. 1947); Linder, *The Joint Employment Doctrine* at 332-45.

31. *See* MARC LINDER, REIFICATION AND THE CONSCIOUSNESS OF THE CRITICS OF POLITICAL ECONOMY: STUDIES IN THE DEVELOPMENT OF MARX' THEORY OF VALUE 151-75 (1975). David Brody, *Time and Work during Early American Industrialism*, 30 LAB. HIST. 5, 14, 27 (1989), undercuts whatever vitality the category may have had historically by characterizing as self-employed unskilled laborers, piece-rate workers, sweated outworkers, and those whose wages and hours were governmentally prescribed.

32. *See* F. SCHERER, INDUSTRIAL MARKET STRUCTURE AND ECONOMIC PERFORMANCE 84 (2d ed. 1980 [1970]); ALFRED CHANDLER, JR., SCALE AND SCOPE: DYNAMICS OF INDUSTRIAL CAPITALISM 27 (1990).

33. Not even MICHAEL PIORE & CHARLES SABEL, THE SECOND INDUSTRIAL DIVIDE: POSSIBILITIES FOR PROSPERITY 303-307 (1984), who advocate "the ideal of yeoman democracy" in "a republic of small holders," take the position

that flexibly specialized craft producers could compete with mass production if they were self-employed solo producers.

34. On how this process also occurred historically in the wholesale and retail trades, see GLENN PORTER & HAROLD LIVESAY, MERCHANTS AND MANUFACTURERS: STUDIES IN THE CHANGING STRUCTURE OF NINETEENTH-CENTURY MARKETING (1989 [1971]).

35. *See* JEFFREY HARROD, POWER, PRODUCTION, AND THE UNPROTECTED WORKER 248-64 (1987).

36. SMALL BUSINESS PROBLEMS at 7-8.

37. GEORGE KENNAN, MEMOIRS 1925-1950, at 7 (1967). Kennan states that none of his American ancestors, who had emigrated to the United States in the eighteenth century and farmed, "had ever been in significant degree an employer of labor; not one had ever sold his own labor to an entrepreneur, to be used for commercial gain." *Id.* at 6-7. However representative Kennan's forebears might have been for the nineteenth century, today's family farmers cannot escape the Marxist "predicament." Pig farmers, for example, who are "driven to indoor pens by the need to keep production prices down," do not earn enough to buy the costly ventilation equipment that would prevent the human health problems caused by the noxious gases produced by decomposing hog waste indoors. Peter Kilborn, *The Perils of Pig Farming Touch Man and Beast*, N.Y. Times, Aug. 25, 1991, § 1, at 1, col. 2, at 14, col. 2 (nat. ed.).

38. As the author of "the most popular" college economics textbook at the turn of the century and future president of Yale remarked:

> It is characteristic of the modern industrial system that a laborer who owns no capital, though nominally free to do what he pleases, must actually find some property owner who will give him enough to keep him alive during the period which must elapse between the rendering of the labor and the sale of the finished product. Under such circumstances, the laborer almost inevitably submits to the direction of the property owner in deciding how his labor shall be applied. Laborers without capital must necessarily work on this basis; even those who have small amounts of capital habitually do so.

ARTHUR HADLEY, ECONOMICS: AN ACCOUNT OF THE RELATIONS BETWEEN PRIVATE PROPERTY AND PUBLIC WELFARE 121 (1896). On Hadley, see 3 JOSEPH DORFMAN, THE ECONOMIC MIND IN AMERICAN CIVILIZATION: 1865-1918, at 258-59 (1949).

39. *See* E.P. Thompson, *Time, Work-Discipline and Industrial Capitalism*, PAST & PRESENT, Dec. 1967, at 56, 60-61.

40. On the splintering of the *Mittelstand*, see GRÜNBERG, DER MITTELSTAND IN DER KAPITALISTISCHEN GESELLSCHAFT at 167.

41. Wright's call for "detailed work histories" has still not been heeded. WRIGHT, CLASS STRUCTURE AND INCOME DETERMINATION at 230.

42. "[T]here can be no watertight legal definition of who is a 'dependent' worker and who is 'independent.'" Bob Hepple, *Restructuring Employment Rights*, 15 INDUS. L.J. 69, 75 (1986).

43. As has been suggested by Patricia Leighton, *Employment Contracts: A Choice of Relationships*, 90 EMPLOYMENT GAZETTE 433, 439 (1982); *idem*, *Employment and Self-Employment: Some Problems of Law and Practice*, 91 EMPLOYMENT GAZETTE 197 (1983); and Hakim, Self-Employment in Britain, at 425.

44. *See* LINDER, THE EMPLOYMENT RELATIONSHIP IN ANGLO-AMERICAN LAW at xii-xiii.

45. *See generally*, RICHARD SCASE & ROBERT GOFFEE, THE ENTREPRENEURIAL MIDDLE CLASS 70-97 (1982). If the point of including such persons in the discussion of self-employment is to gauge their contribution to job creation, the much-touted impact of small employers appears to have been exaggerated. *See* CHARLES BROWN, JAMES HAMILTON, & JAMES MEDOFF, EMPLOYERS LARGE AND SMALL (1990). Or as an Israeli Treasury spokesman asked rhetorically when the self-employed demanded a two percent reduction in national insurance payments that was designed to encourage employment: "'What are they going to do, employ themselves twice?'" Evelyn Gordon, *NII Refutes Self-Employed's Charges*, Jerusalem Post, Aug. 26, 1991 (NEXIS). At the time of the Keogh Bill debates, it was asserted that seven million self-employed had eleven million employees. 108 CONG. REC. 18757 (1962) (Sen. Smathers). The tendency to confuse the self-employed with small capitalists--or owners of firms of any size for that matter--is not restricted to the United States. *See, e.g.*, 7 SVEND AAGE HANSEN & INGRID HENRIKSEN, DANSK SOCIAL HISTORIE: VELFÆRDSSTATEN 1940-78, at 201-205 (1980) (analyzing self-employed [*selvstændige*] in Denmark in the postwar period).

46. ELIOT FREIDSON, PROFESSIONAL POWERS: A STUDY OF THE INSTITUTIONALIZATION OF FORMAL KNOWLEDGE 124 (1986).

47. *See* Wagner, *The Proletarianization of Nursing in the United States*.

48. *See* STARR, THE SOCIAL TRANSFORMATION OF AMERICAN MEDICINE at 420-49.

49. *Id*. at 446. *See also* Dirk Johnson, *Doctors' Dilemma: Unionizing*, N.Y. Times, July 13, 1987, at 21, col. 3 (nat. ed.) (discussing efforts by physicians to form unions); Lisa Belkin, *Doctors Lose Autonomy To Health-Care Networks*, N.Y. Times, Nov. 11, 1991, at A1, col. 1 (nat. ed.) (networks prescribe how much doctors may charge and what procedures they may perform).

50. "[P]our Marx, en 1848-1852, le petit bourgeois, c'est le boutiquier; mieux, *la petite bourgeoisie*, comme classe...c'est 'la boutique.'" BAUDELOT, ESTABLET, & MALEMORT, LA PETITE BOURGEOISIE EN FRANCE at 20.

51. Farmers obviously form a third very large sector of this group. Agriculture has been ignored in this book because the current debate centers on the issue of an alleged resurgence of self-employment; yet no proponent of this thesis argues that the United States or any other advanced capitalist country has witnessed a significant rise in the number of self-employed farmers. Since family farms operated without the use of hired workers represent a significant--albeit dwindling--share of solo self-employed, reference must be made in passing to the debate as to whether such farmers are caught up in the process of proletarianization. *See, e.g.*, John Davis, *Capitalist Agricultural Development and the Exploitation of the Propertied Laborer*, in THE RURAL SOCIOLOGY OF THE ADVANCED SOCIETIES: CRITICAL PERSPECTIVES 133 (Frederick Buttel & H. Newby ed. 1980); INGOLF VOGELER, THE MYTH OF THE FAMILY FARM: AGRIBUSINESS DOMINANCE OF U.S. AGRICULTURE 134, 138-43 (1982); DAVID GOODMAN AND MICHAEL REDCLIFT, FROM PEASANT TO PROLETARIAN: CAPITALIST DEVELOPMENTS AND AGRARIAN TRANSITIONS (1982); *idem, Capitalism, Petty Commodity Production and the Farm Enterprise*, 25 SOCIOLOGIA RURALIS 231 (1985); SUSAN MANN, AGRARIAN CAPITALISM IN THEORY AND PRACTICE (1990). Unfortunately, the controversy has largely been conducted at the level of taxonomy without connection to political consequences.

52. To be sure, in terms of income, a large segment of retailers must be viewed as part of the working class, yet they constitute the group "with the most emphatic petty bourgeois [*Mittelstand*] consciousness." FRITZ MARBACH, THEORIE DES MITTELSTANDES 280 (1942).

53. The judiciary has done obeisance to the ideological function of franchising: "If our economy had not developed that system of operation [franchises subject to close restrictions] these individuals [franchisees] would have turned out to have been merely employees." Susser v. Carvel Corp., 206 F. Supp. 636, 640 (S.D.N.Y. 1962).

54. Hakim, *Self-Employment in Britain* at 425.

55. ARONSON, SELF-EMPLOYMENT at 36.

56. U.S. DEPARTMENT OF COMMERCE, OFFICE OF SERVICE INDUSTRIES, FRANCHISING IN THE ECONOMY 1986-1988, at 1, 3-4 (1988).

57. Only one case appears to have held that alleged franchisees were employees of the franchiser. Mister Softee of Indiana, Inc. v. Oil, Chemical and Atomic Workers Int'l U., 162 N.L.R.B. 354 (1966). *See generally*, HAROLD BROWN, FRANCHISING: REALITIES AND REMEDIES (rev. ed. 1990).

58. *Self-employment: Lots of Loners*, ECONOMIST, Mar. 23, 1985, at 66 (increase in self-employment in Britain due in part to "larger firms'

employment preferences...to reduce labour hassles and costs such as pensions, sickness and holiday pay").

59. WERNER SOMBART, DIE DEUTSCHE VOLKSWIRTSCHAFT IM NEUNZEHNTEN JAHRHUNDERT 455-58 (1954 [1903]).

60. *See, e.g.*, Angela Dale, *Social Class and the Self-Employed*, 20 SOCIOLOGY 430 (1986).

61. *See* GRÜNBERG, DER MITTELSTAND IN DER KAPITALISTISCHEN GESELLSCHAFT at 102, 128-29. Many older workers become self-employed because they lose their strength and control over the pace of work or because their skills become obsolete. *See* ARONSON, SELF-EMPLOYMENT at 23.

62. For 1939 it was estimated that slightly more than three-fifths of all self-employed were nonemployers, ranging from one-fifth in construction to ninety-seven per cent in "independent hand trades." *See* SMALL BUSINESS PROBLEMS tab. 6 at 34. The West German census has developed a separate detailed classificatory system for the isolated ("alleinschaffend"). STATISTISCHES BUNDESAMT, 12 VOLKS- UND BERUFSZÄHLUNG VOM 6. JUNI 1961: ERWERBSPERSONEN IN WIRTSCHAFTLICHER UND SOZIALER GLIEDERUNG 23-24 (1961); *Das neue Schema der Sozio-ökonomischen Gliederung*, in WIRTSCHAFT UND STATISTIK, May 1970, at 247-48.

63. STATISTISCHES BUNDESAMT, 1 VOLKS- UND BERUFSZÄHLUNG VOM 6. JUNI 1961: DIE METHODISCHEN GRUNDLAGEN DER VOLKS- UND BERUFSZÄHLUNG 1961, at 144 (1961) ("[a]usschlaggebend ist die wirtschaftliche Selbständigkeit").

64. John Tierney, *In Tunnel, "Mole People" Fight to Save Home*, N.Y. Times, June 13, 1990, at A1, col. 2, at A20, col. 1 (nat. ed.).

65. SPEIER, DIE ANGESTELLTEN VOR DEM NATIONALSOZIALISMUS at 65.

66. BEVERLY LOZANO, THE INVISIBLE WORK FORCE: TRANSFORMING AMERICAN BUSINESS WITH OUTSIDE AND HOME-BASED WORKERS 11, 12 (1989).

67. *Id.* at 2.

68. *Id.* at 89, 157.

69. HOME-BASED CLERICAL WORKERS: ARE THEY VICTIMS OF EXPLOITATION? H.R. REP. NO. 677, 99th Cong., 2d Sess. 7 (1986).

70. LOZANO, THE INVISIBLE WORK FORCE at 66. *See also* Agis Salpukas, *Trucking-Driving Couple Share Life on the Road*, N.Y. Times, July 25, 1988, at 29, col. 1 (nat. ed.) ("having invested $53,000 in his used truck," driver (and his wife) feel "intense pressure to keep moving" to meet "tight schedule necessary to serve" customers).

71. LOZANO, THE INVISIBLE WORK FORCE at 79. *See also*, Eileen Boris, *Regulating Industrial Homework: The Triumph of "Sacred Motherhood*," 71 J. AM. HIST. 745, 746 (1985).

72. LOZANO, THE INVISIBLE WORK FORCE at 11.

73. *See* Hakim, *Self-Employment in Britain* at 444.

74. As one of the leading nineteenth-century economists put it:

> In most cases, employers take all the risk; that is, they insure regular wages to their hands, whether the work be constant or irregular, lucrative or insufficient to pay the expenses. ... Sometimes, however, the person employed takes the risk, and his Wages, when he is at work, must be high enough to compensate him for occasional necessary idleness.

FRANCIS BOWEN, AMERICAN POLITICAL ECONOMY 192-93 (1969 [1870]).

75. *See, e.g.*, Peter Kilborn, *Tomato Pickers' Hope for Better Life Becomes Victim as Industry Steps In*, N.Y. Times, May 9, 1991, at A10, col. 1 (nat. ed.); Marc Linder, *Petty-Bourgeois Pickle Pickers: An Agricultural Labor-Law Hoax Comes a Cropper*, 25 TULSA L.J. 195, 258-59 (1989).

76. Kilborn, *Tomato Pickers' Hope for Better Life Becomes Victim as Industry Steps In* at A10, col. 4.

77. *See generally*, U.S. WOMEN'S BUREAU, FLEXIBLE WORKSTYLES: A LOOK AT CONTINGENT LABOR (1988).

78. BNA, DAILY LAB. REP., July 18, 1985, at A-3 (LEXIS); GAO, WORKERS AT RISK (HRD 91-56, 1991).

79. *See* Thomas Nardone, *Part-Time Workers: Who Are They?*, MONTHLY LAB. REV., Feb. 1986, at 13. Involuntary part-time workers have been increasing faster than those who prefer part-time employment. *See* Chris Tilly, *Reasons for the Continuing Growth of Part-Time Employment*, MONTHLY LAB. REV., Mar. 1991, at 10.

80. *See* U.S. BLS, INDUSTRY WAGE SURVEY: TEMPORARY HELP SUPPLY, SEPTEMBER 1987 (Bull. 2313, 1988); Wayne Howe, *Temporary Help Workers: Who They Are, What Jobs They Hold*, MONTHLY LAB. REV., Nov. 1986, at 45; Max Carey & Kim Hazelbaker, *Employment Growth in the Temporary Help Industry*, MONTHLY LAB. REV., Apr. 1986, at 37. In 1988, the president of Manpower, Inc., testified before Congress that his company alone employed more than 500,000 people annually. *See Rising Use of Part-Time and Temporary Workers* at 101-102 (statement of M. Fromstein). At least for purposes of workers' compensation, the courts have ruled that firms that "buy some" "temporary help" from entities like Manpower that are "in the business of selling temporary help" are also employers. *See, e.g.*, St. Claire v. Minnesota Harbor Serv., Inc., 211 F. Supp. 521, 523 (D. Minn. 1962).

81. A leasing firm furnishes all the workers a customer-firm requires for a particular operation or project.

82. *Rising Use of Part-Time and Temporary Workers* at 37 (statement of A. Freedman, Conference Bd.).

83. The controversy over the forging of a large contingent of contingent workers recapitulates the statutory struggle in the 1940s over whether so-called nonproductive activities at the beginning and end of the workday were compensable under the Fair Labor Standards Act. *See* Linder, *Class Struggle at the Door* at 59-64.

84. Two decades ago, then Rep. Mikva introduced a remarkable bill that would have partially closed this gap for low-paid, unskilled, manual workers employed through temporary-help services. The Day Laborer Protection Act of 1971 would have included as compensable hours worked under the Fair Labor Standards Act all "travel time between the job site and the temporary help service, time spent at the job site, and one-half the time spent awaiting assignment at the temporary help service prior to being sent to a job site." H.R. 9282, 92d Cong., 1st Sess. § 6(b), 117 CONG. REC. 21,192 (1971). For an unsympathetic assessment of the bill, see Mack Moore, *Proposed Federal Legislation for Temporary Labor Services*, 26 LAB. L.J. 767 (1975). For an extraordinary judicial award of compensation for travel time without express statutory warrant, see Vega v. Gasper, 118 Lab. Cas. (CCH) ¶ 35,474 (W.D. Tex. Apr. 30, 1991).

85. A real-world example will illustrate this point. The owner of a shipping agency-warehouse in Laredo, Texas, instead of rationalizing his operations, pays his loaders/unloaders a piece rate and instructs them to wait outside for the next truck. If the unemployment rate is high enough, an abundant supply of workers with no compensable opportunity costs makes it possible for the employer to pay for a five- rather than an eight-hour workday.

86. "[A] significant portion of the 8.3 million workers who are listed by the Labor Department as self-employed, often contracting with companies for their services, also fall into this category [of full-time temporary workers]." Louis Uchitelle, *Reliance on Temporary Jobs Hints at Economic Fragility*, N.Y. Times, Mar. 16, 1988, at 1, col. 1, 32, col. 1 (nat. ed.).

87. Among those whose usual work was nonagricultural self-employment, part-timers increased from 16.5 per cent in 1970 to 27.5 per cent in 1982. *See* EMPLOYMENT AND EARNINGS, Jan. 1971, tab. A-22 at 130; *id.*, Jan. 1983, tab. 34 at 168.

88. *See, e.g.*, Francis Horvath, *Work at Home: New Findings from the Current Population Survey*, MONTHLY LAB. REV., Nov. 1986, at 31; *Oversight Hearings on the Department of Labor's Proposal to Lift the Ban on Industrial Homework: Hearings Before the Subcomm. on Labor Standards of the House Comm. on Education and Labor*, 99th Cong., 2d Sess. (1986); Bettina Berch, *The Resurrection of Out-Work*, MONTHLY REV., Nov. 1985, at 37. ARONSON, SELF-EMPLOYMENT at 114, underestimates the abuses of industrial homework. Charles Craver, *The Vitality of the American Labor Movement in*

the Twenty-First Century, 1983 U. ILL. L. REV. 633, 641, speaks opaquely of "relatively 'self-employed' individuals working out of their own homes."

89. For the parallel process in Britain, see Catherine Hakim, *Employers' Use of Homework, Outwork and Freelances*, 92 EMPLOYMENT GAZETTE 144 (1984); JAMES ROBERTSON, FUTURE WORK: JOBS, SELF-EMPLOYMENT AND LEISURE AFTER THE INDUSTRIAL AGE (1985).

90. *See* Arno Mayer, *The Lower Middle Class as Historical Problem*, 47 J. MOD. HIST. 409, 425, 432 (1975); GRÜNBERG, DER MITTELSTAND at 102, 28-29. For the outline of an imaginary reconstruction of petty bourgeois petty commodity production, see ROBERTO UNGER, FALSE NECESSITY: ANTI-NECESSITARIAN SOCIAL THEORY IN THE SERVICE OF RADICAL DEMOCRACY 29-30, 181-87, 223-28, 342-47 (1987). For an account of one historical example of such production, see Harriet Friedmann, *Simple Commodity Production and Wage Labour in the American Plains*, 6 J. PEASANT STUD. 71 (1978).

91. Several unsuccessful attempts have been undertaken in Congress to mandate some pro rata pension and group health benefits for contingent workers. *See* H. 2563, 101st Cong., 1st Sess. (1989), in 135 CONG. REC. H 2286 (June 6, 1989); *id.*, E 2013 (June 7, 1989) (Part-Time and Temporary Workers Protection Act of 1989); S. 1309, 100th Cong., 1st Sess. (1987), in 133 CONG. REC. 7475 (June 2, 1987) (Part-Time and Temporary Workers Protection Act of 1987).

92. SMITH, WEALTH OF NATIONS at 83-84.

93. *See generally*, ALLIN COTTRELL, SOCIAL CLASSES IN MARXIST THEORY (1984).

94. Marx, *Questionnaire for Workers* at 200.

95. For an example of modern legislation protecting homeworkers regardless of whether they are "an employe, agent, independent contractor, or any other person," see the Pennsylvania Industrial Homework Law, 43 PA. STAT. ANN. § 491-3 (Purdon 1964). Moreover, at least one federal judge has suggested that "it makes some sense to say that the FLSA [Fair Labor Standards Act] should apply to homeworkers, regardless of the type of work and the contract under which they work." Fegley v. Higgins, 760 F. Supp. 617, 622 (E.D. Mich. 1991).

96. *But see* 32 MARX-ENGELS WERKE 167 (1965) (letter from Marx to Engels (Sept. 26, 1868)) ("A large, the largest part of these shopkeepers suffer all the miseries of the proletariat, in addition the 'anxiety' and 'thraldom to respectability,' and without the compensating self-confidence of the better workers").

97. Employers are clearly engaged in the divide-and-conquer strategy of using contingent workers as "buffers [a]s the tradeoff for granting more employment security to the 'primary' work force." Audrey Freedman, *How*

the 1980's Have Changed Industrial Relations, MONTHLY LAB. REV., May 1988, at 35, 38.

98. *See, e.g.*, CHARLES HECKSCHER, THE NEW UNIONISM: EMPLOYEE INVOLVEMENT IN THE CHANGING CORPORATION (1988); PAUL WEILER, GOVERNING THE WORKPLACE: THE FUTURE OF LABOR AND EMPLOYMENT LAW (1990).

99. Anne Polivka & Thomas Nardone, *On the Definition of "Contingent Work"*, MONTHLY LAB. REV., Dec. 1989, at 9, 10.

100. BNA, DAILY LAB. REP., July 18, 1985, at A-3 (LEXIS) (Audrey Freedman, Conf. Bd.).

101. For an extended theoretical account of these developments, see Jeffrey Pfeffer & James Baron, *Taking the Workers Back Out: Recent Trends in the Structure of Employment*, 10 RES. IN ORGANIZATIONAL BEHAV. 257 (1988).

102. As an example, the largest union in Britain, the General, Municipal, and Boilermakers' Union, has responded to requests from former white-collar members who set up their own businesses with severance-redundancy payments to unionize them. BNA, DAILY LAB. REP., May 28, 1987, at A-12 (LEXIS).

103. Proposals for expanding coverage of mandatory medical insurance in the United States have moved in this direction. *See, e.g.*, HENRY AARON, SERIOUS AND UNSTABLE CONDITION: FINANCING AMERICA'S HEALTH CARE 141 (1991). In Scandinavia the self-employed are eligible for unemployment insurance benefits. *See* LINDER, THE EMPLOYMENT RELATIONSHIP IN ANGLO-AMERICAN LAW at 215, 232 n.167.

104. "With companies and those who work for them increasingly setting up innovative arrangements--flex time, telecommuting, job sharing, three- and four-day weeks, on-call assignments--the old standards defining just who is an employee seem increasingly imprecise." Daniel Woskowitz, *IRS Sharpens Definitions of Who Is an Employee*, Washington Post, Sept. 2, 1991, at F15 (NEXIS). For recognition--at least in the setting of the Third World--of the absence of a "clear-cut dichotomy" between wage labor and self-employment, which, however, fails to conceive of the latter as a reified relationship, see Alison MacEwen Scott, *Who are the Self-Employed?* in CASUAL WORK AND POVERTY IN THIRD WORLD CITIES 105 (R. Bromley & C. Gerry ed. 1979).

105. *See* Alejandro Portes, Manuel Castells, & Lauren Benton, *Conclusion: The Policy Implications of Informality*, in THE INFORMAL ECONOMY: STUDIES IN ADVANCED AND LESS DEVELOPED COUNTRIES 298, 309-10 (A. Portes, M. Castells, & L. Benton ed. 1989).

106. ROBERT DAHL, AFTER THE REVOLUTION: AUTHORITY IN A GOOD SOCIETY 120, 123 (1971 [1970]).

107. For a broad analysis of the evolving political-economic and ideological roles of the state, see ALAN WOLFE, THE LIMITS OF LEGITIMACY: POLITICAL CONTRADICTIONS OF CONTEMPORARY CAPITALISM (1980 [1977]).

108. On the history of the conceptualization of the class relationships between a proletarian core and workers on the periphery, see ADAM PRZEWORSKI, CAPITALISM AND SOCIAL DEMOCRACY 47-97 (1987 [1985]). For a vacuously rhetorical attempt to apply that tradition in the context of the contemporary growth of contingent employment and self-employment, see Chris Gerry, *The Working Class and Small Enterprise in the UK Recession*, in BEYOND EMPLOYMENT: HOUSEHOLD, GENDER AND SUBSISTENCE 288 (N. Redclift & E. Mingione ed. 1985).

109. KARL MARX, DIE KLASSENKÄMPFE IN FRANKREICH 1848 BIS 1850, in I:10 KARL MARX [&] FRIEDRICH ENGELS, GESAMTAUSGABE (MEGA) 119, 187 (1977 [1850]).

Bibliography

Books and Articles

Aaron, Henry. SERIOUS AND UNSTABLE CONDITION: FINANCING AMERICA'S HEALTH CARE (1991)

Aldrich, Howard, and Jane Weiss. *Differentiation within the United States Capitalist Class: Workforce Size and Income Differences*. 46 AM. SOC. REV. 279 (1981)

Altmeyer, A. *Improving Old-Age and Survivors Insurance*. SOC. SEC. BULL., Mar. 1946, at 3

AMERICAN COLLEGE DICTIONARY (1963)

AMERICAN HERITAGE DICTIONARY OF THE ENGLISH LANGUAGE (1969)

Anderson, Margo. THE AMERICAN CENSUS: A SOCIAL HISTORY (1988)

Anderson, W., and Frank Thompson. *Neoclassical Marxism*. 52 SCI. & SOC. 215 (1988)

Archer, Melanie. *The Entrepreneurial Family Economy: Family Strategies and Self-Employment in Detroit, 1880*. 15 J. FAM. HIST. 281 (1990)

------. *Self-Employment and Occupational Structure in an Industrializing City: Detroit, 1880*. 69 SOC. FORCES 785 (1991)

Aronson, Robert. SELF-EMPLOYMENT: A LABOR MARKET PERSPECTIVE (1991)

Aurand, Harold. *Self-Employment: Last Resort for the Unemployed*. INT'L SOC. SCI. Rev., Winter 1983, at 7

Balderston, Lydia. HOUSEWIFERY: A MANUAL AND TEXT BOOK ON PRACTICAL HOUSEKEEPING (1919)

Balkin, Steve. *Self-Employment Assistance Programs in the United States Targeted to Low-Income Disadvantaged People*. 40 INDUS. REL. RES. ASS'N PROC. 356 (1987)

------. SELF-EMPLOYMENT FOR LOW-INCOME PEOPLE (1989)

Ballenger, Louella. *Sole Proprietorship Returns, 1988*. SOI BULLETIN, Summer 1990, at 39

Banks, J. *The Social Structure of Nineteenth Century England as Seen through the Census*, in THE CENSUS AND SOCIAL STRUCTURE: AN

INTERPRETATIVE GUIDE TO NINETEENTH CENTURY CENSUSES FOR ENGLAND AND WALES (Richard Lawton ed. 1978)

Baudelot, Christian, Roger Establet, and Jacques Malemort. LA PETITE BOURGEOISIE EN FRANCE (1981 [1974])

Bauman, Kurt. *Characteristics of the Low-Income Self-Employed.* 40 INDUS. REL. RES. ASS'N PROC. 339 (1987)

Bechhofer, Frank, and Brian Elliott. *The Voice of Small Business and the Politics of Survival.* SOCIOLOGICAL REV., Feb. 1978, at 57

Becker, Eugene. *Self-Employed Workers: An Update to 1983.* MONTHLY LAB. REV., July 1984, at 14

Belkin, Lisa. *Doctors Lose Autonomy To Health-Care Networks.* N.Y. Times, Nov. 12, 1991, at A1, col. 1 (nat. ed.)

Bell, Spurgeon. PRODUCTIVITY, WAGES, AND NATIONAL INCOME (1940)

Belous, Richard. THE CONTINGENT ECONOMY: THE GROWTH OF THE TEMPORARY, PART-TIME AND SUBCONTRACTED WORKFORCE (1989)

Bendick, Marc, and Mary Egan. *Transfer Payment Diversion for Small Business Development: British and French Experience.* 40 INDUS. & LAB. REL. REV. 528 (1987)

Berch, Bettina. *The Resurrection of Out-Work.* MONTHLY REV., Nov. 1985, at 37

Berg, Maxine. THE AGE OF MANUFACTURES: INDUSTRY, INNOVATION AND WORK IN BRITAIN 1700-1820 (1985)

Bernstein, Merton, and Joan Berstein. SOCIAL SECURITY: THE SYSTEM THAT WORKS (1989 [1988])

Bertaux, Daniel, and Isabelle Bertaux-Wiame. *Artisanal Bakery in France: How It Lives and Why It Survives.* In THE PETITE BOURGEOISIE: COMPARATIVE STUDIES OF THE UNEASY STRATUM 155 (F. Bechhofer & B. Elliott ed. 1981)

Beveridge, William. SOCIAL INSURANCE AND ALLIED SERVICES (Cmd. 6404, 1942)

Bischoff, Joachim, et al. JENSEITS DER KLASSEN? GESELLSCHAFT UND STAAT IM SPÄTKAPITALISMUS (1982)

Blau, David. *A Time-Series Analysis of Self-Employment in the United States.* 95 J. POL. ECON. 445 (1987)

Bögenhold, Dieter. DIE SELBSTÄNDIGEN: ZUR SOZIOLOGIE DEZENTRALER PRODUKTION (1985)

Boris, Eileen. *Regulating Industrial Homework: The Triumph of "Sacred Motherhood."* 71 J. AM. HIST. 745 (1985)

Bouriez-Gregg, Françoise. LES CLASSES SOCIALES AUX ÉTATS-UNIS (1954)

Bowen, Francis. AMERICAN POLITICAL ECONOMY (1969 [1870])

Brand, Horst, and Ziaul Ahmed. *Beauty and Barber Shops: The Trend of Labor Productivity.* MONTHLY LAB. REV., Mar. 1986, at 21

Bregger, John. *Self-Employment in the United States.* MONTHLY LAB. REV., Jan. 1963, at 37

Brody, David. *Time and Work During Early American Industrialism.* 30 LAB. HIST. 5 (1989)

Brown, Charles, James Hamilton, and James Medoff. EMPLOYERS LARGE

AND SMALL (1990)

Brown, Harold. FRANCHISING: REALITIES AND REMEDIES (rev. ed. 1990)

Brown, Harold. PERCEPTION, THEORY AND COMMITMENT: THE NEW PHILOSOPHY OF SCIENCE (1979 [1977])

Bullock, Charles. THE ELEMENTS OF ECONOMICS (2d ed. 1913 [1905])

Bureau of National Affairs. DAILY LAB. REP. (various years)

------. PENSIONS & BENEFITS DAILY (1991)

Cantillon, Richard. ESSAI SUR LA NATURE DU COMMERCE EN GÉNÉRAL (Henry Higgs ed. 1931 [1755])

Carey, H. PRINCIPLES OF POLITICAL ECONOMY (1837)

Carey, Max, and Kim Hazelbaker. *Employment Growth in the Temporary Help Industry.* MONTHLY LAB. REV., Apr. 1986, at 37

Carver, Thomas. PRINCIPLES OF POLITICAL ECONOMY (1919)

CHAMBERS 20TH CENTURY DICTIONARY (1987)

Chandler, Alfred, Jr. SCALE AND SCOPE: DYNAMICS OF INDUSTRIAL CAPITALISM (1990)

Clark, De N. *Industrial Law and the Labour-Only Sub-Contract.* 30 MOD. L. REV. 6 (1967)

Clegg, Stewart, Paul Boreham, and Geoff Dow. CLASS, POLITICS, AND THE ECONOMY (1986)

Cohen, G. *Karl Marx and the Withering Away of Social Science.* In MARX, JUSTICE, AND HISTORY 288 (Marshall Cohen et al. ed. 1980 [1972])

Cohen, Wilbur. *Coverage of the Self-Employed Under Old-Age and Survivors Insurance: Foreign Experience.* SOC. SEC. BULL., Aug. 1949, at 11

Comment. *Unemployment Compensation--"Self-Employment."* 1940 WIS. L. REV. 147

Commerce Clearing House. UNEMPLOYMENT INSURANCE REPORTER

Committee on Social Insurance of the American Association for Labor Legislation. *Health Insurance: Tentative Draft of an Act,* 6 AM. LAB. LEGIS. REV. 239 (1916)

Córdova, Efrén. *From Full-Time Wage Employment to Atypical Employment: A Major Shift in the Evolution of Labour Relations?* 125 INT'L LAB. REV. 641 (1986)

Corey, Lewis. THE CRISIS OF THE MIDDLE CLASS (1935)

Cottrell, Allin. SOCIAL CLASSES IN MARXIST THEORY (1984)

Craver, Charles. *The Vitality of the American Labor Movement in the Twenty-First Century.* 1983 U. ILL. L. REV. 633

Cuneo, Carl. *Has the Traditional Petite Bourgeoisie Persisted?* 9 CANAD. J. SOC. 269 (1984)

Dahl, Robert. AFTER THE REVOLUTION: AUTHORITY IN A GOOD SOCIETY (1971 [1970])

Dale, Angela. *Social Class and the Self-Employed.* 20 SOCIOLOGY 430 (1986)

Davis, John. *Capitalist Agricultural Development and the Exploitation of the Propertied Laborer.* In THE RURAL SOCIOLOGY OF THE ADVANCED SOCIETIES: CRITICAL PERSPECTIVES 133 (F. Buttel & H. Newby ed. 1980)

Des Moines Register. July 31, 1991, at 9A, col. 1 (letter)

Devine, Teresa. *The Recent Rise in Female Self-Employment* (unpub. MS,

June 30, 1991)

Dorfman, Joseph. 3 THE ECONOMIC MIND IN AMERICAN CIVILIZATION: 1865-1918 (1949)

Draper, Hal. 2 KARL MARX'S THEORY OF REVOLUTION: THE POLITICS OF SOCIAL CLASSES (1978)

Duncan, Joseph, and William Shelton. REVOLUTION IN UNITED STATES GOVERNMENT STATISTICS, 1926-1976 (U.S. Dep't of Commerce, 1978)

Dupeyroux, Jean-Jacques. *Et maintenant?* DROIT SOCIAL, July-Aug. 1981, at 486

------. SÉCURITÉ SOCIALE (1967)

Eden, Dov. *Self-Employed Workers: A Comparison Group for Organizational Psychology.* 9 OCCUPATIONAL BEHAVIOR AND HUMAN PERFORMANCE 186 (1973)

Elfring, Tom. SERVICE SECTOR EMPLOYMENT IN ADVANCED ECONOMIES: A COMPARATIVE ANALYSIS OF ITS IMPLICATIONS FOR ECONOMIC GROWTH (1988)

Epstein, Abraham. *The Future of Social Security: Needed Amendments in the Present Law.* NEW REPUBLIC, Jan. 27, 1937, at 373

------. INSECURITY: A CHALLENGE TO AMERICA (1933)

Evans, David, and Linda Leighton. SELF-EMPLOYMENT SELECTION AND EARNINGS OVER THE LIFE CYCLE (U.S. Small Bus. Adm'n, Dec. 1987)

------. *Some Empirical Aspects of Entrepreneurship.* 79 AM. ECON. REV. 519 (1989)

Ferguson, Tim. *Elite's Earnings Are Exposed and Taxes...and It's a Scandal?* Wall St. J., May 14, 1991, at A17, col. 3

Fischel, Daniel. *Labor Markets and Labor Law Compared with Capital Markets and Corporate Law*, 51 U. CHI. L. REV. 1061 (1984)

Folbre, Nancy. *Exploitation Comes Home: A Critique of the Marxian Theory of Family Labour.* 6 CAMBRIDGE J. ECON. 317 (1982)

------. *The Unproductive Housewife: Her Evolution in Nineteenth-Century Economic Thought.* 16 SIGNS 463 (1991)

Form, William. DIVIDED WE STAND: WORKING-CLASS STRATIFICATION IN AMERICA (1985)

------. *Self-Employed Manual Workers: Petty Bourgeois or Working Class?* 60 SOCIAL FORCES 1050 (1982)

Freedman, Audrey. *How the 1980s Have Changed Industrial Relations.* MONTHLY LAB. REV., May 1988, at 35

Freidson, Eliot. PROFESSIONAL POWERS: A STUDY OF THE INSTITUTIONALIZATION OF FORMAL KNOWLEDGE (1986)

Friedman, Milton, and Simon Kuznets. INCOME FROM INDEPENDENT PROFESSIONAL PRACTICE (1945)

Friedmann, Harriet. *Patriarchal Commodity Production.* SOCIAL ANALYSIS, Dec. 1986, at 47

------. *Simple Commodity Production and Wage Labor in the American Plains.* 6 J. PEASANT STUD. 71 (1978)

------. *World Market, State, and Family Farm: Social Bases of Household*

Production in the Era of Wage Labor. 20 COMP. STUD. IN SOC'Y & HIST. 545 (1978)

FUNK AND WAGNALL'S NEW STANDARD DICTIONARY OF THE ENGLISH LANGUAGE (1963)

Galbraith, John. ECONOMICS AND THE PUBLIC PURPOSE (1973)

Gerry, Chris. *The Working Class and Small Enterprise in the UK Recession*. In BEYOND EMPLOYMENT: HOUSEHOLD, GENDER AND SUBSISTENCE 288 (N. Redclift & E. Mingione ed. 1985)

Gintis, Herbert, and Samuel Bowles. *Structure and Practice in the Labor Theory of Value*. REV. RADICAL POL. ECON., Winter 1981, at 1

Goleman, Daniel. *Tax Tip: If It's Lump Sum, Cheating Is More Likely*. N.Y. Times, Apr. 13, 1991, at 6, col. 3.

Goodman, David, and Michael Redclift. *Capitalism, Petty Commodity Production and the Farm Enterprise*. 25 SOCIOLOGIA RURALIS 231 (1985)

------. FROM PEASANT TO PROLETARIAN: CAPITALIST DEVELOPMENTS AND AGRARIAN TRANSITIONS (1982)

Goodman, Isidore. *Legislative Development of the Federal Tax Treatment of Pension and Profit-Sharing Plans*. 49 TAXES 226 (1971)

Gordon, Evelyn. *NII Refutes Self-Employed's Charges*. Jerusalem Post, Aug. 26, 1991 (NEXIS)

Gorz, André. ADIEUX AU PROLÉTARIAT (1980)

------. *Allocation universelle: Version de droite et version de gauche*. 41 LA REVUE NOUVELLE 419 (1985)

------. MÉTAMORPHOSES DU TRAVAIL (1988)

Greenberger, Ellen, and Laurence Steinberg. WHEN TEENAGERS WORK: THE PSYCHOLOGICAL AND SOCIAL COSTS OF ADOLESCENT EMPLOYMENT (1986)

Greenough, William, and Francis King. PENSION PLANS AND PUBLIC POLICY (1976)

Grimm, Jacob, and Wilhelm Grimm. 1/10 DEUTSCHES WÖRTERBUCH (1854/1905)

Grünberg, Emil. DER MITTELSTAND IN DER KAPITALISTISCHEN GESELLSCHAFT: EINE ÖKONOMISCHE UND SOZIOLOGISCHE UNTERSUCHUNG (1932)

Gunton, George. PRINCIPLES OF SOCIAL ECONOMICS (1897)

Haber, Sheldon, Enrique Lamas, and Jules Lichtenstein. *On Their Own: The Self-Employed and Others in Private Business*. MONTHLY LAB. REV., May 1987, at 17

Haber, William, and Merrill Murray. UNEMPLOYMENT INSURANCE IN THE AMERICAN ECONOMY: AN HISTORICAL REVIEW AND ANALYSIS (1966)

Habermas, Jürgen. DIE NACHHOLENDE REVOLUTION (1990)

Hacking, Ian. *Biopower and the Avalanche of Printed Numbers*, 5 HUMANITIES IN SOCIETY 279 (1982)

------. *Making Up People*. In RECONSTRUCTING INDIVIDUALISM: AUTONOMY, INDIVIDUALISTS, AND THE SELF IN WESTERN THOUGHT (T. Heller ed. 1986)

------. THE TAMING OF CHANCE (1990)

Hadley, Arthur. ECONOMICS: AN ACCOUNT OF THE RELATIONS BETWEEN PRIVATE PROPERTY AND PUBLIC WELFARE (1896)

------. *Profits*, in 3 CYCLOPAEDIA OF POLITICAL SCIENCE, POLITICAL ECONOMY AND OF THE POLITICAL HISTORY OF THE UNITED STATES 375 (John Lalor ed. 1884)

Hagelstange, Thomas. *Die Entwicklung von Klassenstrukturen in der EG und in Nordamerika (1987)*

------. *Niedergang oder Renaissance der Selbständigen? Statistische Daten zur Entwicklung in der EG und in Nordamerika.* ZEITSCHRIFT FÜR SOZIOLOGIE, Apr. 1988, at 142

Hakim, Catherine. *Census Reports as Documentary Evidence: The Census Commentaries 1801-1951.* 28 SOCIOLOGICAL REV. 551 (1980)

------. *Employers' Use of Homework, Outwork and Freelances.* 92 EMPLOYMENT GAZETTE 144 (1984)

------. *New Recruits to Self-Employment in the 1980s.* 97 EMPLOYMENT GAZETTE 286 (1989)

------. *Self-Employment in Britain: Recent Trends and Current Issues.* 2 WORK, EMPLOYMENT & SOCIETY 421 (1988)

Hale, Robert. *Coercion and Distribution in a Supposedly Non-Coercive State.* 38 POL. SCI. Q. 470 (1923)

------. *Minimum Wages and the Constitution.* 36 COLUM. L. REV. 629 (1936).

Hansen, Svend Aage, and Ingrid Henriksen. 7 DANSK SOCIAL HISTORIE: VELFÆRDSTATEN 1940-78 (1980)

Harris, Abram. *Pure Capitalism and the Disappearance of the Middle Class.* 47 J. POL. ECON. 328 (1939)

Harrod, Jeffrey. POWER, PRODUCTION, AND THE UNPROTECTED WORKER (1987)

Heckscher, Charles. THE NEW UNIONISM: EMPLOYEE INVOLVEMENT IN THE CHANGING CORPORATION (1988)

Heffernan, William. *Social Dimensions of Agricultural Structures in the United States.* 12 SOCIOLOGIA RURALIS 481 (1972)

Hepple, Bob. *Restructuring Employment Rights.* 15 INDUS. L.J. 69 (1986)

Hollander, Samuel. THE ECONOMICS OF ADAM SMITH (1976 [1973])

Hookstadt, Carl. *Reclassification of the United States 1920 Occupation Census, by Industry.* MONTHLY LAB. REV., July 1923, at 1

Horvath, Francis. *Work at Home: New Findings from the Current Population Survey.* MONTHLY LAB. REV., Nov., 1986, at 31

Hourwich, Isaac. *The Social-Economic Classes of the Population of the United States. II.* 19 J. POL. ECON. 309 (1911)

Howe, Wayne. *The Business Services Industry Sets Pace in Employment Growth.* MONTHLY LAB. REV., Apr. 1986, at 29

------. *Temporary Help Workers: Who They Are, What Jobs They Hold.* MONTHLY LAB. REV., Nov. 1986, at 45

International Labour Office. THE PROMOTION OF SELF-EMPLOYMENT (Int'l Lab. Conf., 77th Sess., Rep. VII, 1990)

Jaynes, Gerald. BRANCHES WITHOUT ROOTS: GENESIS OF THE BLACK WORKING CLASS IN THE AMERICAN SOUTH, 1862-1882 (1986)

Jenkins, Robert. PROCEDURAL HISTORY OF THE 1940 CENSUS OF POPULATION AND HOUSING (1985)

Johnson, Dirk. *Doctors' Dilemma: Unionizing.* N.Y. Times, July 13, 1987, at 21, col. 3 (nat. ed.)

Kennan, George. MEMOIRS 1925-1950 (1967)

Keogh, Eugene. *Pensions for the Self-Employed.* 100 EST. & TR. 175 (1961)

Kilborn, Peter. *Novel Program for the Jobless Aims to Create Entrepreneurs.* N.Y. Times, May 16, 1990, at 1, col. 7 (nat. ed.)

------. *Part-Time Hirings Bring Deep Change in U.S. Workplaces.* N.Y. Times, June 17, 1991, at A1, col. 6 (nat. ed.)

------. *The Perils of Pig Farming Touch Man and Beast.* N.Y. Times, Aug. 25, 1991, § 1, at 1, col. 2 (nat. ed.)

------. *Tomato Pickers' Hope for Better Life Becomes Victim as Industry Steps In.* N.Y. Times, May 9, 1991, at A10, col. 1 (nat. ed.)

King, Willford. THE NATIONAL INCOME AND ITS PURCHASING POWER (1930)

Kuznets, Simon. NATIONAL INCOME AND ITS COMPOSITION, 1919-1938 (1941)

Landau, Sidney. DICTIONARIES: THE ART AND CRAFT OF LEXICOGRAPHY (1989 [1984])

Larson, Arthur. *Social Security and Self-Employed Lawyers: A Plea for Re-evaluation.* 39 A.B.A.J. 971 (1953)

Larson, Magali. THE RISE OF PROFESSIONALISM: A SOCIOLOGICAL ANALYSIS (1979 [1977])

Lebergott, Stanley. MANPOWER IN ECONOMIC GROWTH: THE AMERICAN RECORD SINCE 1800 (1964)

Leighton, Patricia. *Employment and Self-Employment: Some Problems of Law and Practice.* 91 EMPLOYMENT GAZETTE 197 (1983)

------. *Employment Contracts: a Choice of Relationships.* 90 EMPLOYMENT GAZETTE 433 (1982)

Leppert-Fögen, Annette. DIE DEKLASSIERTE KLASSE: STUDIEN ZUR GESCHICHTE UND IDEOLOGIE DES KLEINBÜRGERTUMS (1974)

Leveson, Irving. *Some Determinants of Non-Farm Self-Employment.* MONTHLY LAB. REV., May, 1968, at 11

Levy, Marcia. SELF-EMPLOYMENT IN THE COVERED WORK FORCE (Soc. Sec. Adm. Staff Paper No. 19, 1975)

Linder, Marc. Book review of Aronson, SELF-EMPLOYMENT. 98 AM. J. SOC. ___ (1992)

------. *Class Struggle at the Door: The Origins of the Portal-to-Portal Act of 1947.* 39 BUFFALO L. REV. 53 (1991)

------. *Employees, Not-So-Independent Contractors, and the Case of Migrant Farmworkers: A Challenge to "Law and Economics" Agency Doctrine.* 15 N.Y.U. REV. L. & SOC. CHANGE 435 (1986-87)

------. THE EMPLOYMENT RELATIONSHIP IN ANGLO-AMERICAN LAW: A HISTORICAL PERSPECTIVE (1989)

------. EUROPEAN LABOR ARISTOCRACIES: TRADE UNIONISM, THE HIERARCHY OF SKILL, AND THE STRATIFICATION OF THE MANUAL WORKING CLASS BEFORE THE FIRST WORLD WAR (1985)

------. *From Street Urchins to Little Merchants: The Juridical Transvaluation of Child Newspaper Carriers.* 63 TEMPLE L. REV. 829 (1990)

------. *The Involuntary Conversion of Employees into Self-Employed: The Internal Revenue Service and Section 530.* 22 CLEARINGHOUSE REV. 14 (1988)

------. *The Joint Employment Doctrine: Clarifying Joint Legislative-Judicial Confusion.* 10 HAMLINE J. PUB. L. & POL. 321 (1989)

------. *Petty-Bourgeois Pickle Pickers: An Agricultural Labor-Law Hoax Comes a Cropper.* 25 TULSA L.J. 195 (1989)

------. REIFICATION AND THE CONSCIOUSNESS OF THE CRITICS OF POLITICAL ECONOMY: STUDIES IN THE DEVELOPMENT OF MARX' THEORY OF VALUE (1975)

------. *Self-Employment as a Cyclical Escape from Unemployment: A Case Study of the Construction Industry in the United States during the Postwar Period.* In 2 RESEARCH IN SOCIOLOGY OF WORK: PERIPHERAL WORKERS 261 (1983)

------. *Towards Universal Worker Coverage under the National Labor Relations Act: Making Room for Uncontrolled Employees, Dependent Contractors, and Employee-Like Persons.* 66 U. DET. L. REV. 555 (1989)

------. *What is an Employee? Why It Does, But Should Not, Matter.* 7 LAW & INEQUALITY 155 (1989)

------, and John Houghton. *Self-Employment and the Petty-Bourgeoisie: Comment on Steinmetz and Wright.* 96 AM. J. SOC. 727 (1990)

Looking for Tax Breaks? Incorporate Yourself. BUS. WK., Aug. 27, 1984, at 87

Loufti, Martha. *Self-Employment Patterns and Policy Issues in Europe.* 130 INT'L LAB. REV. 1 (1991)

Love, Harold. *Social Security and Retirement Plans for Lawyers: It Need Not Mean Socialism.* 38 A.B.A.J. 463 (1952)

Lozano, Beverly. THE INVISIBLE WORK FORCE: TRANSFORMING AMERICAN BUSINESS WITH OUTSIDE AND HOME-BASED WORKERS (1989)

McCarthy, Philip. SOME SOURCES OF ERROR IN LABOR FORCE ESTIMATES FROM THE CURRENT POPULATION SURVEY (Nat'l Comm'n on Employment and Unemployment Statistics Background Paper No. 15, 1978)

Malamud, Bernard. THE ASSISTANT (n.d. [1957])

Mann, Susan. AGRARIAN CAPITALISM IN THEORY AND PRACTICE (1990)

Marbach, Fritz. THEORIE DES MITTELSTANDES (1942)

Marshall, Alfred. PRINCIPLES OF ECONOMICS (1952 [1890])

Marwick, Arthur. CLASS: IMAGE AND REALITY IN BRITAIN, FRANCE AND THE USA SINCE 1930 (1980)

Marx, Karl. CAPITAL: A CRITICAL ANALYSIS OF CAPITALIST PRODUCTION. In II:9 Karl Marx [and] Friedrich Engels. GESAMTAUSGABE (MEGA) (1990 [1887])

------. 1 CAPITAL (Ben Fowkes tr. 1976)

------. 2 CAPITAL (1974 [1967])

------. 3 CAPITAL (1974 [1967])

------. LE CAPITAL. In II:7 Karl Marx [and] Friedrich Engels. GESAMTAUSGABE (MEGA) (1989 [1875])

------. 1 DAS KAPITAL. In II:5 Karl Marx [and] Friedrich Engels.

GESAMTAUSGABE (MEGA) (1983 [1867])
------. 1 DAS KAPITAL. In 23 MARX-ENGELS WERKE (1962)
------. 2 DAS KAPITAL. In 24 MARX-ENGELS WERKE (1963)
------. 3 DAS KAPITAL. In 25 MARX-ENGELS WERKE (1964 [1894])
------. *Das Kapital (Ökonomische Manuskripte 1863-1865)*. In II:4, Text Pt. 1
    Karl Marx [and] Friedrich Engels. GESAMTAUSGABE (MEGA)
    (1988)
------. DIE KLASSENKÄMPFE IN FRANKREICH 1848 BIS 1850. In I:10 Karl Marx
    [and] Friedrich Engels. GESAMTAUSGABE (MEGA) 119 (1977
    [1850])
------. Letter to Engels (Sept. 26, 1868). In 32 MARX-ENGELS WERKE 167
    (1965)
------. *Ökonomisch-philosophische Manuskripte* (Erste Wiedergabe). In I:2
    Karl Marx [and] Friedrich Engels. GESAMTAUSGABE (MEGA) 187
    (1982 [1844])
------. *Questionnaire for Workers*. In I:25 Karl Marx [and] Friedrich Engels.
    GESAMTAUSGABE (MEGA) 199 (1985 [1880])
------. VALUE, PRICE AND PROFIT. In II:4, Text Pt. 1 Karl Marx [and]
    Friedrich Engels. GESAMTAUSGABE (MEGA) 383 (1988 [1865])
------. *Die Verhandlungen des 6. rheinischen Landtags. Erster Artikel: Debatten
    über Preßfreiheit und Publikation der Landständischen
    Verhandlungen*. In I:1 Karl Marx [and] Friedrich Engels.
    GESAMTAUSGABE (MEGA) 121 (1975 [1842])
------. ZUR KRITIK DER POLITISCHEN ÖKONOMIE (MANUSKRIPT 1861-1863).
    In II:3, Text Pt. 6 Karl Marx [and] Friedrich Engels.
    GESAMTAUSGABE (MEGA) (1982)
------, and Friedrich Engels. MANIFEST DER KOMMUNISTISCHEN PARTEI. In
    4 MARX-ENGELS WERKE 469 (1959 [1848])
Mason, John. SELF-KNOWLEDGE: A TREATISE (1801 [1745])
Mauke, Michael. DIE KLASSENTHEORIE VON MARX UND ENGELS (1973
    [1970])
Mayer, Arno. *The Lower Middle Class as Historical Problem*. 47 J. MOD.
    HIST. 409 (1975)
Melosh, Barbara. "THE PHYSICIAN'S HAND": WORK CULTURE AND CONFLICT
    IN AMERICAN NURSING (1982)
Mill, James. ELEMENTS OF POLITICAL ECONOMY (3d ed. 1826 [1821]). In
    James Mill, SELECTED ECONOMIC WRITINGS 203 (Donald Winch
    ed. 1966)
Mill, John Stuart. PRINCIPLES OF POLITICAL ECONOMY (W. Ashley ed. 1921
    [1848])
Millican, Anthony. *IRS Auditing Harbor Trucking Firms over Status of Drivers*.
    L.A. Times, Aug. 30, 1991, at B3, col. 3 (NEXIS)
Mills, C. Wright. WHITE COLLAR: THE AMERICAN MIDDLE CLASSES (1956
    [1951])
Moberley, Robert. *Temporary, Part-Time, and Other Atypical Employment
    Relationships in the United States*. 38 LAB. L.J. 689 (1987)
Montgomery, David. BEYOND EQUALITY: LABOR AND THE RADICAL
    REPUBLICANS 1862-1872 (1967)

Moore, Mack. *Proposed Federal Legislation for Temporary Labor Services*. 26
    LAB. L.J. 767 (1975)
------. *The Temporary Help Service Industry: Historical Development, Operation,
    and Scope*. 18 INDUS. & LAB. REL. REV. 554 (1965)
Moore, Robert. *Self-Employment and the Incidence of the Payroll Tax*. 36
    NAT'L TAX J. 491 (1983)
Morgan, Daniel, and Yale Goldberg. EMPLOYEES AND INDEPENDENT
    CONTRACTORS (1990)
Moses, Stanley. *Labor Supply Concept: Political Economy of Conceptual
    Change*. In 3 COUNTING THE LABOR FORCE: READINGS IN LABOR
    FORCE STATISTICS. Appendix 96 (Dianne Werneke ed., Nat'l
    Comm'n on Employment and Unemployment Statistics, 1979 [1975])
Mott, Gordon. *Male Models Chase A Dream in Paris*. N.Y. Times, Sept. 30,
    1987, at 19, col. 1 (nat. ed.)
Nardone, Thomas. *Part-Time Workers: Who Are They?* MONTHLY LAB. REV.,
    Feb. 1986, at 13
Nathan, Otto. *Favorable Economic Consequences of the Fair Labor Standards
    Act*. 6 LAW & CONTEMP. PROBS. 416 (1939)
National Ass'n of the Self-Employed. SELF-EMPLOYED AMERICA, Mar.-Apr.
    1991
National Committee on Social Legislation. *The Servicemen's Readjustment Act
    of 1944: "The G.I. Bill of Rights."* 5 LAWYERS GUILD REV. 90 (1945)
Das neue Schema der sozio-ökonomischen Gliederung. WIRTSCHAFT UND
    STATISTIK, May 1970, at 247
NEW REPUBLIC, Aug. 26, 1946, at 218
Nicholson, John. *Pensions for Partners: Tax Laws Are Unfair to Lawyers and
    Firms*. 33 A.B.A.J. 302 (1947)
Note. *Unemployment Insurance--A Discussion of the Eligibility Requirements
    and the Voluntary Leaving Disqualification*. 17 GEO. WASH. L. REV.
    447 (1949)
Oliver, Allen. *Lawyers and Social Security: No Need for Change*. 40 A.B.A.J.
    586 (1954)
Oxenfeldt, Alfred. NEW FIRMS AND FREE ENTERPRISE: PRE-WAR AND POST-
    WAR ASPECTS (1943)
OXFORD ENGLISH DICTIONARY (1933; 2d ed. 1989)
Parris, Addison. THE SMALL BUSINESS ADMINISTRATION (1968)
Perry, Arthur. PRINCIPLES OF POLITICAL ECONOMY (1891)
Peterson, Richard, John Schmidman, and Kirk Elifson. *Entrepreneurship or
    Autonomy? Truckers and Cabbies*. In VARIETIES OF WORK 181 (P.
    Stewart & M. Cantor ed. 1982)
Pfeffer, Jeffrey, and James Baron. *Taking the Workers Back Out: Recent
    Trends in the Structure of Employment*. 10 RES. IN ORGANIZATION
    BEHAV. 257 (1988)
Philipps, J., J. McNider, and D. Riley. *Origins of Tax Law: The History of the
    Personal Service Corporation*. 40 WASH. & LEE L. REV. 433 (1983)
Phillips, Joseph. THE SELF-EMPLOYED IN THE UNITED STATES (1962)
Piore, Michael. BIRDS OF PASSAGE: MIGRANT LABOR AND INDUSTRIAL
    SOCIETIES (1979)

------, and Charles Sabel. THE SECOND INDUSTRIAL DIVIDE: POSSIBILITIES
    FOR PROSPERITY (1984)
Polivka, Anne, and Thomas Nardone. *On the Definition of "Contingent Work."*
    MONTHLY LAB. REV., Dec., 1989, at 9
Porter, Glenn, and Harold Livesay. MERCHANTS AND MANUFACTURERS:
    STUDIES IN THE CHANGING STRUCTURE OF NINETEENTH-CENTURY
    MARKETING (1989 [1971])
Portes, Alejandro, Manuel Castells, & Lauren Benton. *Conclusion: The Policy
    Implications of Informality.* In THE INFORMAL ECONOMY: STUDIES
    IN ADVANCED AND LESS DEVELOPED COUNTRIES 298 (A. Portes,
    M. Castells, & L. Benton ed. 1989)
Przeworksi, Adam. CAPITALISM AND SOCIAL DEMOCRACY (1987 [1985])
Pyle, David. TAX EVASION AND THE BLACK ECONOMY (1989)
QUELLEN ZUR BEVÖLKERUNGS-, SOZIAL- UND WIRTSCHAFTSSTATISTIK
    DEUTSCHLANDS   1815-1875.   QUELLEN   ZUR   BERUFS-UND
    GEWERBESTATISTIK   DEUTSCHLANDS   1816-1875:   PREUBISCHE
    PROVINZEN (Antje Kraus ed. 1989)
Rabban, David. *Distinguishing Excluded Managers from Covered Professionals
    under the NLRA.* 89 COLUM. L. REV. 1775 (1989)
Rand School of Social Science. 6 THE AMERICAN LABOR YEAR BOOK (1925)
RANDOM HOUSE DICTIONARY OF THE ENGLISH LANGUAGE (1969 [1966]; 2d
    ed. 1987)
Ratner, Sidney. TAXATION AND DEMOCRACY IN AMERICA (1967 [1942])
Ray, Robert. A Report on Self-Employed Americans in 1973. MONTHLY
    LAB. REV., Jan. 1975, at 49
Reagan Michael. THE MANAGED ECONOMY (1970 [1963])
Reddy, William. MONEY AND LIBERTY IN MODERN EUROPE: A CRITIQUE
    OF HISTORICAL UNDERSTANDING (1987)
Reubens, Beatrice. *Unemployment Insurance in Western Europe: Responses to
    High Unemployment, 1973-1983.* In UNEMPLOYMENT INSURANCE:
    THE SECOND HALF-CENTURY 173 (W. Hansen & J. Byers ed. 1990)
Reverby, Susan. ORDERED TO CARE: THE DILEMMA OF AMERICAN
    NURSING, 1850-1945 (1987)
Reynolds, Lloyd. *Cutthroat Competition.* 30 AM. ECON. REV. 736 (1940)
Rifkin, Glenn. *From Unemployment into Self-Employment.* N.Y. Times, Sept.
    19, 1991, at C1, col. 4 (nat. ed.)
Robertson, James. FUTURE WORK: JOBS, SELF-EMPLOYMENT AND LEISURE
    AFTER THE INDUSTRIAL AGE (1985)
Rodgers, Daniel. THE WORK ETHIC IN THE UNITED STATES 1850-1920 (1978)
Roemer, John. A GENERAL THEORY OF EXPLOITATION AND CLASS (1982)
------. *New Directions in the Marxian Theory of Exploitation and Class.* In
    ANALYTICAL MARXISM 81 (J. Roemer ed. 1985 [1982])
Rosen, Jan. *Your Money: Caution Is Urged On Retiring Early.* N.Y. Times,
    June 8, 1991, at 18, col. 1 (nat. ed.)
Rothstein, Mervyn. *From Cartoons to a Play About Racism.* N.Y. Times, Aug.
    17, 1991, at 11, col. 1 (nat. ed.)
Rubinow, I. *Standards of Sickness Insurance. I.* 23 J. POL. ECON. 221 (1915)
------. *Compulsory Old-Age Insurance in France,* 26 POL. SCI. Q. 500 (1911)

Rudick, Harry. *More about Professions for Partners: A Better Solution Than Pension Plans?* 33 A.B.A.J. 1001 (1947)

Samuelson, Paul. ECONOMICS (9th ed. 1973 [1948])

Sapulkas, Agis. *Trucking-Driving Couple Share Life on the Road.* N.Y. Times, July 25, 1988, at 29, col. 1 (nat. ed.)

Scase, Richard, and Robert Goffee. THE ENTREPRENEURIAL MIDDLE CLASS (1982)

Scherer, F. INDUSTRIAL MARKET STRUCTURE AND ECONOMIC PERFORMANCE (2d ed. 1980 [1970])

Scott, Alison. *Who Are the Self-Employed?* In CASUAL WORK AND POVERTY IN THIRD WORLD CITIES 105 (R. Bromley & C. Gerry ed. 1979)

Self-Employment in OECD Countries. OECD EMPLOYMENT OUTLOOK, Sept. 1986, at 43

Self-employment: Lots of Loners. ECONOMIST, Mar. 23, 1985, at 66

Senior, Nassau. AN OUTLINE OF THE SCIENCE OF POLITICAL ECONOMY (1939 [1836])

Sensat, Julius. *Methodological Individualism and Marxism.* 4 ECON. & PHIL. 189 (1988)

------. *Reification as Dependence on Extrinsic Information* (unpub. MS, 1991)

Simon, Carl, and Ann Witte. BEATING THE SYSTEM: THE UNDERGROUND ECONOMY (1982)

Slichter, Sumner. THE CHALLENGE OF INDUSTRIAL RELATIONS: TRADE UNIONS, MANAGEMENT, AND THE PUBLIC INTEREST (1947)

Smith, Adam. AN INQUIRY INTO THE NATURE AND CAUSES OF THE WEALTH OF NATIONS (E. Cannan ed. 1937 [1776])

Solow, Robert. THE LABOR MARKET AS A SOCIAL INSTITUTION (1990)

Sombart, Werner. DIE DEUTSCHE VOLKSWIRTSCHAFT IM NEUNZEHNTEN JAHRHUNDERT (1954 [1903])

Speier, Hans. DIE ANGESTELLTEN VOR DEM NATIONALSOZIALISMUS: EIN BEITRAG ZUM VERSTÄNDNIS DER DEUTSCHEN SOZIALSTRUKTUR 1918-1933 (1989 [1977])

Starr, Paul. THE SOCIAL TRANSFORMATION OF AMERICAN MEDICINE (1982)

Stein, Robert. *New Definitions for Employment and Unemployment.* EMPLOYMENT AND EARNINGS AND MONTHLY REPORT ON THE LABOR FORCE, Feb. 1967, at 3

Steinmetz, George, and Erik Wright. *The Fall and Rise of the Petty Bourgeoisie: Changing Patterns of Self-Employment in the Postwar United States.* 94 AM. J. SOC. 973 (1989)

------. *Reply to Linder and Houghton.* 96 AM. J. SOC. 736 (1990)

STENOGRAPHISCHER BERICHT ÜBER DIE VERHANDLUNGEN DER DEUTSCHEN CONSTITUIERENDEN NATIONALVERSAMMLUNG ZU FRANKFURT AM MAIN (F. Wigard ed. 1848-49)

Stinson, John, Jr. *Multiple Jobholding up Sharply in the 1980s.* MONTHLY LAB. REV., July 1990, at 3

Storch, Henri. 1 COURS D'ÉCONOMIE POLITIQUE (J. B. Say ed. 1823 [1815])

Sullivan, Teresa, Elizabeth Warren, and Jay Westbrook. AS WE FORGIVE OUR DEBTORS: BANKRUPTCY AND CONSUMER CREDIT IN AMERICA (1991 [1989])

Szymanski, Albert. CLASS STRUCTURE: A CRITICAL PERSPECTIVE (1983)

Taussig, Frank. WAGES AND CAPITAL: AN EXAMINATION OF THE WAGES FUND DOCTRINE (1896)

Therborn, Göran. WHY SOME PEOPLES ARE MORE UNEMPLOYED THAN OTHERS: THE STRANGE PARADOX OF GROWTH AND UNEMPLOYMENT (1986)

Thompson, E. *Time, Work-Discipline and Industrial Capitalism*, PAST & PRESENT, Dec. 1967, at 56

Tilly, Chris. *Reasons for the Continuing Growth of Part-Time Employment.* MONTHLY LAB. REV., Mar. 1991, at 10

Times (London). Aug. 13, 1976, at 13, col. 7

Tierney, John. *In Tunnel, "Mole People" Fight to Save Home.* N.Y. Times, June 13, 1990, at A1, col. 2 (nat. ed.)

Tishler, Hace. SELF-RELIANCE AND SOCIAL SECURITY, 1870-1917 (1971)

Treble, James. URBAN POVERTY IN BRITAIN 1870-1914 (1979)

Uchitelle, Louis. *The New Surge in Self-Employed.* N.Y. Times, Jan. 15, 1991, at C2, col. 1 (nat. ed.)

------. *Reliance on Temporary Jobs Hints at Economic Fragility.* N.Y. Times, Mar. 16, 1988, at 1, col. 1 (nat. ed.)

Unger, Roberto. FALSE NECESSITY: ANTI-NECESSITARIAN SOCIAL THEORY IN THE SERVICE OF RADICAL DEMOCRACY (1987)

Vogeler, Ingolf. THE MYTH OF THE FAMILY FARM: AGRIBUSINESS DOMINANCE OF U.S. AGRICULTURE (1982)

Volkov, Shulamit. THE RISE OF POPULAR ANTIMODERNISM IN GERMANY: THE URBAN MASTER ARTISANS, 1873-1896 (1978)

Wagner, David. *The Proletarianization of Nursing in the United States, 1932-1946.* 10 INT'L J. HEALTH SERVICES 271 (1980)

Walker, Francis. *American Industry in the Census.* 24 ATL. MONTHLY 689 (1869)

------. *The Source of Business Profits.* 1 Q.J. ECON. 265 (1887)

Webster, Noah. A DICTIONARY OF THE ENGLISH LANGUAGE (1828)

WEBSTER'S NEW COLLEGIATE DICTIONARY (1961)

WEBSTER'S NEW INTERNATIONAL DICTIONARY OF THE ENGLISH DICTIONARY (2d unabridged ed. 1947 [1934])

WEBSTER'S NEW TWENTIETH CENTURY DICTIONARY (unabridged ed. 1962)

WEBSTER'S NINTH NEW COLLEGIATE DICTIONARY (1983)

WEBSTER'S SEVENTH NEW COLLEGIATE DICTIONARY (1965)

WEBSTER'S THIRD NEW INTERNATIONAL DICTIONARY OF THE ENGLISH DICTIONARY (unabridged ed. 1969 [1961])

Weiler, Paul. GOVERNING THE WORKPLACE: THE FUTURE OF LABOR AND EMPLOYMENT LAW (1990)

Weitzman, Martin. THE SHARE ECONOMY: CONQUERING STAGFLATION (1984)

Wendt, Laura. *Census Classifications and Social Security Categories.* SOC. SEC. BULL., Apr. 1938, at 3

Weyforth, William. THE ORGANIZABILITY OF LABOR (1917)

Williams, Raymond. THE YEAR 2000 (1983)

Wilson, John. *The Political Economy of Contract Farming.* REV. RADICAL

POL. ECON., Winter 1986, at 47

Wolder, Victor. *The Forgotten Man of Taxes.* 24 TAXES 970 (1946)

Wolfe, Alan. THE LIMITS OF LEGITIMACY: POLITICAL CONTRADICTIONS OF CONTEMPORARY CAPITALISM (1980 [1977])

Wolman, Leo. THE GROWTH OF AMERICAN TRADE UNIONS 1880-1923 (1924)

Wood, James. EMPLOYMENT EXPERIENCE OF PATERSON BROAD-SILK WORKERS, 1926-36: A STUDY OF INTERMITTENCY OF EMPLOYMENT IN A DECLINING INDUSTRY (WPA Nat'l Research Proj. 1939)

Woskowitz, Daniel. *IRS Sharpens Definition of Who Is an Employee.* Washington Post, Sept. 2, 1991, at F15 (NEXIS)

Woytinsky, W. LABOR IN THE UNITED STATES: BASIC STATISTICS FOR SOCIAL SECURITY (1938)

------. THE LABOR SUPPLY OF THE UNITED STATES: OCCUPATIONAL STATISTICS OF THE 1930 CENSUS (1936)

------. DIE WELT IN ZAHLEN: DIE ARBEIT (1926)

Wright, Erik. CLASS STRUCTURE AND INCOME DETERMINATION (1979)

------. CLASSES (1985)

Government Publications

Belgium

Institut national d'assurances sociales pour travailleurs indépendants. 50 ANS D' ALLOCATIONS FAMILIALES, 30 ANS DE PENSIONS, 20 ANS DE STATUT SOCIAL (1988)

VINGT ANS AU SERVICE DE CLASSES MOYENNES (Institut Belge d'Information et de Documentation ed. 1974)

France

Ministère du Commerce. Direction du travail. Service du recensement professionnel. 4 RÉSULTATS STATISTIQUES DU RECENSEMENT GÉNÉRALE DE LA POPULATION EFFECTUÉ LE 24 MARS 1901: POPULATION PRÉSENTE. RÉSULTATS GÉNÉRAUX (1906)

Germany

Statistisches Bundesamt. 1 VOLKS- UND BERUFSZÄHLUNG VOM 6. JUNI 1961: DIE METHODISCHEN GRUNDLAGEN DER VOLKS- UND BERUFSZÄHLUNG 1961 (1961)

------. 12 VOLKS- UND BERUFSZÄHLUNG VOM 6. JUNI 1961: ERWERBSPERSONEN IN WIRTSCHAFTLICHER UND SOZIALER GLIEDERUNG (1961)

Great Britain

1 ABSTRACT OF THE ANSWERS AND RETURNS: ENUMERATION ABSTRACT (1831)
------. ABSTRACT OF THE ANSWERS AND RETURNS: OCCUPATION ABSTRACT, M.DCCC.XLI. Part 1: ENGLAND AND WALES (1844)
------. CENSUS OF ENGLAND AND WALES FOR THE YEAR 1861: GENERAL REPORT (1863)
------. CENSUS OF ENGLAND AND WALES, 1891: GENERAL REPORT (C.--7222, 1893)
------. II:1 CENSUS OF GREAT BRITAIN, 1851. POPULATION TABLES: AGES, CIVIL CONDITION, OCCUPATIONS, AND BIRTH-PLACE OF THE PEOPLE (1854)
------. House of Commons. 4 PARL. DEB. (5th ser.) (1909)
------. House of Commons. 419 PARL. DEB. (5th ser.) (1946)
------. House of Commons. 445 PARL. DEB. (5th ser.) (1947)
------. House of Commons, 91 PARL. DEB. (6th ser.) (1986)

United States

Advisory Council on Social Security. FINAL REPORT: DECEMBER 10, 1938. Sen. Doc. No. 4. 76th Cong., 1st Sess (1939)
------. RECOMMENDATIONS FOR SOCIAL SECURITY LEGISLATION. Sen. Doc. No. 208. 80th Cong., 2d Sess. (1949)
Bureau of Economic Analysis. BUSINESS STATISTICS, 1961-88 (26th ed. 1989)
------. THE NATIONAL INCOME AND PRODUCT ACCOUNTS OF THE UNITED STATES, 1929-82: STATISTICAL TABLES (1986)
Bureau of Labor Statistics. CONCEPTS AND METHODS USED IN LABOR FORCE STATISTICS DERIVED FROM THE CURRENT POPULATION SURVEY (Rep. No. 463, 1976)
------. CURRENT POPULATION SURVEY (unpub. 1972-1991)
------. EMPLOYMENT AND EARNINGS (1967-1991)
------. HANDBOOK OF LABOR STATISTICS (Bull. 2340, 1989)
------. IMPACT ON WORKERS AND COMMUNITY OF A PLANT SHUTDOWN IN A DEPRESSED AREA (Bull. No. 1264, 1960)
------. INDUSTRY WAGE SURVEY: TEMPORARY HELP SUPPLY, SEPTEMBER 1987 (Bull. 2313, 1988)
------. LABOR FORCE STATISTICS DERIVED FROM THE CURRENT POPULATION SURVEY, 1948-87 (Bull. 2307, 1988)
------. LABOR FORCE STATISTICS DERIVED FROM THE CURRENT POPULATION SURVEY: A DATABOOK (Bull. 2096, 1982)
Bureau of the Census. CENSUS OF POPULATION: 1950. CHARACTERISTICS OF THE POPULATION. Pt. 1: UNITED STATES SUMMARY (1953)
------. CENSUS OF POPULATION: 1970. 1 CHARACTERISTICS OF THE POPULATION. Pt. 1: UNITED STATES SUMMARY (1973)
------. CENSUS OF POPULATION: 1970. DETAILED CHARACTERISTICS. FINAL REPORT PC(1)-D1: UNITED STATES SUMMARY (1973)
------. CENSUS OF POPULATION: 1970. SUBJECT REPORTS. FINAL REPORT PC(2)-7A: OCCUPATIONAL CHARACTERISTICS (1973)
------. CENSUS OF POPULATION: 1970. SUBJECT REPORTS. FINAL REPORT

PC(2)-7F: OCCUPATIONS OF PERSONS WITH HIGH EARNINGS (1973)

------. CENSUS OF POPULATION: 1980. 1 CHARACTERISTICS OF THE POPULATION. CHAPTER C: GENERAL SOCIAL AND ECONOMIC CHARACTERISTICS. Pt. 1: UNITED STATES SUMMARY (1983)

------. CENSUS OF POPULATION: 1980. 1 CHARACTERISTICS OF THE POPULATION. CHAPTER D: DETAILED POPULATION CHARACTERISTICS. Pt. 1: UNITED STATES SUMMARY (1984)

------. CURRENT POPULATION REPORTS: LABOR FORCE (Ser. P-50, No. 1, July 11, 1947)

------. CURRENT POPULATION REPORTS: LABOR FORCE (Ser. P-50, No. 30, Mar. 13, 1951)

------. CURRENT POPULATION REPORTS: LABOR FORCE (Ser. P-50, No. 88, Apr. 1959)

------. CURRENT POPULATION REPORTS: LABOR FORCE BULLETIN: LABOR FORCE, EMPLOYMENT, AND UNEMPLOYMENT IN THE UNITED STATES, 1940 TO 1946 (Ser. P-50, No. 2, Sept. 11, 1947)

------. CURRENT POPULATION REPORTS: MONTHLY REPORT ON THE LABOR FORCE: AUGUST, 1947 (Ser. P-57, No. 63, Sept. 4, 1947)

------. THE CURRENT POPULATION SURVEY: DESIGN AND METHODOLOGY (Technical Paper 40, 1978)

------. HISTORICAL STATISTICS OF THE UNITED STATES, COLONIAL TIMES TO 1970 (bicentennial ed. 1975)

------. INTERVIEWER'S MANUAL: CURRENT POPULATION SURVEY (CPS-250, rev. July 1989)

------. MONEY INCOME OF HOUSEHOLDS, FAMILIES, AND PERSONS IN THE UNITED STATES: 1987 (Curr. Pop. Rep., Ser. P-60, No. 162, 1989)

------. 1987 CENSUS OF CONSTRUCTION INDUSTRIES. INDUSTRY SERIES. UNITED STATES SUMMARY: ESTABLISHMENTS WITH AND WITHOUT PAYROLL (1990)

------. 1987 CENSUS OF CONSTRUCTION INDUSTRIES. SUBJECT SERIES: LEGAL FORM OF ORGANIZATION AND TYPE OF ORGANIZATION (1990)

------. 1987 CENSUS OF RETAIL TRADE. NONEMPLOYER STATISTICS SERIES: NORTHEAST (1990)

------. 1987 CENSUS OF RETAIL TRADE. SPECIAL REPORT SERIES: SELECTED STATISTICS (1991)

------. 1987 CENSUS OF SERVICE INDUSTRIES: GEOGRAPHIC AREA SERIES: UNITED STATES (1989)

------. 1987 CENSUS OF SERVICE INDUSTRIES: NONEMPLOYER STATISTICS SERIES: MIDWEST (1990)

------. 1987 CENSUS OF SERVICE INDUSTRIES. SUBJECT SERIES: ESTABLISHMENTS AND FIRM SIZE (INCLUDING LEGAL FORM OF ORGANIZATION) (1990)

------. 1982 CENSUS OF RETAIL TRADE. INDUSTRY SERIES: ESTABLISHMENT AND FIRM SIZE (INCLUDING LEGAL FORM OF ORGANIZATION) (1985)

------. 1982 CENSUS OF SERVICE INDUSTRIES. GEOGRAPHIC AREA SERIES: UNITED STATES (1984)

------. 1977 CENSUS OF RETAIL TRADE. SUBJECT STATISTICS (1981)

------. 1977 CENSUS OF SERVICE INDUSTRIES: 1 SUBJECT STATISTICS (1981)

------. 1972 CENSUS OF CONSTRUCTION INDUSTRIES: 1 INDUSTRY AND SPECIAL STATISTICS (1976)

------. 1972 CENSUS OF CONSTRUCTION INDUSTRIES. SPECIAL REPORT SERIES: TYPE OF OPERATION AND LEGAL FORM OF ORGANIZATION (1975)

------. 1972 CENSUS OF RETAIL TRADE: SUMMARY AND SUBJECT STATISTICS (1976)

------. 1972 CENSUS OF SELECTED SERVICE INDUSTRIES. 1 SUMMARY AND SUBJECT STATISTICS (1976)

------. 1967 CENSUS OF BUSINESS. 1 RETAIL TRADE--SUBJECT REPORTS: U.S. SUMMARY (1971)

------. 1967 CENSUS OF BUSINESS. SELECTED SERVICES. AREA STATISTICS: UNITED STATES (1970)

------. SIXTEENTH CENSUS OF THE UNITED STATES: 1940. 2 POPULATION: CHARACTERISTICS OF THE POPULATION. Pt. 1: UNITED STATES SUMMARY (1943)

------. SIXTEENTH CENSUS OF THE UNITED STATES: 1940. 3 POPULATION: THE LABOR FORCE OF THE POPULATION. Pt. 1: UNITED STATES SUMMARY (1943)

------. SPECIAL REPORTS: OCCUPATIONS AT THE TWELFTH CENSUS (1904)

------. STATISTICAL ABSTRACT OF THE UNITED STATES (110th ed. 1990)

------. SUPPLEMENT TO THE MONTHLY REPORT ON THE LABOR FORCE (No. 58-S, May 12, 1947)

------. THIRTEENTH CENSUS OF THE UNITED STATES TAKEN IN THE YEAR 1910. 4 POPULATION: OCCUPATIONAL STATISTICS (1914)

------. 200 YEARS OF U.S. CENSUS TAKING: POPULATION AND HOUSING QUESTIONS, 1790-1990 (1989)

Commissioner of Internal Revenue. STATISTICS OF INCOME FOR 1916. H. Doc. No. 1169. 65th Cong., 2d Sess. (1918)

Commissioner of Labor. TWENTY-FOURTH ANNUAL REPORT OF THE COMMISSIONER OF LABOR: WORKMEN'S INSURANCE AND COMPENSATION SYSTEMS IN EUROPE (1911).

Congress. 90 CONG. REC. (1944)

------. 94 CONG. REC. (1948)

------. 97 CONG. REC. (1951)

------. 98 CONG. REC. (1952)

------. 100 CONG. REC. (1954)

------. 108 CONG. REC. (1962)

------. 111 CONG. REC. (1965)

------. 117 CONG. REC. (1971)

------. 131 CONG. REC. (1985)

------. 132 CONG. REC. (1986)

------. 133 CONG. REC. (1987)

------. 135 CONG. REC. (1989)

------. 136 CONG. REC. (1990)

------. 137 CONG. REC. (1991)

180 *Bibliography*

Dep't of Commerce. Bus. Conditions Dig. (various years)

------. Survey of Current Bus. (various years)

------. Office of Federal Statistical Policy and Standards. An Error Profile: Employment as Measured by the Current Population Survey (Statistical Working Paper 3, 1978)

------. Office of Service Industries. Franchising in the Economy 1986-1988 (1988)

Dep't of Labor. From Homemaking to Entrepreneurship: A Readiness Training Program (1985)

------. *Report of the Subcomm. on the Foreign Experience of the Task Force on Economic Adjustment and Worker Dislocation: Evaluation of Programs to Assist Displaced Workers in Foreign Industrialized Countries*. In Economic Adjustment and Worker Dislocation in a Competitive Society: Report of the Secretary of Labor's Task Force on Economic Adjustment and Worker Dislocation (1986)

------. Women's Bureau. Flexible Workstyles: A Look at Contingent Labor (1988)

General Accounting Office. Tax Administration: Information Returns Can Be Used to Identify Employers Who Misclassify Workers (GGD-89-107, Sept. 25, 1989)

------. Tax Administration: Missing Independent Contractors' Information Returns Not Always Detected (GGD-89-110, Sept. 1989)

------. Workers at Risk: Increased Numbers in Contingent Employment, Lack Insurance, Other Benefits (HRD-91-56, Mar. 1991)

House of Representatives. H. Rep. No. 1418: Providing Federal Govenrment Aid for the Readjustment of Returning World War II Veterans. 78th Cong., 2d Sess. (1944)

------. H. Rep. No. 378: Self-Employed Individuals Tax Retirement Act of 1961. 87th Cong., 1st Sess. (1961)

------. H. Rep. No. 677: Home-Based Clerical Workers: Are They Victims of Exploitation? 99th Cong., 2d Sess. (1986)

------. H. Rep. No. 754. 99th Cong., 2d Sess. (1986)

------. H. Conf. Rep. No. 760. 97th Cong., 2d Sess. (1982)

------. Comm. on Education and Labor. *Day Laborer Protection Act of 1971: Hearings Before the Special Subcomm.* 92d Cong., 1st Sess. (1972)

------. Comm. on Education and Labor. *Oversight Hearings on the Department of Labor's Proposal to Lift the Ban on Industrial Homework: Hearings Before the Subcomm. on Labor Standards.* 99th Cong., 2d Sess. (1986)

------. Comm. on Foreign Affairs. *Micro-Enterprise Development Legislation: Hearing Before the Subcomm. on International Economic Trade and Policy.* 100th Cong., 1st Sess. (1988)

------. Comm. on Government Operations. *Rising Use of Part-Time and Temporary Workers: Who Benefits and Who Loses? Hearing Before a Subcomm.* 100th Cong., 2d Sess. (1988)

------. Comm. on Government Operations. *Employee-Independent Contractor Issues: Hearing Before the Subcomm. on Commerce, Consumer, and Monetary Affairs.* 101st Cong., 1st Sess. (1989)

------. Comm. on Government Operations. *Children at Risk in the Workplace: Hearings Before the Employment and Housing Subcomm.* 101st Cong., 2d Sess. (1990)

------. *Exploiting Workers by Misclassifying Them as Independent Contractors: Hearing Before the Employment and Housing Subcomm..* 102d Cong., 1st Sess. (1991)

------. Comm. on Ways and Means. *Revenue Revisions, 1947-48: Hearings.* 80th Cong., 1st Sess. (1947)

------. Comm. on Ways and Means. *Postponement of Income Tax Set Aside for Retirement: Hearings.* 82d Cong., 2d Sess. (1952)

------. Select Comm. on Hunger. *Self-Employment for the Poor: The Potential of Micro-Enterprise Credit Programs: Hearings.* 100th Cong., 2d Sess. (1988)

Internal Revenue Service. Gen Couns. Mem. 39,553 (Feb. 2, 1986)

------. SOI BULLETIN (various years)

------. STATISTICS OF INCOME--1979-1980 SOLE PROPRIETORSHIP RETURNS (1982)

------. SOURCE BOOK: SOLE PROPRIETORSHIP RETURNS 1957-1984 (1986)

------. Tech. Adv. Mem. 86-25-003 (Feb. 28, 1986)

National Commission on Employment and Unemployment Statistics. COUNTING THE LABOR FORCE (1979)

President. THE MIDYEAR ECONOMIC REPORT OF THE PRESIDENT: TO THE CONGRESS, JULY 30, 1948 (1948)

President's Committee to Appraise Employment and Unemployment Statistics. MEASURING EMPLOYMENT AND UNEMPLOYMENT (1962)

Senate. S. REP. NO. 992: SELF-EMPLOYED INDIVIDUALS TAX RETIREMENT ACT OF 1961. 87th Cong., 1st Sess. (1961)

------. S. REP. NO. 317. 99th Cong., 2d Sess. (1986)

------. Comm. on Finance. *Individual Income Tax Reduction: Hearings.* 81st Cong., 1st Sess. (1947)

------. Comm. on Finance. *Pension Plans for Owner-Managers of Corporations: Hearings.* 86th Cong., 2d Sess. (1960)

------. Comm. on Finance. *Self-Employed Individuals' Retirement Act: Hearings.* 87th Cong., 1st Sess. (1961)

------. Comm. on Finance. *Social Security Revision: Hearings.* 81st Cong., 2d Sess. (1950)

------. Special Comm. to Study Problems of American Small Business. SMALL BUSINESS PROBLEMS: SMALL BUSINESS WANTS OLD-AGE SECURITY. 78th Cong., 1st Sess. (Sen. Comm. Print No. 17, 1943)

Small Bus. Adm'n. STATE OF SMALL BUSINESS 1989 (1989)

------. STATE OF SMALL BUSINESS: A REPORT OF THE PRESIDENT (1990)

------. THE STATE OF SMALL BUSINESS: A REPORT OF THE PRESIDENT (1986)

Social Sec. Bd. COMPARISON OF STATE UNEMPLOYMENT COMPENSATION LAWS AS OF DECEMBER 31, 1945 (Employment Sec. Memorandum No. 8, rev. Dec. 1945)

------. Unemployment Comp. Div. MANUAL OF STATE EMPLOYMENT SECURITY LEGISLATION (Employment Sec. Memorandum No. 13, rev. Nov. 1942)
SOCIAL SEC. BULL. ANNUAL STATISTICAL SUPPLEMENT. 1989

Statutes and Regulations

Belgium

Arrêté royal instituant au ministère de l'industrie et du travail un Office des classes moyennes, Jan. 15, 1906, No. 10, at 65
Arrêté royal portant réglement organique du Ministère des Affaires économiques et des Classes moyennes, Dec. 11, 1939, No. 865, at 6252
Recueil des lois et arrêtés royaux, June 15, 1954, No. 494, at 2818-21
Arrêté royal organisant le statut social des travailleurs indépendants, July 27, 1967, No. 1053, at 3236

United States

Federal

Ch. 531, §§ 202(a)(1) and 210(a) and (b), 490 Stat. 620 (1935) (Social Security Act)
Ch. 619, §165, 56 Stat. 798 (1942) (Revenue Act of 1942)
Ch. 268, §§ 503, 902, 58 Stat. 284 (1944) (Servicemen's Readjustment Act of 1944)
Ch. 120, § 101, 61 Stat. 140 (1947) (Labor Management Relations Act)
Ch. 809, § 104(a), 64 Stat. 492 (1950) (Social Security Act Amendments)
Pub. L. No. 87-792, 76 Stat. 809 (1962) (Self-Employed Individuals Tax Retirement Act of 1962)
Pub. L. No. 97-248, Title II, § 250(a), 96 Stat. 528 (1982) (TEFRA)
Pub. L. No. 99-496, 100 Stat. 1261 (1986) (Joint Training Partnership Act Amendments of 1986)
Pub. L. No. 100-203, 101 Stat. 1330 (1987) (Omnibus Budget Reconciliation Act of 1987)
7 U.S.C. § 2014(f)(1)(A) (Supp. 1991) (Food Stamp Act of 1977)
26 U.S.C. §§ 1 and 11 (1976, 1982, and 1988)
26 U.S.C. § 32(c)(2)(A)(ii) (Supp. 1991)
26 U.S.C. § 269A(b)(1) and (2) (1988)
26 U.S.C. §§ 401(c)(1)(A) and (4) (Supp. 1991)
26 U.S.C. §§ 1401-1403 (1988) (Self-Employment Contributions Act)
26 U.S.C. §§ 3101-3128 (1989) (Federal Insurance Contributions Act)
26 U.S.C. §§ 3301-3311 (1989) (Federal Unemployment Tax Act)
29 U.S.C. § 1651(a)(1)(A) & (B) (Supp. 1991)
42 U.S.C. § 403(b) (Supp. 1991) (Social Security Act)
38 C.F.R. § 36.514 and §§ 36.525-532 (Supp. 1944)

20 C.F.R. § 631.3(c) (1990)
26 C.F.R. § 1.43-2(c)(2)(iii) (1991)
26 C.F.R. § 1.269A-1 (proposed), in 48 Fed. Reg. 13,438 (1983)
Rev. Rul. 74-44, 1974-1 C.B. 287

State

Ala. Code § 25-4-78 (1990)
1917 Cal. Stat. ch. 586, §§ 8(b) and 57(b)
Cal. Unemp. Ins. Code §§ 708 & 708.5 (West Supp. 1991 & West 1986)
1937 Iowa Acts ch. 4, § 5(c) at 516
1939 Iowa Acts ch. 64, § 2 at 93
Iowa Code § 14.13.2 (1991)
Iowa Code §§ 96.5.3 and 96.19.18 (1991)
Pa. Stat. Ann. tit. 43 § 491-3 (Purdon 1964) (Industrial Homework Law)
Pa. Stat. Ann. tit. 43 § 802(h) (Purdon 1991)
1931 Wis. Laws ch. 20, § 108.01(1) and 108.04(5)(f) (Spec. Sess.)
Wis. Stat. § 108.04(5)(g) (1937)

Cases

Germany

Annalen des Königl. Sächs. Oberappellationsgerichts, 1, No. 44, 1 Apr. 1859
    (1860)

United States

Bakery & Pastry Drivers and Helpers Local 802 of Teamsters v. Wohl, 315
    U.S. 769 (1942)
Bautista v. Jones, 25 Cal. 2d 746, 155 P.2d 343 (1945)
Bolles v. Appeal Bd. of the Mich. Employment Security Comm'n, 361 Mich
    378, 105 N.W.2d 192 (1960)
Boro Park Sanitary Live Poultry Market, Inc. v. Heller, 280 N.Y. 481, 21
    N.E.2d 687 (1939)
Bunch v. Schweiker, 681 F.2d 249 (4th Cir. 1982)
Campbell Soup Co. v. Wentz, 172 F.2d 80 (3d Cir. 1948)
Carlsen v. California Unemp. Ins. App. Bd., 64 Cal. App. 3d 577, 134 Cal.
    Rptr. 581 (1976)
Cooperman v. California Unemployment Ins. App. Bd., 49 Cal. App. 3d 1,
    122 Cal. Rptr. 127 (1975)
Cumming v. District Unemployment Compensation Bd., 382 A.2d 1010 (D.C.
    1978)
Delno v. Celebrezze, 347 F.2d 159 (9th Cir. 1965)
Department of Lab. & Indus. v. Unemployment Compensation Bd. of
    Review., 203 Pa. Super. 183, 199 A.2d 475 (1964)
Dumont v. Hackett, 390 A.2d 375 (R.I. 1978)
Employers' Liability Assur. Corp. v. Industrial Accident Comm'n, 187 Cal.

615, 203 P. 95 (1921)

Fegley v. Higgins, 760 F. Supp. 617 (E.D. Mich. 1991)

F.E. Hazard, Ltd. v. Moffitt, 303 N.L.R.B. No. 130, 1991-92 NLRB Dec. (CCH) ¶ 16,768

Feist Publications, Inc. v. Rural Telephone Service Co., 59 U.S.L.W. 4251 (No. 89-1909, Mar. 27, 1991)

Fugazy Continental Corp., 231 N.L.R.B. 1344 (1977), *enforced*, 603 F.2d 214 (2d Cir. 1979)

General Investment Corp. v. United States, 823 F.2d 337 (9th Cir. 1987)

Hanke v. International Bhd. of Teamsters, Local 309, 33 Wash.2d 646, 207 P.2d 206 (1949)

Hearst v. Iowa Dep't of Revenue & Fin., 461 N.W.2d 295 (Iowa 1990)

Heinrich Motors, Inc. v. NLRB, 403 F.2d 145 (2d Cir. 1968)

International Bhd. of Teamsters, Local 309 v. Hanke, 339 U.S. 470 (1950)

Joseph Radtke, S.C. v. United States, 712 F. Supp. 143 (E.D. Wis. 1989), *aff'd*, 895 F.2d 1196 (7th Cir. 1990)

Local 777, Democratic Union Org. Comm. v. NLRB, 603 F.2d 862 (D.C. Cir. 1978)

Ludeking v. Finch, 421 F.2d 499 (8th Cir. 1970)

McLaughlin v. Seafood, Inc., 867 F.2d 875 (5th Cir. 1989)

Martin v. Unemployment Compensation Bd. of Review, 174 Pa. Super. 412, 101 A.2d 421 (1953)

Miller v. Director, Ala. Dep't of Indus. Rel., 460 So.2d 1326 (Ala. 1984)

Miller v. Tobin, 70 N.Y.S.2d 36 (1947)

Mississippi Employment Security Comm'n v. Medlin, 171 So.2d 496 (Miss. 1965)

Mister Softee of Indiana, Inc. v. Oil, Chemical and Atomic Workers Int'l U., 162 NLRB 354 (1966)

Packard Motor Co. v. NLRB, 330 U.S. 485 (1947)

Pavlonis v. Commonwealth Unemployment Compensation Bd. of Review, 426 A.2d 215 (Pa. Commw. 1981)

Peckham v. Board of Trustees of the Int'l Bhd. of Painters, 653 F.2d 424 (10th Cir. 1981)

Phillips v. Unemployment Compensation Comm'n, 323 Mich. 188, 35 N.W.2d 237 (1948)

Powell v. Appeal Bd. of Mich. Employment Security Comm'n, 345 Mich. 455, 75 N.W.2d 874 (1956)

St. Claire v. Minnesota Harbor Serv., Inc., 211 F. Supp. 521 (D. Minn. 1962)

Sargent v. Commissioner, 93 T.C. 572 (1989)

Sargent v. Commissioner, 929 F.2d 1252 (8th Cir. 1991)

Senn v. Tile Layers Protective Union, Local No. 5, 222 Wis. 383, 268 N.W. 270 (1936)

Senn v. Tile Layers Protective Union, Local No. 5, 301 U.S. 468 (1937)

Shell Oil Co. v. Marinello, 63 N.J. 402, 307 A.2d 598 (1973), *cert. denied*, 415 U.S. 920 (1974)

Simon v. Unemployment Ins. App. Bd., 193 Cal. App. 3d 1076, 238 Cal. Rptr. 589 (1987)

Slocum Straw Works v. Industrial Comm'n, 232 Wis. 71, 286 N.W. 593 (1939)

Spicer Accounting, Inc. v. United States, 66 A.F.T.R.2d 90-5806 (9th Cir. 1990)

State v. Sherlock Auction & Realty, Inc., 235 Kan. 232, 678 P.2d 630 (1984)

Suchodolski v. American Fed'n of Labor, 127 N.J.Eq. 511 (1940)

Sun Shipbuilding & Dry Dock Co. v. Unemployment Compensation Bd. of Review, 160 Pa. Super. 501, 52 A.2d 362 (1947)

Sun Shipbuilding & Dry Dock Co. v. Unemployment Compensation Bd. of Review, 358 Pa. 224, 56 A.2d 254 (1948)

Susser v. Carvel Corp., 206 F. Supp. 636 (S.D.N.Y. 1962)

Unemployment Compensation Bd. of Review v. Kessler, 365 A.2d 459 (Pa. Commw. 1976)

Vega v. Gasper, 118 Lab. Cas. (CCH) ¶ 35,474 (W.D. Tex. Apr. 30, 1991)

Walling v. Twyeffort, Inc., 158 F.2d 944 (2d Cir.)

U.S. Soc. Sec. Bd. Unemployment Compensation Interpretation Service: Benefit Series (1938-1974)

Index

About the Author

MARC LINDER teaches labor law at The University of Iowa and has written numerous books on political economy and law, including *The Employment Relationship in Anglo-American Law* (Greenwood, 1989). Before becoming a legal services attorney representing migrant farm workers, he received a Ph.D. in political science and taught at universities in Germany, Denmark, Mexico, and the United States.